Structuring Poverty in the Windy City

Structuring Poverty in the Windy City

AUTONOMY, VIRTUE,
AND ISOLATION IN
POST-FIRE CHICAGO

Joel E. Black

 University Press of Kansas

Published by the University Press of Kansas (Lawrence, Kansas 66045), which was organized by the Kansas Board of Regents and is operated and funded by Emporia State University, Fort Hays State University, Kansas State University, Pittsburg State University, the University of Kansas, and Wichita State University.

Library of Congress Cataloging-in-Publication Data Names: Black, Joel E., author.
Title: Structuring Poverty in the Windy City : Autonomy, Virtue, and
    Isolation in Post-Fire Chicago / Joel E. Black.
Description: Lawrence, Kansas : University Press of Kansas, 2019. | Includes
    bibliographical references and index.
Identifiers: LCCN 2018058813
    ISBN 9780700628001 (hardback)
    ISBN 9780700628018 (paperback)
    ISBN 9780700628025 (ebook)
Subjects: LCSH: Poor—Illinois—Chicago. | Chicago (Ill.)—History—19th century. |
    Chicago (Ill.)—History—20th century. | BISAC: HISTORY / United States /
    19th Century. | POLITICAL SCIENCE / Public Policy / Social Policy.
Classification: LCC HV4046.C36 B53 2019 | DDC 305.5/69097731109034—dc23
LC record available at https://lccn.loc.gov/2018058813.

British Library Cataloguing-in-Publication Data is available.

Printed in the United States of America

10 9 8 7 6 5 4 3 2 1

The paper used in this publication is recycled and contains 30 percent postconsumer waste. It is acid free and meets the minimum requirements of the American National Standard for Permanence of Paper for Printed Library Materials Z39.48-1992.

Contents

Illustrations

Acknowledgments

Books that were dissertations require many thank-yous. This one is no exception. The ideas behind it grew out of a legal history course that I took with Elizabeth Dale at the University of Florida's Levin College of Law in 2006; subsequent iterations would benefit from the support and encouragement of a terrific doctoral committee that included Joseph Spillane, Danaya Wright, William Link, and Dan Smith. The final project won honorable mention in the Richard J. Milbauer Award competition for best dissertation. As I discovered in graduate school, not everybody gets to like his or her school or dissertation director. I did. It is my enormous good fortune to have been trained by Elizabeth Dale, who taught me how to think about law and how to use it to interpret meaningful pasts. I am grateful for her.

Travel to Chicago to research the book was supported by the Milbauer Fund, a Bertram Wyatt-Brown Dissertation Research Award, and numerous small travel grants from the History Department, the College of Liberal Arts and Sciences, and the Graduate Student Council. They all helped. The book also benefited from several professional opportunities. Invitations to participate in the Institute for Constitutional Studies summer research seminar The Economic Constitution: Coercion or Freedom? at George Washington University in 2010 and the graduate student workshop at the Law and Society Annual Meeting in Chicago that same year supplied important intellectual support. Academic journals did too. In fact, I developed small parts of this book into article manuscripts and published them as "A Theory of African-American Citizenship: Richard Westbrooks, the Great Migration, and the *Chicago Defender*'s 'Legal Helps' Column," *Journal of Social History* 46 (2013): 896–915; "Space and Status in Chicago's Legal Landscapes," *Journal of Planning History* 12 (2013): 227–244; and "Citizen Kane: The Everyday Ordeals and Self-Fashioned Citizenship of Wisconsin's 'Lady Lawyer,'" *Law and History Review* 33 (February 2015), 201–230.

The book also benefited from feedback I received at several national conferences at Wayne State University, the Organization of American Historians, the Business History Conference, and the American Society for Legal History.

I would like to thank David Congdon at the University Press of Kansas. David has been a staunch advocate for the book, and I am grateful for his support. I am also appreciative of outside reviewers who provided helpful comments on the manuscript. "Thank you" is also in order for the staff members and special collections librarians at the Chicago History Museum, the University of Illinois in Chicago and Urbana, the University of Chicago, and the Chicago Public Library, who helped to identify sources at the project's beginning and then helped to secure permissions as it neared its end. The staff in the Archives Department of the Clerk of the Circuit Court of Cook County—where the only surviving, microfilmed papers from Chicago's municipal court are housed—were particularly gracious with their time and assistance.

I have lived with this book through changes in location, job status, residency, and family structure. Over the years, many people have helped me to move the book forward by reading all or parts of it. I appreciate Erin Cunningham, William Davenport Mercer, Courtney Thorsson, Matthew Sandler, Scott Catey, Heather Bryson, Elizabeth Dale, Ellen Herman, Risa Goluboff, and anonymous readers for their helpful comments. Others—including my mom, Janet Black; my sister, Thea Black; and my uncle, aunt, in-laws, nieces, and nephews—did not read any part of the book. But, like my friends Evan and Greg, with whom I recently hiked—ill-advisedly—up British Columbia's notoriously steep Grouse Mountain, they provided valuable relief from the exile of revision.

My greatest debt is to my immediate family. I met my wife, Erin Cunningham, nearly twenty years ago in Victoria, British Columbia, and after living together in Vancouver, Winnipeg, and Montreal, we drove a rusty 1970 Volkswagen bus off our map and into the Deep South, directly to Gainesville, Florida. We arrived just after the beginning of the fall term of 2004 and spent a wonderful six years there. In

2016, after six years in Eugene, Oregon, we jumped at the opportunity to return to Gainesville. This time it was with our two-year-old daughter, Josephine, in tow. Throughout these years, this book ate up time that I was permitted to have. I am enormously grateful for Erin and for Josephine, with whom extraordinary things have been made possible. With enormous gratitude and love, this book is dedicated to them.

It is my hope that the reader finds some value and enjoyment in the pages ahead.

Gainesville, Florida
December 2018

Introduction: Structures of Poverty

On October 8, 1871, Chicago was on fire. The conflagration destroyed twenty-six hundred acres, "burned out" eighty thousand dwellers, and left tens of thousands without housing, food, fuel, or clothing. In its immediate post–Great Fire issue, the *Chicago Tribune* detailed the fire's path—to the city's west, north, and south—where it eviscerated buildings such as the *Tribune* building and the courthouse building, whose remnants are depicted on this book's cover. It enumerated lives lost, such as that of the anonymous woman engulfed at State and Taylor, the "drunken man" incinerated while trying to escape the flames on Michigan Avenue, and Jacob Wolf, who "roasted to death in his house." It issued pleas for information about the whereabouts of the missing (and presumed living), such as ten-year-old Tommy Jackson and seven-year-old Thomas O'Brien. And it credited aid pledges, mostly from other midwestern cities—Cleveland and St. Louis. In addition to registering panic and alarm in Chicago, the *Tribune* would spell out the city's path to renewal. It reported Governor John Palmer's meeting with prominent Chicagoans and state legislators and their vow to "take action." It described how churches and public schools offered food, water, and shelter. "Cheer up!" the *Tribune* editorialized. "Chicago will rise again!" One-term mayor Roswell Mason—preparing to leave office—was more pragmatic. On October 13—less than one full week after the Great Fire—he handed all relief duties to the commercial elite at the Chicago Relief and Aid Society. It was a critical decision, one that ensured that Chicago's physical rebuilding would be accompanied by an equally ambitious "rebuilding" of the city's impoverished men and women, as reformers, social scientists, and journalists set out to interpret and define the city's jobless, wayward, and migrating. In the process, it galvanized new expressions of social and quasi-governmental authority based on poverty.[1] That authority is the subject of this book.

By rooting its authority over city life in the conditions of the poor, the Relief and Aid Society took a position that many Americans would embrace more fully decades later. In the process, it inaugurated one of the great stories of modern America. Since President Franklin Roosevelt's New Deal for beleaguered workers and manufacturers and President Lyndon Johnson's Great Society and War on Poverty three decades later, public officials have used poverty to justify their authority—and to institute a new order, or governance.[2] In fact, fifty years after Johnson's domestic "war," poverty continues to structure debate over national policy. In his 2014 State of the Union address, for instance, President Barack Obama offered aid to poor residents living in "promise zones."[3] Republicans responded with an antipoverty plan crafted by House Speaker Paul Ryan. This plan stressed affordability and self-sufficiency, while it limited aid and proposed a major transfer of federal funds to state governments, where antipoverty initiatives were set to unfold.[4] In 2017, federal officials deepened their claims about the individual causes of poverty when Housing and Urban Development secretary Ben Carson described poverty as a "state of mind." The following year, President Donald Trump endorsed work requirements for food stamp recipients and then in 2018 proposed that food stamps disqualify recipients from citizenship.[5] Intriguingly, the Republican plan's twenty-first-century innovation replicates two features of nineteenth-century poverty administration coordinated by the Relief and Aid Society. First, it champions hierarchies. In its penchant for abstractions—such as "freedom" and "self-sufficiency"—it organizes the poor into rankings of "worth" and "worthlessness" and in the process reduces the multivalences of scarcity to expressions of individual value. Second, it endorses local jurisdiction, subjecting the poor to the rigors—and the prejudices—of local, rather than federal, oversight. Both point to poverty's enduring influence in the making of authority.

This book uses the lives of Gilded Age "strumpets," Progressive Era "tramps," and Southern Black migrants to tell a story about governance and poverty in Chicago in the era *before* Franklin Roosevelt and the New Deal.[6] It locates these origins in catastrophe—in the Great Fire and in the Relief and Aid Society's attempts to rebuild the city afterward. In their haste to restore Chicago, Relief and Aid Society officials did more than oversee the building of houses, streets, and hubs; they also coordinated shared interpretations of poverty, elements of which would be absorbed by reformers, socials scientists, and journalists. For instance, Relief and Aid Society officials systematically denied all aid to able-bodied men, insisting that they work for wages instead. This mandate was enforced through conspicuous oversight: upon requesting aid, able-bodied men were issued "certificates of character," which they presented to employment bureau officials. According to the society, the returned certificate attested to an individual's "worth," while the unreturned certificate silently confirmed "that the bearer [chose instead] to eat the bread of idleness."[7] The Relief and Aid Society interpreted white women in search of paid work as similarly unresponsive.[8] In fact, in the decades after the Chicago Fire, the process begun by the Relief and Aid Society would expand outward from jobless men to include workingwomen and southern Black migrants. Each would define, and be defined by, poverty.

As this book demonstrates, the Relief and Aid Society's attempt to eliminate poverty in Chicago after the Fire gave rise to new theories—generated by intellectuals and reformers—about what it meant to be poor. Their theories, or views, which are described in this book, form the basis of what I call structures of poverty, a term that is already standard in the literature and that I use to embrace the idea that poverty, or the condition of being impoverished, is the result of structures, or overriding patterns, of authority that are beyond the individual's control.[9] They arose, I argue, through compulsions that were cemented in shared interpretations of autonomy, virtue, and isolation—interpretations that did not initially communicate an order. Instead, these observations intersected with myriad claims about industrialization and urbanization that were remaking life in late nineteenth-century America. But over time, these statements would amount to something more than random observation—they would amount to an order based on poverty. By the turn of the twentieth century, the overlapping views of authorities described in this book converged in a common language of compulsion that promoted autonomy, virtue, and isolation. In Chicago these compulsions formalized in public studies of vice, crime, and race and in everyday courtroom hearings.[10] This book traces this process of calcification, from social claim to legal decree.

It also distinguishes between different perspectives and demonstrates that things that do not appear to be an order can impose order. From above, the seemingly uncoordinated views expressed by reformers, social scientists, and journalists might appear to represent an assortment of opinions and viewpoints. But as revealed in recent protests by Black Lives Matter activists—who have observed in the complicated patterns of urban policing an architecture of structural racism that permits the brutalization of African Americans—the view is different from below. For tramps, sex workers, and migrants thirteen decades ago, these seemingly uncoordinated views ratified compulsions—described in this book as autonomy, virtue, and isolation—that directly impacted them. Because they experienced reformers', social scientists', and journalists' claims and observations intimately and immediately, they were well positioned—as today's Black Lives Matter activists are well positioned—to recognize public declarations of compulsion instantaneously as structural. This book is devoted to unveiling these structures of poverty—to describing their rise, their fall, and their impact on formal authority in Chicago in the period between the Great Fire and the New Deal. In the process, it outlines the ideas these structures mobilized, the resistance that they engendered, and the legitimacies they forged.

INTERVENTIONS

Structuring Poverty in the Windy City engages scholars across a broad spectrum of enterprises to tell a story about authority. Legal historians and social scientists have discussed authority in terms of the nation-state.[11] And while they tend to disagree over the size and scope of that state, a recent spate of landmark studies on capitalism, work, and citizenship confirm the state's role in authority making.[12] Recognizing the importance of these formal expressions of authority, this book also looks beyond them to explore informal expressions of authority that are rooted in accounts of popular justice, where legal ideas and outcomes are debated by nonexperts—and where constitutional meaning is derived from everyday social interactions rather than through constitutional decree alone.[13] Building on the vitality of these accounts, this book interprets figures such as Hull House founder Jane Addams, *Chicago Defender* journalist Richard Westbrooks, and Chicago School sociologist Robert Park as benefactors of a legal order. By describing populations moving to Chicago, seeking and abandoning work, sleeping in privies, boardinghouses, and parks, and trading in physical and sexual labor, informal authorities—such as Addams, Westbrooks, and Park—used poverty as a justification for their oversight. As this book's chapters demonstrate, their opinions would profoundly influence claims made by courts and city commissions. In this way, the ordeals of Chicago's tramps, "chippies," and migrants became the premises of new deployments of urban authority. In describing how these figures encountered and contested compulsory autonomy, virtue, and isolation, this book makes four interventions into fields of everyday life, work, law, and current battles. Each deepens our understanding of the structures that define poverty.

Structuring Poverty in the Windy City tells a story about everyday life. In the process, it takes us beyond welfare policies and practices that have shaped approaches to the impoverished in America.[14] By examining conditions on the ground, it focuses on everyday ordeals and interactions, often involving work and housing, to reveal individuals who were defined by absences: legally, vagrants are without jobs and homes; morally, sex workers are without currency; socially, migrants are without standing—each is described as a member of a despised and outlying community. However, if absences separated, they also united, as compulsory autonomy, virtue, and isolation—rooted in everyday interaction—would find expressions in reformers', social scientists, and journalists' observations.[15] Here, past itinerant populations—passing through or settling in Chicago; moving between parks, boardinghouses, and saloons; working in domestic service, clerking, meatpacking, harvesting, or cutting ice—shape our understanding of city life a century ago. Their ordeals and grievances reveal that poverty is a created condition: from their perspective, they were *impoverished*, or *made* poor, their status produced by policies and practices generated by reformers, social scientists, and journalists looking to establish their own authority on the backs of white men who fail to work continuously, of white women who fail to stay at home, and of African American migrants who dared to leave *their* part of town. In this way, the present study points to ways that historically we have accepted—and continue to accept—conceptions of poverty that overlook structures to stress individual failings.

Structuring Poverty in the Windy City tells a story about work. Historians often filter their accounts of labor through the Civil War, the abolition of slavery, and the emergence of free labor to describe a labor model that is at once "free" but also infused with the legacy of enslavement. They describe the sweeping influence of unfree, antebellum-era workers "scraping by," whose labors set the course of American capitalism or, as legal historian Christopher Tomlins claims, set the course for early-American law.[16] But the "just and generous . . . system, which opens the way for all" envisioned by President Abraham Lincoln ultimately bore little "of the freedom it promised," according to historian Eric Foner. Instead, free labor, as expressed in accounts of "coolie," convict-lease, contract, and padrone regimes, might instead be understood to authorize enslavement in the era after slavery was prohibited.[17] By focusing on how poor workers chased harvests, cut ice, slaughtered livestock, sweated in factories, swept streets, and toiled in domestic, needle, and clerical work, this book extends the narrative of unfree labor beyond workplaces into the twentieth century, where it was the basis of an order built upon the work and housing practices of the least powerful.

Structuring Poverty in the Windy City also tells a story about law and courts, through the rise of liberty of contract doctrine. Its peri-odization—from the Great Fire to the New Deal—straddles a critical transformation in American law, from legal form to social context, fu-eled by anxiety about law's ability to manage the forces of industrial-ization and urbanization that were transforming life in the Progressive Era city.[18] Scholars tell us that the liberty of contact—the unrestricted contracting of labor as a property right—emerged from a sequence of United States Supreme Court legal opinions that began with Jus-tice Stephen Field's famous dissenting opinion in the *Slaughter-House Cases*—a landmark ruling testing the authority of the New Orleans legislature to restrict butchers, and their labors, to one facility: the Crescent City Livestock Landing and Slaughter-House Company.[19] Michael Ross, Ronald Labie and Jonathan Laurie, Wendy Parmet, and Randy Barnett deepen our understanding of the *Slaughter-House Cases* by more closely examining the worldview of Justice Field, by explor-ing the political and constitutional implications of the opinion and by criticizing the merits of the narrative to which it has given rise.[20] But as this book demonstrates, the liberty of contract was more than doc-trine—it was also reflected in social practices, most conspicuously in reformers', social scientists', and journalists' observations that the poor were unequal. How could a socially unequal person equitably contract employment? This question—about how social practices shape legal outcomes—absorbed legal theorists a century ago. Botanist and future Harvard University Law School dean Roscoe Pound famously chris-tened the term "sociological jurisprudence" to describe law's role in the regulation of "everyday rights and wrongs."[21] In fact, Pound would go a step further—to blast legal doctrines that failed to accommodate social realities. For instance, in a 1909 article that he published dur-ing the short period that he lived in Chicago, Pound excoriates the liberty of contract as an aberration, writing "there has *never* been at common law any such freedom of contract," adding that the concept itself threatened to "*impair* the authority of the court."[22] In stressing the social dimension of legal doctrine—the liberty of contract—that reduced workers to units of economic power, this book argues that marginal urban figures and their structural poverty were central to a legal order that cultivated inequality under spumes of liberty.

Finally, *Structuring Poverty in the Windy City* speaks to current battles over incarceration and marginalization. Social scientists investigating the relationship between capitalism and social inequality in the twentieth century have described how neoliberal policies have eroded rights, flooded labor markets with temporary and irregular workers, sponsored robust commitments to privatization and market-based problems, and demeaned government intervention in the economy— most notably on behalf of populations they believe to be individually responsible for their poverty.[23] In response, they assert the existence of structural patterns that impoverish and that have been captured alternatively in the experiences of a class of workers that economist Guy Standing has termed "the precariat," legal sociologist Katherine Beckett has termed the "banished," and French sociologist Loïc Wacquant has described in terms of the criminalization of the poor.[24] This current debasement of the impoverished—at work, by warehousing, through surveillance—resonates in the ordeals experienced a century ago by the migrating, marginal, and displaced. By stressing everyday ordeals, the primacy of work, and legal compulsion and innovation, *Structuring Poverty in the Windy City* builds directly on the claims of Standing, Beckett, and Wacquant about workers today to describe ways that marginal populations of workers experienced the disruptions and consequences of an order and rejected expression of power predicted on the abasement of the least powerful.

ORGANIZATION

Chicago provides a template for how we understand Progressive Era urban life.[25] In part, this is because it is a city of "firsts": it pioneered the nation's first municipal court system; social scientists developed in Chicago new approaches to the study of urban life; and landmark Chicago commissions on vice, crime, and race pointed to a new role for the city in studying itself. And, in part, this is because records describing these "firsts" are well preserved in its archives and embedded in its grand architecture. But it is also because Chicago is familiar, particularly to historians of Progressive Era life. Drawing from newspapers, municipal court records, social scientific studies, arrest records, case studies, poems, pamphlets, ethnographies, private investigations, commissions, and arrest records, *Structuring Poverty in the Windy City* invites us to look at this familiar city in a new light. In Progressive Era Chicago, men and women identifying alternatively as unemployed, provisionally employed, or vagrant, as wageworkers or sex workers, as migrants or "home guard" moved in and out of city courts, street, workplaces, boardinghouses, parks, shelters, and neighborhoods. Reformers, social scientists, and journalists recount populations transitioning between city and country, between jobs, between home and the road, and between wage and sex work in accounts that seemed random and disorganized. But as this book points out, observers such as judges Harry Olson and McKenzie Cleland, academics Robert Park, Charles Merriam, and Grace and Edith Abbott, and reformers Jane Addams and Louise deKoven Bowen were more than documenters of city life. They were purveyors of an order that arranged strikebreakers, clerks, meat packers, needleworkers, launderers, porters, and manufacturers—individuals living unsettled lives of migration and settlement, domesticity and homelessness, vagrancy and occupation—into shared conceptions of poverty. Their uncoordinated accounts cataloged experiences and outlined compulsions that—from the perspective of the impoverished—made poverty structural. However, because the impoverished left so few records, this book is forced to rely on claims made by reformers, social scientists, and journalists who may not have fully understood the impact of the compulsions they endorsed or the order those compulsions composed.

This book is organized in three sections that describe the rise, the application, and the fall of an order fostered by structures of poverty. In the first chapter, I describe its origins in the efforts by reformers, social scientists, and journalists to define poverty in Chicago after the

Great Fire of 1871 through categories of joblessness and homelessness that already existed in the city's vagrancy law. Although judges on Chicago's new municipal court—opened in late 1906—would wrestle with its meaning, they would also adopt many of its terms. The book's three middle chapters each describe the application of a separate compulsion. In this vein, each chapter follows a similar outline, in which compulsory autonomy, virtue, and isolation are asserted, resisted, and ultimately ratified by formal authorities: courts and commissions. Chapter 2 describes efforts to compel white men to autonomy and to criminalize joblessness. Jobless and homeless men in Hobohemia, the Hobo College, and at the *"Hobo" News* shot back from landscapes of resistance that frustrated the efforts of local courts to compel autonomy. Chapter 3 describes efforts to compel white workingwomen to virtue—to make them dependent. As vice commissioners acted to criminalize sex work for white women, judges struggled to create a legal justification for virtue but actively encouraged their participation in domestic duty and marriage—institutions that weakened their ability to earn. Chapter 4 takes a different turn. Whereas conceptions of autonomy compelled white male breadwinning and conceptions of virtue compelled white women to dependency, conceptions of isolation—based on notions of racial difference—compelled migrants to be separate within the spaces of the city. This chapter examines the ordeals of southern Black migrants in the era of World War I, who encountered stifling compulsory isolation in Chicago. This isolation stalled the momentum—the hope—of the Great Migration and forced African Americans into work spaces and neighborhoods that entrenched their poverty in separate spaces—and that did so at the moment of their most auspicious mobility. As these chapters reveal, the sexual and racial distinctions that degraded and elevated men and women would coordinate an order in which they were unequal. The book's final chapter tracks the decline of that order in the 1920s and early 1930s as the figure of the "gangster tramp," the "contracting workingwoman," and the "New Negro" undermined the social and legal enforcement of long-standing compulsions—and disrupted the authority upon which they were built. But as the book's epilogue points out, the structures developed through the Gilded Age and Progressive Era would reemerge in the New Deal Programs of the 1930s, where they would present as crucial—albeit neglected—forerunners to the "new" policies of New Deal America.

This book traces the social, economic, and legal dimensions of poverty in modern America. It positions the ordeals of marginal and outlying men and women—who were among the least organized, least protected, and most unequal workers—at the center of urban life. It reveals that amid dramatic and spontaneous fluctuations in the city's growth between the Great Fire and the Great Depression, marginality became a permanent feature of urban life. With this book, I aim to belie arguments that poverty was an individual choice and to provide concrete testimony to the interconnectedness of work and domesticity that preserved attributes of slavery and inequality in America long after the Civil War. In the era before national relief inaugurated by the New Deal, the perceived need to manage impoverished men and women was used to justify expressions of authority. Work in America has historically been used to enslave, confine, and degrade men and women of modest means. A century and a half after structures of poverty were reared in the embers of Chicago's horrific fire, work would continue to denote the incomplete and fractured statuses of the men and women who make up our nation's workforce.[26] This book tells this story. At the same time, *Structuring Poverty in the Windy City* invites us to look beyond topics examined in this book—labor history, social practices, and legal and economic relationships—to engage more comprehensively with issues of citizenship, ethnicity, politics, and sexuality and the orders they encounter. Their stories, some glimpsed in the pages ahead, still need to be written.

1. Rise: Vagrancy, Poverty, and the Makings of an Order

To see complex systems of functional order as order, and not as chaos, takes understanding. The leaves dropping from the trees in the autumn, the interior of an aeroplane engine, the entrails of a dissected rabbit, the city desk of a newspaper, all appear to be chaos if they are seen without comprehension. Once they are understood as systems of order, they actually look different.

— Jane Jacobs[1]

In the days of leather badges, police at the Lake Street Squad patrolled the upper Loop — "the fashionable retail thoroughfare of the city" between Van Buren Street, the Chicago River, and Lake Michigan. At night their patrol expanded to include railroad depots, steamship landings, and public halls. These patrols, designed to regulate mobility, brought them into contact with the city's margins — its reserves of indigent, peripatetic men registered in the squad's oversized arrest book as "vagrants."[2] However, despite its widespread use in everyday policing, vagrancy law would be the subject of intense public scrutiny. At least this was the case in May 1897, when the *Chicago Tribune* upbraided local police — likely performing a type of patrol similar to that of a Lake Street Squad officer — after they arrested a "man of means and influence" who had fallen unconscious in an outdoor hallway and charged him with vagrancy. "Booked like a hardened disreputable," the *Tribune* complained, this anonymous figure was sentenced by a magistrate to serve sixty days in the "Bridewell" — an English term that officials in Chicago used to describe their local jail. In its coverage of the story, the *Tribune* omitted the man's name, his occupation, and his home state — explaining vaguely that he was from a "western town." Instead, the *Tribune* used his story to argue that Chicago officials were putting the wrong people in jail. In the same story, the paper identified

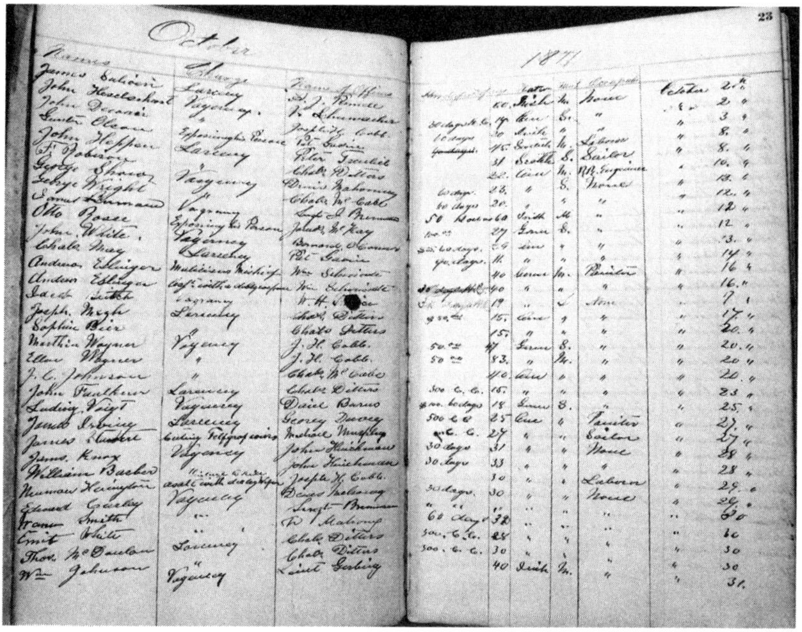

Figure 1.1. The Lake Street Squad's oversized arrest book lists names, charges, ages, and case dispositions. This page shows arrests from October 1877. Seventeen of the thirty-two arrests were for vagrancy. Chicago Police Department, Chicago Police Department Collection (manuscript), 1866–1969, Chicago History Museum.

Sarah McGinty, "drunk and making a disturbance on State Street," as the right kind of people. Her reputation was not cloaked in anonymity, and her sentence was not an "indignation for which there is no adequate redress."[3] Together these accounts — printed in Chicago's leading daily — help us to track the emergence of shared interpretations of poverty generated by reformers, social scientists, and journalists in the late nineteenth century. Like Jane Jacobs's "system of order," structures of poverty described in this book announced an order that would express itself through compulsion — that white men be autonomous, that white women be virtuous, and that southern Black migrants be isolated. For observers of poverty and for the men and women subject to its decrees, the structures it generated were conspicuous. They would make the poor visible in new ways.

As police arrest books attest, vagrancy law was a highly prized tool of the late nineteenth-century poverty administration. But in Chicago — where only a small number of men and women experienced a vagrancy arrest and trial from 1878 to 1893 — the law was often deeply symbolic.[4] This symbolic meaning was enriched by a lengthy history. In the Middle Ages, it punished absent workers; in colonial North America, it regulated settlers and settlement. In Gilded Age Chicago, it was used to justify expanded policing in response to fears that the city's laws were too "loose and lax," that Chicago was becoming a "tramp mecca," or that jobless, indigent men posed a danger to the "property and perhaps the lives of decent, reputable citizens."[5] In fact, Chicago's impoverished would experience the overlapping claims of reformers, social scientists, and journalists as a kind of feudal lord and the city as a sort of feudal manor — in both cases they were subjected to continuous oversight. As this chapter reveals, the modern conception of poverty that would define life on the margins in urban America evolved out of older, feudal commitments, even as they altered and modified them to fit new circumstances.

Categories of joblessness and homelessness help to sort and organize the complex interactions and relationships that emerged out of vagrancy law to form structures of poverty in the decades after the Great Fire.[6] In fact, these categories would formalize in the new Municipal Court of Chicago, which was created in 1906 as a testament to Progressive Era optimism that law could resolve the ills unleashed by urbanization and industrialization. But what emerged in the place of this new, formal, legal understanding of the impoverished was a divided municipal court. Its judges were torn between commitments to business efficiency on the one hand and the plight of the poor on the other. Judges eager to enforce autonomy, virtue, and isolation would be frustrated to discover that imprisoning impoverished men and women only deepened problems it was meant to abate: persistent joblessness and homelessness, or dependence on a pimp. Instead, the new court would serve a different purpose: justification. And it did so in a couple of different ways. In exchange for adopting the ideas expressed by reformers, social scientists, and journalists — and elevating their claims to the status of law — the court would legitimize its authority. In the process, it adopted and fortified structures of poverty; concerns about domestic relations were formalized in a new court in 1911, as were concerns about morals two years later in 1913. The consequences for the impoverished were immediate: punishment for the failure to be autonomous, or virtuous, or isolated was no longer censure; the courts made them criminals. As municipal court judges looked past the divisions and conflict that existed between social claims and law to stress the ways they reinforced each other, they transformed opinion about the impoverished into a new legal imperative.

VAGRANCY

Historically, sovereigns — from monarchies to congresses — have used vagrancy law to regulate the impoverished in moments of crisis involving labor, commerce, or general security. The precepts of vagrancy law harken back to fourteenth-century plagues known as the Black Death, when feudal officials attempted to control workers by fixing their wages and restricting their mobility.[7] We know that vagrancy was again used to stabilize commerce in the sixteenth century, when English statutes kept workers in place by allowing employers to pay them once annually and compelled them to labor under threat of gruesome, violent punishment.[8] In sixteenth-century England, idle but able-bodied men risked a whipping and a branding "burnt through the gristle of the right ear" after a first vagrancy conviction; they faced a two-year indenture after a second conviction.[9] This progressively brutal Elizabethan punishment scheme prefigured developments in eighteenth-century English vagrancy statutes, in which "idle and disorderly persons" could be sentenced to one month's incarceration, "rogues and vagabonds" were whipped and incarcerated for up to six months, and "incorrigible rogues" were whipped and possibly incarcerated for two years.[10] By the nineteenth century, English vagrancy law not only protected markets but also redefined joblessness, in the words of English jurist William Blackstone, as a "high offense against the public economy" and as a legal justification for brutal treatment.[11]

Colonial officials would accommodate the brutal provisions of English vagrancy law to the challenges of early-American life.[12] For instance, the Massachusetts Bay Colony — which boasted one of English North America's earliest constitutional orders — punished poverty in its legal code when it defined "common coasters, unprofitable fowlers and tobacco takers" as threats to the settlement.[13] Meanwhile, in colonial Virginia, security was a higher priority — men charged with vagrancy were impressed into service in imperial wars.[14] Farther south, in South Carolina, colonial authorities commonly enlisted white jobless men to neutralize another feature of colonial life: "negro insurrection."[15] Scholars have also pointed to the ways that the pressures of the Revolutionary and early national eras variegated the meaning of vagrancy law. Work, for instance, acquired political meaning, fueled by Ben Franklin's brassy aphorisms — such as "at the workingman's house hunger looks in but never enters" — and was enshrined in the First Constitutional Convention's exclusion of "vagabonds" from membership in the incipient confederation, which again emplaced the poor in a constitutional order by enshrining their repugnance to that order.[16] In fact, as American republicanism came to define the era after the founding, constitutional moment, the impoverished were recast as an offense to a political order that attempted to incorporate all white men into a single, united, national "will."[17] In colonial America, as in early modern England, vagrancy law was as proximate to new and unfamiliar challenges as it was to the systems of authority to which they gave rise.

In America conceptions of poverty were reflected in new ideological commitments to freedom. In early national-era America, vagrancy law parsed a complicated labor market cluttered with free, indentured, and bound workers. Evolving conceptions of work — and specifically the idea that workers should be made free and independent through their labors — were reflected in powerful ideological shifts that historians have identified in concepts of poverty, freedom, and belonging.

Just as the physical spaces of the antebellum plantation represented a tidy counterpoint to the "free" northern workshop, historian Edmund Morgan reveals that the "unfree" nature of African slavery helped to define the "free" nature of wage work.[18] Legal historian Robert Steinfeld corroborates Morgan's claim by pointing to the demise of the indentured laborer in the 1830s — a figure who was neither free nor slave, Black nor white, but intermediary.[19] In short, American republicanism supervised commitments to individual autonomy and political freedom that profoundly shaped thinking about poverty as an outlier of early nineteenth-century life.

In the decades before the Great Fire — before the Civil War — Chicago lawmakers upheld vagrancy law in the city's police courts.[20] Evidence suggests that officials viewed the poor, such as Cornelius Kennedy, as agents of disorder; he was convicted of vagrancy after he "was proved to be prowling about in a manner to cause suspicion" and fined twenty-five dollars. When he could not pay the fine, "he was again committed."[21] Officials also interpreted the impoverished as powerless in a bizarrely circular argument in which they reasoned that they could be forced to work for free *because* they had elected to not work for wages. "Could not these persons be made to work at some useful and profitable employment?" the *Tribune* editorialized. "Are there no streets or alleys to clean, no crossings to sweep, no parks to be kept in order?" the paper queried, implying that for some people — and not only the enslaved — work need not be compensated.[22] Officials likened this joblessness to crime. This was the case with Eugene Sullivan, an "idle, drinking fellow" accused of intoxicating Chicago's newest and "greenest" residents — and then robbing them blind.[23] Judges described thief John Smith as a vagrant; he was convicted after he was discovered to be "in possession of a large number of master keys."[24] Finally, Chicago officials equated vagrancy with vice. This was the case with E. W. Stetson, who was convicted of vagrancy after he was found in a "house of ill fame."[25] As these cases suggest, Chicago officials used vagrancy law broadly, as a catchall, to criminalize a range of practices associated with city life and their attempts to regulate it.

For women, "vagrancy" was a watchword for "vice."[26] In an era of coverture — a common-law concept that denied independent legal personhood to married women — vagrancy law was typically used to regulate the virtue of women who were unmarried, widowed, or working. Margaret Rollins and Catherine Dorsey were both arrested for vagrancy in Chicago in the mid-1850s after they were discovered, in separate incidences, to be sleeping in the streets.[27] In early 1856, "Wild Willie," who may have been a prostitute, was arrested for vagrancy after attempting to stab saloonkeeper "Humble Stu." Faced with the prospect of an unpleasant jail sentence, "Willie" sought to deflect blame when she stabbed herself with a penknife. It did not work. She was apprehended and taken to "the ward for the insane" instead.[28] Mary Ann Smith, who also was likely a prostitute, was convicted of vagrancy in Chicago in 1857 and fined five dollars and sentenced to forty days in jail.[29] Meanwhile, Catherine Forbes, known to be a "common prostitute," was convicted of vagrancy in the 1860s only because the judge could find no other way to punish her.[30] In late 1859, a Chicago police court judge fined Mary Jane Kenefick and Joanna Leonard, "two drunken night walkers," twenty-five dollars each for vagrancy.[31] That same year, thirteen-year-old Catherine Courtney was charged with vagrancy after she was discovered sleeping in the coal closet on the upper floor of one of the city's courthouses.[32] For children and women, vagrancy law — which helped officials criminalize vice — also punished their failure to live domestically.

If "vagrancy" was a watchword for "autonomy" for white men and for virtue for white women, for African American migrants vagrancy was a shibboleth for racial isolation. Before the Civil War, Black Americans were legally barred from living in Illinois and from testifying in its courts. Chicagoan Georgiana Wentworth benefited from the law — which technically made African Americans legally invisible in Illinois — after she robbed a "colored man and woman of $20" and was acquitted because under state law "colored persons could not give evidence against a White individual."[33] In instances where African Americans were convicted of vagrancy, the law provided that their labor could be auctioned off, a judicial innovation that reduced them through their labors to the status of a slave — despite the constitutional prohibition on slavery. For instance, after "Nelson (a mulatto)" was convicted of being Black in Illinois in the early 1860s, he appealed, arguing that the law under which he was convicted contradicted the state's ban on involuntary servitude. This argument prompted an appellate judge to explain that because the reduction in the individual's status was only "for a limited time," the punishment was more like vagrancy law, which was legal, and less like slavery, which was not.[34] For African Americans in Illinois, vagrancy law also pointed to the deprivations and exclusions that would only intensify their isolation in subsequent decades.

A brief overview of vagrancy law reveals that by the mid-nineteenth century, it was more than a tool to insulate markets and regulate workers and more than a mechanism of community membership and political "freedom." Rather, its loose and varied criminalization of joblessness and homelessness would ultimately lend support to reformers', social scientists', and journalists' insistence that men be autonomous, women be virtuous, and migrants be isolated. From the perspective of the impoverished, these claims were tantamount to compulsions that marked them — singled them out — in the larger community. Reared in conflagration, these structures of poverty would announce themselves in two ways: through the criminalization of joblessness and the criminalization of homelessness. Each is taken up in subsequent sections.

JOBLESSNESS

In the late nineteenth century, the administration of poverty varied by region. In the post–Civil War South, for instance, Black Codes recalled vagrancy law when they criminalized freedmen's mobility and restricted their participation in waged employment.[35] In states located along the Pacific coast, authorities used vagrancy-type laws to exclude Mexican and Chinese workers from competitive, waged employment — to prop up the wages of white workers.[36] As in the South

and West, the systematic regulation of joblessness in Chicago focused — first and foremost — on work.[37] This would become the focus
of the Chicago Relief and Aid Society. Once it assumed command of
relief duties after the Great Fire, the society instituted a robust system
of oversight that made joblessness — and the male dependency it associated with joblessness — into a marker of its authority.[38] In the process,
the society would enroll a well-established tenet of vagrancy law — that
all men should work for wage.

The Great Fire devastated Chicago in the fall of 1871. It consumed
more than twenty-one hundred acres, or three and one-eighth square
miles, destroying seventy-three miles of streets, eighteen thousand
nonresidential buildings — hotels, theaters, churches, schools, and
railroad depots — and roughly one hundred thousand private homes.[39]
Surviving Relief and Aid Society records describing "the stifling clouds
of dust, smoke, and cinders" amid the muggy "confusion and utter
chaos" of a night that was "lurid with flames" offer glimpses of the
Fire's devastation. Observers recalled the Fire's awesome brutality, "the
hissing and crackling of the flames, and the deafening roar of the gale,
the pelting cinders and brands, and the crumbling materials that gave
tragic coloring to the scene." These sounds and gusts unfurled, the Relief and Aid Society added, against an inky backdrop that made "the
night memorable in the minds of those who witnessed it."[40] In the jour-
nalism of the moment, the Relief and Aid Society's florid accounts of
the conflagration were supplemented by descriptions of the following
day's light, when the memory of "hissing, crackling" flames succumbed
to thoughts of renewal.

According to Fire historian Karen Sawislak, the Relief and Aid Society sustained two typologies of "worth" among survivors: Fire victims
were either hardworking but unlucky, or they were lazy and deceitful.[41]
These hierarchies of worth — venerating pluck and effort — deepened
existing commitment to principles of self-sufficiency. As historian
James Brown notes, the society engineered relief amid changes in official approaches to poverty. For instance, in the era before the Fire,
authorities tended to lump dependents together, treating populations

of sick, injured, and poor men, women, and families in much the same way, warehousing them in the same almshouse facilities. But this uniform response to the poor began to fragment in the late 1860s as new county hospitals opened in 1866 and 1869 distinguished between types of dependency and argued that some dependents were criminal, while others were not. By the early 1870s, officials on the Committee on Poverty and Pauperism sounded the alarm over "assumed pauperism" and demanded that men who were able-bodied be denied aid outright.[42] This committee's denunciation of poverty — which would be reflected in the Relief and Aid Society's existing hierarchies of worth and then later described by British reformer Charles Booth, who also classified the impoverished in an influential 1888 report — filter urban problems through men's capacity to perform labor.[43] At the same time, these facilities, which were created to respond to different problems, suggested that men were dependent for different reasons.

While the Relief and Aid Society envisioned men as autonomous, it would promote a view of women as their dependents. According to Sawislak, able-bodied men and boys, automatically disqualified from aid, were sent to the society's employment bureau, where they were expected to accept and perform any work available.[44] By contrast, for able-bodied women dependency only strengthened *their* relief claim. Of course, the Relief and Aid Society provided "exceptions." Dry goods entrepreneur Alexander T. Stewart, for instance, made sewing machines available to some women.[45] But seamstress work — a labor that seldom made any workers autonomous — only deepened women's dependency outside the home and only intensified women's reliance on men. Journalists ratified this gender distinction. The *Tribune* cautioned less than two weeks after the Fire that "work is a necessity" and then urged the Committee on Poverty and Pauperism to "cut off all deadbeats."[46] According to the *New York Times,* aid — defined here as support during the absence of work — threatened to make Chicago's "unworthy" into a permanent dependent class.[47]

Compulsory autonomy proved durable — even desirable — despite evidence of corruption and structural instability in the job market.

Committee on Poverty and Pauperism reformers broadcast their view that the impoverished should never be "too comfortable" or their food "too abundant," while they stared down accusations of their own lavish spending, petty graft, and surreptitious trading in "pauper bodies," charges that exposed the enduring absurdity of their abstemious approach to the impoverished.[48] According to Sawislak, unfettered "access to stockpiles of wealth proved too tempting."[49] But structures of poverty were not always, or only, intended to conceal largesse; sometimes they were designed to foster arguments about labor conditions that focused on the faults of individuals. For instance, sustained economic panics in 1873, 1882, and 1893 disrupted labor markets and sent unemployment rates in Chicago into the double digits, even as high as 40 percent in some cases; historians have suggested that marginal and unskilled workers experienced these panics earliest, deepest, and longest.[50] Numbers help to tell this story. The reports of the Illinois State Bureau of Labor Statistics point out that in periods of stability work was uneven and irregular. For instance, according to the bureau, in 1884 brick makers worked thirty-eight of fifty-two weeks (73 percent), while coopers worked forty-two weeks (80 percent), stonecutters worked thirty-five weeks (67 percent), and cigar makers worked forty-five weeks (87 percent).[51] Skilled workers were also vulnerable to wage cuts. For example, blacksmiths, slaughterers, carpenters, joiners, teamsters, painters, cabinetmakers, foundry men, and packers experienced wage cuts of from 12 to 22 percent from 1882 to 1886.[52] Despite the corruption of charities' officials and regular periods of unemployment, advocations of compulsory autonomy persisted. Their impact was to make work into a thing that more closely reflected conditions in prison, where work was decidedly unfree, than into a thing that reflected conditions in the market, where theoretically at least work was free.[53]

Well-known episodes of labor unrest in Chicago's Haymarket Square in 1886 and in Pullman, Illinois, a decade later would intensify arguments about the criminalization of not working. When a bomb exploded in Haymarket Square in May 1886, killing seven police officers, the *Tribune* castigated demonstrators as "professional agitators" rousing "idle men" and as "Shouting Amazons"—habitually neglectful mothers and wives.[54] Journalists echoed this criticism. The *New York Star* advised workers "to recognize [strikers] as their enemies," the *New York Times* advised that sympathy would be "worse than wasted on these ruffians," and the *Chicago Tribune* envisioned—enthusiastically—"the dawn of a new era [of repression] in Chicago for their kind."[55] It was in this vein that journalists described workers who struck in Pullman—a company town twelve miles south of Chicago—as "unruly and defiant" a decade later, after their wages were cut but their rent (in homes also owned by the company) was not.[56] In fact, social scientist had long been troubled by the completeness of the town's ownership by one man: George Pullman. When Richard Ely visited for *Harper's Magazine* in 1885, he detailed what he considered to be "rank and benevolent, well-wishing feudalism" that made workers tenants in perpetuity.[57] But Ely was in the minority. The Relief and Aid Society found that its views were reiterated by federal labor commissioner Carroll D. Wright, who decreed the Pullman strikers "not justified"; with the criticism, he helped to bake the society's tenets into an order.[58] Despite instances of corruption and evidence of unevenness in the job market, the Relief and Aid Society would play a critical role in extending vagrancy law into a loose coterie of insights about poverty coordinated by reformers, social scientists, and journalists.

HOMELESSNESS

The 1871 Great Fire transformed the meaning of housing in Chicago overnight as the impermanent and provisional wooden structures that lined the city's shores and banks were incinerated; the Relief and Aid Society vowed to replace them with uniform, stable housing.[59] However, as the weather cooled in the fall of 1871, hastily assembled buildings would frame more than sleeping quarters; they would encase moral anxieties about the populations they were designed to shelter. For instance, lumber baron Turlington Harvey chaired the Relief and

Aid Society's Shelter Committee, where he oversaw the warehousing of tenement dwellers in rough, temporary barracks that the society associated with "promiscuous and involuntary associations"; they were built to shelter roughly one thousand families in separate, partitioned units.[60] Fears about "idleness, disorder and vice" would fuel the society's ambition to redefine the city's poor through housing.[61] Like joblessness, housing evolved from vagrancy law into a tenet of compulsory autonomy. Galvanized in the Great Fire, its influence would endure over several decades.

In Chicago, pre–Great Fire authorities classified homelessness with old age, poor health, insanity, unemployment, dissolution, and poverty.[62] Historians have described these unskilled, antebellum workers who lived in persistent slum communities on the city's physical periphery.[63] In these communities, abandoned, lone women and children were housed alongside the provisionally employed, sex workers, immigrants, and other destitute families and marginal figures.[64] In fact, land economist Homer Hoyt classified Chicago's slum quarters, vice districts, and workingmen's quarters — and the people living in them — together, rather than separately, when he described the decade before the Fire.[65] The Fire would hasten the process of separating out these populations. As with the hospitals, asylums, and almshouses, post-Fire housing was remade by new attempts to manage the poor and make them self-sufficient — to define them by the housing they occupied.[66] When Chicago city booster James Parton boasted in the 1860s that "thrifty workmen" could own their own homes in Chicago, while the not-so-thrifty could "still hire a whole house," he also registered distinctions between types of work and housing — pointing out that in the city's "shanty" districts the large populations of occasionally employed and provisionally housed men and women were not actually "workers" and that their dwellings were not actually "homes."[67] As Parton appears to suggest, low-grade housing was a threat to Chicago.

In the era after the Fire, homelessness would embroider a sequence of temporary and provisional living experiences in Chicago.[68] White women who worked for wages faced few housing options. By 1880, roughly half of them lived under the surveillance of host families, as supervised members of putative family economies — where their low pay was justified by their membership in an economic unit, the family. But by 1910, the year reformers, social scientists, and journalists set out to study vice in the city, that number would fall to 30 percent. Historian Joanne Meyerowitz points to this decline when she describes the widespread alarm that developed over young women living "adrift," ostensibly unsupervised, and potentially immoral existences as nondomestic self-supporters in Progressive Era Chicago.[69] Meanwhile, white men, who were less directly ensconced in the moral panics of the day, enjoyed a greater range of cheap-housing options. For five cents, men could rent a "double decker, iron bedstead" with "dirty" bedding encased in "indescribably foul" air. A dime bought the same but with nominal privacy, while fifteen to twenty-five cents secured a private room, sectioned off by "corrugated iron or wooden partitions."[70] Those who had spent their last nickel on beer might sleep on a bar stool or a saloon floor, while the forsaken and nickel-less could turn to local police stations — where "wretched homeless wanderers may kennel themselves for the night" — or to city parks and city streets.[71] Meanwhile, African American migrants — particularly after the First Great Migration began in 1914 — faced widespread exclusion from temporary housing and were typically forced to lodge in private homes.[72] After the 1880s, reformers at Chicago's Improved Housing Association — the precursor to the Chicago Homes Association — complained that this temporary housing was a "menace to public health" and tantamount to homelessness.[73]

Considering this communal slumbering in houses, in police stations, and on barroom floors, it is not surprising that health concerns would drive housing reform.[74] According to Chicago historian Bessie Louise Pierce, inadequate housing included "rear-lot shacks without plumbing," an untold number of "privy vaults," and "dank and darkly shadowed cellars" that had been "converted into sleeping rooms"; each was an unpleasant reminder of Chicago's prodigious economic boom.[75] "It is very true that good sewers do not supply the sum total of necessities for a good living and healthy life," the Chicago Board of Health admitted in 1877, "but in large cities they are the most important factor." The subject of some of the city's first housing regulations, privies remained common across Chicago in the late 1880s, even in areas that had access to public sewers.[76] Decrepit housing and ubiquitous privies were accompanied by a putrescent stench that announced that industry was nearby. Pierce summarizes these conditions neatly: "The river stinks, the air stinks. People's clothes stink." The intolerable "offensive odors" emanating from "garbage strewn alleys, stockyards, rendering plants, oil-burning rolling mills, soap, glue and fertilizer factories" transformed Chicago — one of the "smelliest places in the country" — into a repugnant sensory experience.[77] Men and women who were poor lodged amid this acrid stench. It was here that *their* housing helped to underwrite the compulsions to autonomy or virtue — compulsion from which they must have felt so far removed.

Reformers' concerns about health, economy, and industry assembled in targeted morals campaigns that focused on housing. In his influential 1890 study of New York City's "Other Half," Jacob Riis described poor housing as the root cause of urban poverty, crime, and immorality.[78] This argument was given a midwestern orientation in 1900 by Indiana-born reformer Robert Hunter, who joined the Chicago Homes Association in the late 1890s and wrote *Tenement Conditions in Chicago*, a book that dealt with issues similar to those treated by Riis.[79] In his book, Hunter expanded upon the Relief and Aid Society's claim that bad housing bred pauperism, crime, and disease, producing "reduced industrial efficiency," promoting "weariness," and "increas[ing] the number of men who are unable continuously to make a living."[80] According to Hunter, Chicago's poor were not just badly housed — they were homeless. "The fact is," Hunter explained, "that the mass of people in tenements have not what people commonly call a home" but rather a "place of shelter for the sleeping hours of the night."[81] In 1900, social scientist Frances Embree endorsed Hunter's assessment that tenements were not homes but rather instances of homelessness, when she argued that "the home and not the saloon is responsible for a large part of the

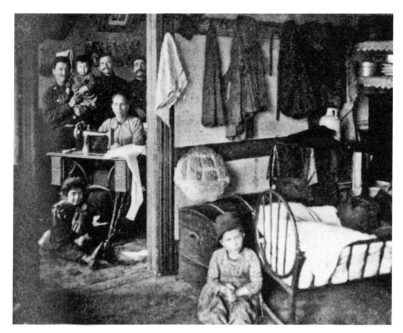

Figures 1.2A and 1.2B. House and street views of dilapidated tenement conditions in Chicago were popularized when they were published in *Tenement Conditions in Chicago*—a midwestern version of Jacob Riis's landmark *How the Other Half Lives*. Reprinted from *Tenement Conditions in Chicago* by Robert Hunter, published in 1901 by the Chicago Homes Association.

drunkenness of the poor."[82] Reformers such as Riis, Hunter, and Embree would reclassify men, women, and children living in dilapidated and provisional housing as "unhoused."[83]

By organizing the particularized and varied experiences of marginal men and women into definite, uniform categories of joblessness and homelessness, reformers, social scientists, and journalists fostered shared insights about poverty that centered, overwhelmingly, on their efforts to change the practices and habits of the poor. In the process, they transformed the fluid expressions of joblessness and homelessness into stable and uniform metrics of urban law and life. The impoverished would feel these structures and compulsions most intensely.

A NEW COURT

Claims about the impoverished that were derived from vagrancy law and adopted by post-Fire aid services were formalized by judges on Chicago's new municipal court, which opened in 1906. Justifications for the new court were grounded in three primary arguments about the dysfunction of nineteenth-century urban law and courts. First, the old police court system was obsolete — too "antiquated and ancient" for "the present needs of the city"; journalists argued that it was a "barnacle of jurisprudence," a "cancer," and a "mill," as well as "petty," "infamous," "malignant," and "pernicious."[84] In these rhetorical nods, the progress of local law that was realized by the new municipal court was not just aspirational — it was axiomatic. In fact, claims about law's progressive, forward march would be popular decades after the municipal court opened. Instances of magistrates' counseling "unfortunate women" to "go and sin no more" only confirmed the paternalism and "village" mentality that recent scholarship has ascribed to Gilded Age courts.[85] Second, old law was corrupt. Magistrates' salaries were notoriously derived from the fines they assessed — which made them vulnerable to accusations that their decisions were not impartial but corrupt, mired in graft and the buying and selling of justice.[86] Third, journalists liked to point to the police court's inability to mete out justice. The *Tribune* pointed to a trio of cases from November 1903. Robert Murray was charged with stealing hats, Edward Powers was charged with stealing a horse and buggy, and John Williams was charged with larceny and threatening to kill. However, despite enormous variety in the facts of each incident, each man was convicted of disorderly conduct and fined fifty dollars. These blanket convictions called into question the police court's ability to administrate life in a major city.[87]

With these justifications in place, officials turned their attention to the substance — the form — of the new court in 1905. According to leading Municipal Court of Chicago historian Michael Willrich, local attorney Hiram T. Gilbert led the charge. He collected and assembled the preliminary proposals put forth by charter convention and committees, each convened to reform local law.[88] Armed with committee minutes and a mandate for professional salaried judges, Gilbert fashioned two distinct reform plans. The first plan went furthest by proposing an overhaul of the entire court. The second, more modest plan called for a restructuring of the justice of the peace system — the police court — which would allow it to better "meet the demands of a poor man's court."[89] When it was passed by the state legislature in 1905, the Municipal Court Act ratified the first plan — complete overhaul.[90] However, despite Gilbert's leadership in orchestrating the new municipal court, Cook County prosecutor Harry Olson would become its first chief justice.[91] Behind Olson, twenty-seven judges presided at locations throughout Chicago.

The new court — efficient, professional, urban, and forward-looking — reveled in its acclaimed novelty.[92] In the new municipal court, elected judges no longer took a portion of the fines they assessed. Instead, they received multiyear appointments and monthly salaries. In the new court, judges were armed with robust discretion to "effect any reform or adopt any new business method."[93] The new municipal court was businesslike or, in Hiram Gilbert's words, "conducted on business principles."[94] According to John Wigmore, dean of the Northwestern University School of Law, "efficient" law was "probably the best justice

Figure 1.3. The Municipal Court used the building at 116 South Michigan Avenue, which was located beside the Illinois Athletic Club at 112 South Michigan Avenue, circa 1908–1910. Chicago. Detroit Publishing Company Photograph Collection, Library of Congress, Prints and Photographs Division, LC-DIG-det-4a22848.

in the United States."[95] Roscoe Pound, elaborated upon this view when he equated "doing things that are wholly unnecessary" with a "denial of justice." According to this calculus, the municipal court's remedy was simple: it parceled out justice.[96] On the municipal court itself, Chief Justice Harry Olson described himself as a general manager and embraced speedy trials, strict bail, and the "prompt dispatch" of justice. Each, he claimed, amounted to the efficient conduct of "public business."[97]

For all its self-congratulatory business acumen, the new court's orientation toward social problems fit awkwardly with turn-of-the-century legal doctrine. In the eighteenth century, William Blackstone had identified "idleness in any person [as a] high offense against the public economy."[98] In the late nineteenth century, libertarian legal theorists Christopher Tiedeman and Ernst Freund modified Blackstone's claim when they argued that "this offense" only punished the poor, while it ignored wealthy individuals who could afford to live without work.[99] "To produce something," Tiedeman elaborated, "is not one of those duties [to the state], nor is it to have a fixed permanent home."[100] The gist of the offense, Tiedeman added, is wandering with no visible means of support.[101] But the municipal court — efficient, professional, forward-looking — was saying something very different. It was saying, as Roscoe Pound explained, that individual freedoms endangered larger social interests: that courts had to deal with the problems of urbanization and industrialization and that if, while dealing with these problems, the poor were harmed or their rights impinged upon, that was acceptable.[102] This was the part that Chicago attorney Robert McMurdy was getting at when he asked if the new municipal court would be able to address the "day to day causes of the poor" or if it would become an "engine for [their] oppression."[103] This tension between social questions and legal doctrine would point to more fundamental questions: Could local courts acting under the auspices of a legal theory — such as liberty of contract — enforce compulsions to be autonomous and provide, to be virtuous and domestic, and to be isolated and segregated? Or did the courts need to better reflect the contingencies they encountered in their environment? At root, these compulsions were not legal but social, and they would require — as Tiedeman pointed out — that judges acknowledge that poverty is not uniform and that laws governing it probably should not be either. The result was conflicting views of law on the court.

DISCORD

While vagrancy law helped to shape the compulsions underwriting structures of poverty, the law would also divide judges over how to best manage the impoverished. A battle over the state's vagrancy law in the late 1870s illustrates this point. In the summer of 1877, African American sex worker Hattie Brooks was imprisoned under a sweeping new state vagrancy law that granted police broad authority to arrest on sight without a warrant.[104] Brooks's appeal of her detention reveals divisions over the validity of preemptive arrests. Judge William King McAllister found it "hopelessly unconstitutional" because it placed the "liberties of the honest poor entirely at the mercy of the police."[105] This ruling, that vagrancy law criminalized poverty, would put him at odds with local police: Superintendent Michael Hickey wanted to use the law as an instrument — to "transfer [the vagrant's] labor to the House of Correction" as a "remedy for the evil." McAllister's interpretation also put him in conflict with mainstream journalists, who imagined that — unchecked — "the evil" of male dependency "will grow to such a size as to defy laws." Some journalists even accused McAllister of ignoring the "perils of the unemployed poor."[106] Finally, it put him in conflict with fellow jurists. Sitting Peoria County Circuit Court judge J. McCulloch publicly accused McAllister of deliberately misinterpreting the amendment to the vagrancy law, which he felt was intended to streamline the prosecution of the poor, of women like Hattie Brooks.[107] Tellingly, the conflict over vagrancy law — over efforts to encase in law social anxieties about the impoverished — would continue to impact

Brooks, whose name appeared again in 1879 when she was arrested in a separate event, also alongside "inmates."[108]

Chief Justice Harry Olson, who was born in Chicago in 1867 but reared on a Kansas farm from age three, sought to streamline poverty's legal meaning for the municipal court. Olson worked as a teacher and public school principal before he earned his law degree from the Union College of Law — later the Northwestern University School of Law — in 1891. According to the *Tribune*, when his friend Charles Deneen was elected state's attorney for Cook County in 1896, he invited Olson to work as assistant state's attorney. A decade later, Olson was elected in his own right to be chief justice of the new municipal court that Hiram T. Gilbert had just put together.[109] In this position, he endorsed the values — autonomy, self-sufficiency — cultivated by the Relief and Aid Society, which he interpreted as "clear[ing]" the "scum of the earth" — jobless men — from the city and forcing "crooks and loafers" to "work at honest labor."[110] It was in this vein that he worked with lawmakers to review early drafts of legislation for Senate Bill 293, which, in the spring of 1907, proposed to streamline the arrests of jobless and homeless men by allowing police to detain them without a warrant — a power that recalled the showdown over Hattie Brooks's arrest in the summer of 1877.[111] Journalists praised the chief justice and called the new law a "mechanism of redemption."[112] Social scientists also applauded Olson's truculence, and some even predicted that it would single-handedly bring an "end to the tramp era in Chicago."[113] Aside from municipal court judge Hosea Wells — who was uncomfortable convicting people without their "actually having committed an offense" and who rejected police chief George Shippy's orders to "drive undesirables out of Chicago" — the judges on the municipal court appeared to embrace Olson's view of poverty.[114] In fact, in 1907, the same year Senate Bill 293 was passed, municipal court judges even debated the merits of a "City Farm Colony," a sprawling outdoor space dedicated to the criminal detention and "correction" of "vagrants" by compelling them to menial labor.[115]

McKenzie Cleland was an exception. Like Olson's, Cleland's trek to Chicago followed the well-worn routes of late nineteenth-century migration and urbanization. According to the *Tribune,* the reformer judge was born in upstate New York in the 1860s and moved west to rural Minnesota as a child. He earned a law degree from St. Louis's Washington University in 1884 and moved to Chicago, where he married, had children, and practiced law.[116] On the municipal court bench, Cleland's goals differed from Olson's: he sought to make himself — and the court — more responsive to the needs of the impoverished. "Let Us Do Justice to the Wrong-Doer, But No Injustice to His Family," he proposed in a 1909 election campaign poster.[117] Imprisoning jobless and provisionally employed men, Cleland would argue, only punished family members dependent upon them; as a legal strategy, he found it "more than useless."[118] The men and women he encountered in his courtroom hailed from the West Side's troubled and downcast Maxwell Street community, which was characterized by "tumbled down stairways, defective plumbing, overflowing garbage boxes [and] unclean streets and alleys."[119] Cleland, who interacted with impoverished Chicagoans as directly as any judge, understood the challenges involved in realizing its compulsions — the ways that autonomy and virtue broke down when courts disrupted families with jail terms. In response, he rejected the blanket criminalization of poverty. Instead, he promoted a system of adult probation in which courts administered poverty "without imprisonment," doing so by modifying the terms of the most pervasive compulsion: asserting instead that men seek, if not actually occupy, steady work.

Cleland's probation plan relied on input from the community, most notably from wives. For instance, women appeared regularly in court to swear that their husbands were sober or seeking work or supporting homes. For men such as Joseph Levi, Emil Hejinalec, and Ludwig Krestenach — who were among hundreds to benefit from this probation system — their wives' testimony kept them out of jail. "Unless you help me to keep this man straight," Judge Cleland told Mrs. Levi, "I can't do anything to make him better." Cleland instructed her to "come back

Figure 1.4. Judge McKenzie Cleland, pictured in the portrait, viewed himself as helping the working poor, while also looking down on them—not unlike on the person captured in this image looking up at his portrait in a courtroom. Chicago, 1909. Chicago History Museum, *Chicago Daily News* negatives collection, DN-0007005.

[again] in two weeks" to update her husband's status.[120] Leo Szulczaski's failure-to-support case illustrates wives' legal role. Stella Szulczaski had her husband — employed as a "rod man at a steel mill" — tried
and convicted in the municipal court in August 1914 of contributing to
the dependency of their two juvenile children. Leo was put on probation and ordered to support his children or face jail time, an obligation
about which Stella was invited to attest.[121] With these hearings, Cleland made families complicit in compulsory autonomy; by identifying
the ways they operate as mothers and wives, he distinguished them as
both consumers of law and as purveyors of a legal order. For instance,
Michael Fitzgerald was returned to jail after his wife complained in
February 1907 "that he had lapsed into his old habits and beaten her
again."[122] Unsurprisingly, businesses were also intrigued by Cleland's
flexible adult probation plan, which drew employers and politicians to
his West Side courtroom. Reportedly, city aldermen, comptrollers, and
even Mayor Edward Dunne stopped in to watch the proceedings and
lend their support.[123] As city leaders likely perceived, because probation
could only end with steady employment, it made the compulsion to
autonomy even more forceful and insidious.

Cleland's flexibility — his legal innovation — annoyed Olson, whose
private letters reveal that he was frustrated with Cleland's adult probation plan — a system Olson rejected because it had no statutory basis.[124]
In early January 1908, Olson sparked a minor uproar among local business, civil, and religious leaders when he transferred Cleland from the
Maxwell Street neighborhood to another court on Michigan Avenue.
The complaint letters that poured in identified the diverse stakeholders
in adult probation. Letters such as the one from attorney Daniel Forbes
claimed the probation system fought crime and saved hundreds from
"the penitentiary." Attorney Samuel Packard considered probation "a
great movement for the reclamation of the criminal classes." Leggings
manufacturer E. C. Cook pointed to probation's benefits to industry.
Normal Park Baptist Church pastor F. L. Anderson claimed to speak
for "more than a hundred in my congregation" when he asked Olson
pointedly, "Will you kindly state the reason for the transfer?" Even Chi-

cago Commons Settlement House founder Graham Taylor expressed support for adult probation. Settlement house leaders promoted Cleland's enormous social value, adding the district "never had the proper attention paid it" by legal officials until "the advent of McKenzie Cleland," who is "revered by the people."[125]

Olson resisted what appeared to be an outpouring of support for Cleland's plan. He shot back at dentist Frank Buckley — who had written on behalf of First Congregationalist pastor William Barton — that while "great good has been accomplished by Cleland," judges were typically transferred annually. Besides, he added, Cleland's adult probation plan had no basis in Illinois law — implying that he may have moved Cleland to punish him. Olson's letter to Buckley was nearly an exact replica of the missive he sent manufacturer John Lenox, in which he explained, "We should all respect the laws as they are."[126] Olson's frustration with Cleland spilled into a personal letter, in which he criticized Cleland directly for vacating judgments against lower-level criminal offenders, protesting, "This is exactly what you did at Maxwell Street," and adding, "As you are well aware there is no adult probation law in force in Illinois." Olson even threatened to remove Cleland from the municipal court entirely, apparently oblivious to the ways that his probation complemented Olson's own position on male autonomy: "If you are not willing to wait until you get the authority of the law, and attempt to circumvent the law by use of unwarranted discretion, it will be my imperative duty as Chief Justice of this court to remove you from the trial of criminal cases."[127] As the Olson-Cleland conflict reveals, attempts to translate the structures of poverty into law would divide judges in their interpretation of autonomy, virtue, and isolation — and in their understanding of the circumstances of the impoverished.

A LEGAL ORDER

The Municipal Court of Chicago would ultimately grow and develop in ways that ratified Olson's approach to poverty over Cleland's, particularly as it developed new courts to administrate compulsory autonomy, virtue, and isolation — to elevate private sins into public harms. The municipal court's Court of Domestic Relations, which opened on April 3, 1911, promoted stability by compelling husbands and fathers to work steadily and support wives and children.[128] In fact, the court's mission was outlined in the municipal court's 1910 annual report: "The family is the unit around which all else that is good must be built," and "anything that destroys that unit works evil to the public good."[129] In addition to promising to regulate family life, the same annual report identified joblessness as "the greatest problem now confronting the Court" because it imperiled individual autonomy.[130] The order the new court espoused was reflected in commitments to liberty-of-contract doctrine compelling stable homes and steady jobs as testaments of freedom and evidence of equality.

As Cleland did with adult probation, the Court of Domestic Relations authorized impoverished women to act like wives and mothers "who have heretofore suffered in silence" and to seek relief in the courts for the misdeeds of their husbands. Desertion cases dominated the court's early caseload. In fact, of the 3,699 cases disposed of in its second year of operation, 1912–1913, 2,432 were for wife and child abandonment and failure to support, transforming the court into a proverbial clearinghouse for weekly maintenance and child-support payments.[131] The probations of Charles Matter, a twenty-five-year-old foreman, George Bowing, a thirty-seven-year-old Marshall Field's employee, and Thomas Cayton, a twenty-four-year-old unskilled laborer, are only a few of thousands of instances in which men were processed by the court and compelled by law to create self-sufficient domestic units.[132] Meanwhile, the physical staging of domestic space in the court's antechambers replicated compulsory virtue. Here wives and mothers were invited to rock in chairs next to "proper reading materials," and children were prompted to use kindergarten supplies or to sleep in a "small bed." The milk made available to children only seemed to reinforce the wholesomeness of the enterprise.

Figure 1.5. Replicating domesticity in legal space. A view of Michael L. Rosina, Cook County assistant state's attorney in the Court of Domestic Relations, sitting in the courthouse in 1917 with an unidentified boy. Chicago History Museum, *Chicago Daily News* negatives collection, DN-0067522.

The enterprise also happened to double as a research lab. Mothers and wives in the antechamber were invited to fill out questionnaires designed to help municipal court officials better understand the causes of domestic breakdown. While the questionnaires ratified existing structures of poverty — that dependent men and autonomous women were criminal — they drilled down on the perils encountered by impoverished women outside the home. According to the questionnaires, in the 499 bastardy actions brought before the municipal court's Morals Court in its first year — 1911 — work was a leading cause of poverty, as most women worked for wages, half of the women were employed as domestics, and one-fifth were employed in factories and less than 10 percent in sales.[133] Meanwhile, in just over half of the questionnaires, women identified "broken marriage promises" as the principal reason for their pregnancy, or "downfall."[134] If sex outside marriage and work for wages cultivated "ruin," then, judges reasoned and the questionnaires seemed to confirm, virtue might operate as a counter and ensconce them safely in domestic spaces, insulated from harm.

The Morals Court and the short-lived Vagrancy Court deepened the municipal court's commitment to the compulsions developed by reformers, social scientists, and journalists. Opened in 1913, just two years after the Court of Domestic Relations, the Morals Court punished women accused of trading in sex outside of married domestic spaces, either occasionally or professionally.[135] In compelling women to the duties of wives and mothers, Morals Court judges would minimize the economic pressures that drove women to wage or sex work. Meanwhile, the court's short-lived Vagrancy Court was created in response to the *Report of the City Council Committee on Crime,* published in 1915.[136] In the court, which existed in the first half of 1918, judges erased distinctions between men as they classified jobless men alongside other types of low-level criminals: pickpockets, confidence men, shoplifters, "safe blowers," "jack rollers," "purse snatchers," and "wagon thieves."[137] This focus on criminalization represented a dramatic departure from Judge Cleland's efforts to use law to moderate the legal compulsions experienced by jobless men and working women. Instead, the ancillary courts sided with Judge Olson and his claim that jobless men should be sent to the "rock pile."[138] Together, they dutifully governed the sexual and racial convictions outlined by structures of poverty — evolved from vagrancy law, forged in the Chicago Fire, and then manifest in the Chicago Municipal Court's ambition to "cause that class" not acting like husbands and fathers, mothers and wives "to leave Chicago."[139] For the men and women subject to this oversight, these compulsions would have felt like an order — systematically regulating their everyday conduct, simultaneously holding out the threat of their punishment and the promise of their redemption.

CONCLUSION

In his 1907 exposé for *McClure's Magazine,* muckraking journalist George Kibbe Turner characterized Chicago as venal and vice addled, and he blamed the city's "archaic police magistrate courts" for its enduring crookedness.[140] In the same breath, he praised its new municipal court. That court's authority would derive as much from businesslike efficiency as from its supposed capacity to administer the ordeals of impoverished men and women, whom Turner described as predatory, disorderly, and "savage."[141] It was in this facility that judges claimed they could distinguish "real" criminal dependents, such as Sarah McGinty, from "false" criminals, such as the "man of means" whose arrest story is recounted at the beginning of this chapter. In the process of wresting with these distinctions, they announced structures and embraced patterns that fell most heavily on the poor. The failure to be autonomous, virtuous, and isolated was punished as a petty crime, as a minor violation that prompted continuous oversight. This book tells the story of this crime and punishment, which evolved in society and in law — often in different ways. From the men (and women) encamped in Grant Park or in the West Side's Hobohemia to the women (and men) laboring in the Loop's Levee Vice District to the migrants traveling to Chicago either along paths laid out from the eastern and southern states or along the routes that connected the towns and communities that made up Chicago's vast, midwestern hinterland, these figures without resources, jobs, or homes who flooded turn-of-the century Chicago would reinforce, interrupt, confront, and evade prevailing interpretations of poverty and governance in the city.[142] Their stories and ordeals form the basis of the next three chapters. We begin with jobless men, or "tramps."

2. Autonomy: Compelling "Tramps" to Jobs and Homes

Everywhere about you there is work . . . and here you are idle. . . . The policeman on the crossing in his slouching uniform . . . [represents] the outstretched hand of the law ready to lay hold upon you should you violate in your despair the rules of social order. Behind him you see the patrol wagon and the stationhouse and the courts of law and the state's prison and enforced labor, the whole elaborate process by means of which society would reassimilate you, an excrement, a non-social being as a transgressor of law, into the body politic once more, and set you to fulfilling a functional activity as a part of the social organism.

— Walter Augustus Wyckoff[1]

Famed private eye Allan Pinkerton registered a rose-tinted encounter with a "tramp" during the Great Upheaval railroad strike of 1877. He described the man's disposition as "careless, happy-hearted" and his appearance as "grizzly, bronzed, weather-beaten." The anonymous tramp was unbound, Pinkerton gushed; he wandered because, the man said, he "couldn't live no other way." The tramp boasted that his roaming armed him with an understanding of the world better than that of "a dozen of yer big city men." Pinkerton's tramp was really a renaissance man who could "not be chained down to one kind of plodding."[2] Pinkerton's account differed dramatically from that of Chicago school sociologist Nels Anderson, recorded forty years later on a downtown Chicago street corner. This figure was urban and immobile, and his chronicler — Anderson — a professional observer and recorder of city life. Anderson laments the man's gambling and attributes his poems and song not to his wide-ranging interest but to profligacy — he shirked work![3] For our purposes, Pinkerton's and Anderson's views of tramps chart a transition from harmless romantic roamer to criminal indigent. In the decades after the Chicago Fire, reformers, social scientists, and journalists would embrace Anderson's view over Pinkerton's to make compulsory autonomy into the centerpiece of a legal order built upon poverty. The alienation that sociologist Walter Wyckoff observed in this chapter's epigraph also stressed the anxiety the jobless experienced as they registered the mechanisms — courts, laws, prisons — designed to enforce compliance with an order they interpreted as omnipresent and spelled out in a duty to provide.

The figure of the tramp preoccupies our historical imagination and has long-intrigued bards, moralists, and scholars. For historians, the struggles of jobless and homeless men in the Gilded Age and the Progressive Era confirm striking accounts of itinerant rovers passing in and out of the labor market, trekking midwestern landscapes, hitching rides on passing locomotives, forming temporary communities — propelled forward by the prospect of work and settlement, restrained only by the violence and perilousness they encountered in workplaces and in "jungles," on conveyances, and along roads.[4] In cities where they were connected and classified by shared geographies of homelessness and joblessness — of criminal dependency — men identified by vagrancy law as "idle" or "dissolute" also defined the late nineteenth-century landscapes they traveled.[5] But unlike historical accounts that align tramps with community building, political activism, policymaking, criminal mobility, and "contested terrains," the structures of poverty described in this book interpreted tramps as the basis of informal urban authority.[6] This bête noire of industrial capitalism became a flash point in a larger conversation over dependency that justified legal, economic, and moral condemnation.

As this chapter demonstrates, the figure of the tramp might be understood as more than poverty and the failure to work steadily but as the cornerstone of a legal order. "Taxonomy of Poverty," the chapter's first section, reveals how reformers, social scientists, and journalists organized the tramp's figure into three general categories — criminal, indigent, and mobile. Highly visible and heavily reported in newspapers and magazines, the tramp was a constant reminder of the dangers accompanying urbanization and industrialization. However, as the chapter's second part reveals, tramps would resist these characterizations in the newspaper the *"Hobo" News,* published in St. Louis and Cincinnati but widely available in Chicago, and at the Hobo College, brainchild of physician-to-the-poor Ben Reitman. In the process, they inserted their voices into a conversation about poverty that was already crowded with industrialists, social reformers, journalists, judges, and policymakers. By rejecting compulsory autonomy and spurning criminal joblessness and homelessness, tramps challenged the merits of the claims made by reformers, social scientists, and journalists. The chapter's final section examines how these views of poverty were formalized on the Municipal Court of Chicago and in the pages of *The Report of City Council Committee on Crime.*[7] By folding social claims about work into law, the courts and the crime committee embraced claims about the criminalization of joblessness. In the process, they endorsed compulsions that were already spelled out in vagrancy law and in the presumptive equality of the liberty of contract — that men work steadily and provide a stable home — and that predicated these allegiances on a larger order.

TAXONOMY OF POVERTY

Chicago was a point of departure, return, and settlement for white men without steady work and stable homes in the second half of the nineteenth century. Whereas the Civil War amplified their ordeals and cast them as free laborers remediating the nation's slave past, the 1871 Fire and 1873 Panic would curb that promise and point to the ways the absence of steady work disparaged them and marked them as tramps.[8] Chicago's post-Fire rebuilding concentrated this degradation. The *New York Times* described "paupers who would not even do the work offered to them," as men who had lost all "sense of the degradation usually attach[ed] to absolute and involuntary dependence."[9] To elaborate upon this low status, reformers, social scientists, and journalists deployed a taxonomy of poverty that focused on three figures — the criminal tramp, the indigent tramp, and the mobile tramp. Together they assembled a diversity of opinions about poverty; these opinions found common ground where they enlisted men to work steadily and maintain homes. From the perspective of jobless and homeless men — the targets of these enlistments — this aggregation of opinions would assume the authority of an order.

The Criminal Tramp

The figure of the modern tramp emerged as a legal category in the 1870s and was promptly criminalized. In the summer of 1876, *Harper's Weekly* announced that "dangerous stragglers have of late become a recognized class in our community," frequently "alarming women and children" who are "subject to these vagabonds."[10] *Scribner's Magazine* elaborated on this criticism in 1878, when it described "tramps" who "set forest fires and commit burglary and murder whenever it may be desirable."[11] These types of breathless indictments were also reflected in more concrete statements. Chicago police superintendent Michael Hickey cited 3,535 vagrancy arrests in 1877, leading him to complain that "tramps require the attention of police at all times."[12] That same year, Chicago lawmakers labeled dependent men a "danger to society" and sought to broaden the city's vagrancy law "to cover pretty much all varieties of the dangerous and vicious" and allow police to arrest "on sight without warrant."[13] Men who did not labor steadily were criminalized as tramps.

The tramp figure would transmit two conflicting views of work that divided journalists and other authorities.[14] The first view was that they were a threat and that communities needed to bolster their laws to punish them and to protect women and children from them. "The law appears to be almost helpless against them," *Harper's Weekly* lamented in 1876.[15] *Harper's* reiterated this claim six months later when it reported on the "incipient criminality" of jobless men, which it claimed had increased "within [the past] three to four years." The magazine then detailed a new antitramp law, which included a workhouse "where they will be compelled to support themselves."[16] In Chicago in 1892, Mayor Hampstead Washburne claimed that the vagrancy laws were "so faulty as to impede conviction" and that they protected jobless men "at the expense of the property and perhaps the lives of the decent and reputable citizens."[17] The following year, police chief Robert McClaughry demanded a new ordinance, explaining, "Scores of well-known crooks are coming to the city, but we cannot arrest them [because] we cannot prove them thieves."[18] Journalists bemoaned Chicago's status as a "Tramp Mecca" one month after the World's Columbian Exposition closed.[19] In 1896, Chief McClaughry imagined a new legal solution in which "those unwilling to work should be imprisoned and compelled to work and kept at it until the habit [of not working] is broken."[20] According to this first view, existing laws punishing the homeless and jobless needed to be strengthened.

The second view, which conflicted with the first, was that it was nearly impossible to distinguish between the marauding, criminal tramp and the hapless, unemployed workingmen who sought work. The latter figure was venerated in *Harper's Weekly* as missing work "even more than the money he earns by it."[21] How were authorities to identify and punish those who, in the words of *Scribner's Magazine* editor Josiah Gilbert Holland, "would not work at any wages if they could" when they looked just like those who *would* work at any wage if they could?[22] According to journalist Samuel Leavitt, this failure to distinguish between the two figures fostered "total unconsciousness" of the "misery" experienced by the "poorer classes"; he describes an obligation to help the jobless clean up and find food rather than to force them to perform hard labor, as was required by Illinois law.[23] Reformers the Reverend William Stead and Jane Addams endorsed Leavitt's view that some workers need to be protected, possibly reflecting the influence of English reformer Charles Booth, whose landmark 1887 English survey graded London's poor from worthy to unworthy, from Class A to Class D.[24]

Formal calls from lawmakers to "get up some work for these idle hands" drowned out this ambiguity — that idea that not all men without work were the same.[25] Ohio put tramps on chain gangs. Towns in New Jersey deported the homeless by enticing them into empty railroad cars at night, sealing the cars, and then towing them to the remote corners of the state. Wisconsin and California even threatened unemployed men with a public whipping — a practice that only recently had been used to punish enslaved men and women.[26] *Scribner's Magazine* editor Josiah Gilbert Holland argued that a job seeker "has no rights but those which the society may see fit of its grace to bestow upon him" and "no more rights than the sow which wallows in the gutter." He proposed servitude or banishment as punishment for chronic unemployment and homelessness, mirroring existing state-level proposals.[27] His approach also reflected a recent notorious Supreme Court opinion in which Justice Roger Taney asserted that different people could have different statuses — that an individual "might justly and lawfully be reduced to slavery for his benefit."[28] Relief and Aid Society administrators Nathaniel Fairbanks and Turlington Walker (T. W.) Harvey — operating in Illinois and Chicago — aligned with this view when they classified the jobless as criminal, unworthy of aid.[29]

The Indigent Tramp

Reformers, social scientists, and journalists employed the expert tools of social science — empirical and verifiable observation — to support their claims that tramps were permanently indigent. Pioneering sociologist William Graham Sumner argued in *What Social Classes Owe Each Other* that it was every man's duty "to take care of himself and his family." Sumner rejected all forms of aid, including public assistance to the poor, which he considered a "siege" on the propertied and a tax on their "rightful earnings."[30] Marginal men and women, their families, and anyone else in the "gutter," Sumner reasoned coldly, are "just where [they] ought to be."[31] Yale University's Francis Wayland echoed this view in a speech he gave to the Social Science Association in 1877. Branding poverty an intractable and systematic "problem," Wayland described three aid proposals — distribute taxes through paid municipal officers, distribute taxes through a municipal board, and collect and distribute voluntary donations; he considered only the latter viable. That option, Wayland explained, discouraged the "idea [that] the state [or government] is responsible for the idle poor" and rejected "indiscriminate giving," which he considered a "danger to society."[32] The poor were "unfit" and "degenerate" by individual choice, Wayland reasoned, and not because of structural forces: "technological change and the erratic demand for labor within American industry."[33] In fact, as historian of American social sciences Dorothy Ross asserted, and as Sumner and Wayland would substantiate, poverty — which presented in the late nineteenth century as an individual flaw — was crucial to new system of knowledge making.[34] This knowledge — Robert Park, renowned sociologist and one-time secretary to Booker T. Washington, pointed out — was crucial not only to the study of the city but also to the intervention into it.[35]

Studies deepened popular, social scientific understanding of the tramp figure and strengthened claims about his indigence. Trinity College sociologist J. J. McCook published his "tramp census" in 1893 amid a deep, nationwide economic panic.[36] The study, among the first of its kind, offered homeless men accommodations in exchange for their responses to survey questions. This important early composite defined the tramp figure as young, healthy, skilled, mobile, literate, and law-abiding — qualities that were replicated in late nineteenth-century Chicago police arrest records.[37] Ten years after the publication of McCook's study, in 1903, Chicago reformer Alice Solenberger began collecting information for her study *One Thousand Homeless Men,* which she published in 1911. All of those studied were men who visited the Chicago Bureau of Charities.[38] The thousand men Solenberger studied shared demographic properties with McCook's tramps, including age, marital status, and skill level; they also were largely young, unmarried, and unskilled.[39] While her study would announce a social benefit to the empirical study of joblessness and homelessness — to restore tramps to self-sufficiency — it would also reveal that the tramp demographic, at least in the Northeast and Midwest, was relatively stable.

McCook's and Solenberger's empirical studies would also advocate solutions to the poverty they defined. McCook advised police to stop opening their stations to homeless men in times of turbulent weather. However, it was not clear that this recommendation — which deprived jobless men of access to facilities that sociologist Walter Wyckoff described as containing a "coiling mass of reeking humanity" — necessarily inspired the greater autonomy that social scientists desired or just left vulnerable men out in the cold.[40] A half dozen years later, the Improved Housing Association of Chicago described how city police stations continued to house lodgers: approximately 163,000 annually and 7,000 a night in severe winter weather.[41] McCook also promoted a new registration system, by which tramps were permitted to travel only after obtaining a stamp in a personal passbook. This strategy of conspicuous surveillance involving passbooks or discharge papers, which resembled practices commonly applied to freedmen in the southern states after the Civil War and to Mexican and Chinese migrant workers along the Pacific coast in the late nineteenth century, reflected an overriding commitment to the presumptive criminalization of indigence.[42]

Building on English reformer Charles Booth's characterizations, Alice Solenberger distinguished between the "worthy" — temporarily dependent men who "could again become self-sufficient" — and the "unworthy" — "parasite[s]" and "chronic beggar[s], local vagrant[s, or] wanderer[s]."[43] In their everyday practice, however, marginal men would frustrate this distinction. Solenberger recalls the confession of one jobless man, "overcome" — in her words — by "some odd streak of honesty." "I have this peg leg," the anonymous man began, "and I could get work enough any time, without any help from you folks . . . if I wanted to, but I don't. You've treated me white so I thought it wouldn't be honest not to tell you, but there's no use pretending I'm going to give up drinking, the way I promised you and go back to work, for I'm not."[44] "He was apparently good to his word," Solenberger recorded; "Within a week he was reported to the office as begging."[45] In another exchange, a Bureau of Charities worker implored a man to think of the future and encouraged him "to take the ice [cutting] work, on the grounds he could save a little money if he did so." The ice cut from the lake, which refrigerated meat shipped from Chicago's slaughterhouses, was often grossly polluted; its putrescence was known to overwhelm workers, historian William Cronon explained.[46] Crucially, the exchange brought the anonymous jobless man and Solenberger into conflict over the purpose of steady work. "What should I save for?" he reportedly asked her:

> I don't need to. I have no one but myself to look after. If I was a married man and had children it would be different. A man with a family *ought* to work all the year 'round. . . . I'm real sorry to disappoint you, Miss, since you seem so set on the idea of me working on the ice, but to tell you the truth I really wouldn't think it was *right* to do it. I'd just be taking the work away from some poor fellow who needs it, and it wouldn't be right for a man to do that when he has plenty of money in his pocket.[47]

For figures such as Solenberger and McCook, the indigence framed explanations as it justified interventions.

The Mobile Tramp

Mobility constituted a third branch in the taxonomy of poverty that reinforced structures of poverty. In their studies, social scientists depicted lone men in search of work, living in philanthropic hotels, cheap lodging houses, or hobo jungles, as occupying spaces without women.[48] In these spaces, absences — of women, of breadwinning, of home — encoded "perversion" as a byproduct of mobility.[49] According to the *Social Evil in Chicago* — which called for a morals court to regulate women's sexual practices — male prostitutes were dangerous for the same reasons as female prostitutes: they threatened a domestic order characterized by "virtuous" wives, healthful homes, and cared-for children.[50] But the commission would also claim that male sex workers were distinct for at least two other reasons. First, they failed to perform steady work. Second, it accused them of being feminine: of forming surreptitious "colonies," of preaching men's nonassociation with women, and of "affecting the carriage, mannerism, and speech of women" they were otherwise enlisted to protect.[51] This gender arithmetic combined two principal duties of manhood, linking the prescribed duties of husband and father with the equally prescribed duties of breadwinner and then imposing both on men who clearly demonstrated little interest in either.

Several of these claims were replicated in case studies, in which social scientists identified "perversion" as a counterpoint to "the purity and wholesomeness of the normal sexual relations" and then argued that mobility — or the road — facilitated "depravity."[52] The case studies that sociologist Nels Anderson compiled in the early 1920s echoed the claims of the vice commission a decade earlier by identifying homosexuality as a feature that distinguished communities of homeless and jobless men. Anderson described young men who sought out the protection of older men, or "wolves," while on the road, and he depicted instances of solicitation, of male rape in hobo jungles, and what he considered exaggerated effeminate behavior, along with instances of consensual sex between men, which he characterized as foreign and abnormal. Anderson's histories also suggested that mobility undermined men's ability to perform the duties of a breadwinner. He described how men who held multiple same-sex relationships on the road would often live informally with women for long periods when they settled and worked steadily or returned to the heterosexual patterns of the family farm.[53] In Anderson's accounts, the search for work was at the root of the sexual instability he ascribed to jobless men; it propelled them through sites — the road, the jungle, and the park. Reproducing the claims of the vice commission, he argued that it took them away from the home and the family to places that were devoid of women and lacked the steady jobs that made them chaste. But at the same time, this mythic road, infused with "perversion" and freighted with sorrow, was crucial. It connected these men to the work and camps that populated the nation's vast West, where resource extraction carried the promise of settlement and domestic duty, even temporarily, among the uprooted. Alongside claims of criminality and indigence, mobility — expressed through sexual practices and through the road — would help to justify compulsory autonomy. As with men classified as indigent, criminal, or mobile, the liberty-of-contract doctrine — based on a presumption of equality — would trigger important questions when applied to populations made unequal by "perversion" or mobility, populations characterized by reformers, social scientists, and journalists as fundamentally different.

HOBOHEMIA

By the early twentieth century, the "down and out of West Madison" Street rejected a taxonomy of poverty that defined them as criminals and indigents.[54] The region along West Madison Street, between Desplaines and Jefferson Streets, housed Chicago's Hobohemia: the social, economic, and cultural hub to the city's jobless population in the opening decades of the twentieth century.[55] Appointed with parks, saloons, and its own college, Hobohemia was a flexible — but prominent — urban space that catered to a sizable settled "home guard" and also accommodated hundreds of thousands of "migratory men" who passed through it each year.[56] In Hobohemia, joblessness, itinerancy, and homelessness were shared attributes that substantiated a larger community through claims to belonging in that community. The "contested" geographical and ideological territories generated by jobless and homeless men in Hobohemia recall the resistance they practiced from the late nineteenth century in response to compulsions they interpreted in claims made by reformers, socials scientists, and journalists.[57]

Historians locate the genesis of the tramp in the Civil War, which instituted new, sweeping commitments to wage work and equipped men without work with survival skills, such as foraging for food, traveling in small groups, setting up temporary camps, and enduring extreme weather, hunger, and loneliness.[58] The Chicago Fire of 1871 and the economic Panic of 1873 only compounded wartime pressures — to work, forage, roam, and prevail — while it enlisted free labor into battles over aid in the city. Journalists would describe jobless men in the labor presses in the 1870s as road-weary "lost sons" who were excluded from relief services reserved for married men with children. At work sites, these figures might encounter informal seniority systems that protected the jobs of breadwinners and "provided for the laying off of single men during depression periods."[59] Recalling particularly bleak conditions in the winter of 1875, one anonymous subscriber, "hopelessly in search of work," described life outside the formal wage-work economy as "footsore, heartsick, shivering in the bleak winds of a severe winter."[60] In contrast to the social scientists, reformers, and journalists who recorded criminal dependency, labor presses tended to register heartbreak. "The world is a desert to us. I have no friends," an anonymous itinerant complained. "I have no roof to live under, no table to eat at, no clothes to distinguish me from thieves."[61] Elsewhere, men described life on the road in search of work as lonely and isolating. "I wish I was a married man," a young miner outside Braidwood, Illinois, admitted, recounting the incentives available to married men.[62] Men without jobs and homes experienced the aches of poverty and isolation acutely and — as described in the labor presses — often alone.

By the end of the nineteenth century, poverty was increasingly an urban experience. In *The Workers,* his classic 1897 study, Princeton University sociologist Walter Wyckoff observed the powerful allure of the city — and the fearful isolation many found within it — while traveling through Chicago: "The men are not physically incapable of work, nor are they habitually tramps, nor yet the beggars of the pavements. . . . By an attraction which is apparently irresistible to them they are drawn to congested labor markets, and there they cling, preferring instinctively a life of want and squalor in fellowship with their kind to one of comparative plenty in the intolerable loneliness of the country."[63] Job seekers on the West Side's Hobohemia, a region that sociologist Nels Anderson disparaged as "Chicago to the down and out," would also exchange comfort for community.[64] If Hobohemia was organized internally by scarcity, precariousness, and mobility, it was shaped externally by the patronage of philanthropists such as James Eads How, who established the International Brotherhood Welfare Association (IBWA) in 1905 to help the urban poor.[65] How, who famously traded his economic privilege for a rootless existence, would devote his time and energies to aiding men without homes and jobs.[66]

If Hobohemia provided a community from which jobless men could resist the structures of poverty, the Hobo College would institutionalize and invigorate that resistance. The Hobo College, born of Ben Reitman's 1907 stopover in St. Louis, grew out of his desire "to do something to stop the police and the sheriff from picking up men and sending them to jail for vagrancy."[67] Originally named the "Reitman College for Vagrants," the college's aims were twofold: to "show society that the vagrant is a large part of it" and to demonstrate "that he can be made a useful member by education." Targeting "habitual vagrants *only*" — men defined by the Relief and Aid Society as ineligible for assistance and men excluded from the progressive rehabilitation schemes championed by social scientists such as McCook and Solenberger — Reitman imagined a two-week matriculation in which students who lived "room and board free" would "learn their lessons" from experts who reflected facets of the world job seekers encountered.[68] The original plan for Reitman's college built out from the ordeals and obstacles experienced by the urban poor and rejected their criminalization.

When the Hobo College officially opened in 1908, Reitman ran it. Historians point out that it quickly became a staple of Hobohemia and "always remained on or close to West Madison," with a footprint "large enough to accommodate one hundred persons."[69] Surviving accounts bring these facilities to life. University of Chicago student Charles Allen reported in 1923 that its entrance was marked by an "almost indiscernible sign with the words: United Brotherhood College printed on it, and over [those] words scribbled — 'Hobo College.'"[70] In 1917, journalist Harry Beardsley described the college's interior spaces, including "a narrow staircase [that led] from the street to [a] second floor," with a "lounging room" and an IBWA office where "the IWW [International Workers of the World] congregate to discuss the labor question." A second "circular and narrow" staircase, Beardsley recalled, led to a third

Figure 2.1. Ben Reitman, circa 1910–1915. Bain Collection, Library of Congress, Prints and Photographs Division, LC-DIG-ggbain-12108.

floor that boasted an auditorium "with calico curtains, a stove, a piano and a hundred or so camp chairs"; it was walled off from a "dining hall–library–kitchen" area where "meals are served at cost" and reading material is made available.[71]

Descriptions of its curriculum survive as well. It included classes in economics for workers, public speaking, English composition, literature, and law — the latter a class in which jobless men were "taught the [vagrancy] statutes in various states and cities, and [were] informed of new legislation which affected them."[72] This focus on the poor and jobless replicated the original ambition of Reitman's "College for Vagrants." And by the end of its first decade, its focus would remain on those sent to jail for violating vagrancy law. "The great flaw in the average vagrancy legislation," municipal court judge Harry M. Fisher explained in a lecture he gave at the college in spring 1917, "lies in the fact that the law punishes individuals not for the actual omission or commission of any act, but for being in a condition, which in many cases the individual cannot help."[73] By contrast, the college's curriculum and its physical spaces reflected an overall commitment to addressing the structures of poverty that impacted all marginal men.

The *"Hobo" News* — an eclectic sixteen-page circular containing poems, essays, travelogues, columns, and editorials praising the jobless that was printed weekly — represents a second plank in jobless men's repudiation of structures of poverty.[74] Copies sold for ten cents; sellers kept half. "You got to catch their eye," one enterprising peddler explained. "If you catch their eye, you got them."[75] Its most crucial function, however, was as a forum where provisionally employed men discussed the criminality, indigence, and mobility that they experienced as an order.[76]

In the *News,* mobility — the road — was not deviant but was dignified as earnest roaming. In E. J. Irvine's words:

In every land but Russia, You meet him on the street
  A lean and hungry creature, With swollen, weary feet
He'll split his last crust with you, He'll rise to heights untold
  Yet on the auction block of life, This son of God is sold.[77]

Columnists such as Louis Young disputed the claims outlined by reformers, social scientists, and journalists, announcing, "It seems to be
taking the average person a long time to learn that the hobo is not
a bum or a lazy shiftless person" but a job seeker.[78] W. B. Lamb announced, "We are the salt of the earth!"[79] Poet Henry Knibbs argued
that poverty was ennobling:

> We are the true nobility!
>> Sons of rest and outdoor air!
> Knights of the tie and rail are we!
>> Lightly meandering everywhere.[80]

According to the jobless, performing work—steady employment—was "of questionable value" and probably criminal. In the
"Hobo" News, itinerant men struck out against attempts to criminalize
joblessness. *News* journalist J. J. O'Connell called on "every intelligent
worker" to denounce the compulsion to work steadily and instead "to
think and act for the uplift of his class" and "voice his opinions on the
economic and political field for that purpose."[81] Wage work was really
"wage slavery," journalist Dan O'Brien explained in the *News,* and as
such a "violation of natural liberties" that degraded the jobless.[82] Sociologist Nels Anderson recalled having an elderly itinerant explain
to him that wage work actually hurt workers: "If you go out and work
for thirty cents an hour all you do is add one more man to the boss'
cause. That is what they want."[83] When the University of Chicago Press
published Anderson's master's thesis as a book, *The Hobo,* in the early
1920s, it was roundly criticized in the *News.*[84] It turned out that the
News did not need Anderson's book to interpret laws governing wage
work. "How much justice do we find when the waged working class
of this country enjoys NO LEGALLY RECOGNIZED RIGHT to work for a
living," *News* journalist D. H. Horn explained, "and yet our politicians
make it a crime of VAGRANCY when a man, through no fault of his
own, is without work and without food?"[85] Work "as performed today
under our present industrial system," columnist Bill Quirks argued, "is

degrading and demoralizing," a subterfuge. "Who is it," he asked, "that howls most about the 'dignity of labor?'"[86]

Quirks's critique responded to the structures of poverty generally and to Warren Harding's presidential campaign specifically. Recorded on the front page of the *News,* Quirks argued that Harding's pledge to "return to normalcy" in 1920 read more like a plan to eliminate valuable wartime labor benefits.[87] "How full of promise were those rhapsodies about the new world of labor," Elmer T. Allison wrote in the summer of 1920, adding that "conditions ha[d] grown more precarious" since. Allison proposed that instead of working more often, the provisionally employed should work less: "Let us enjoy the world we have made," Allison pleaded, "instead of making it a . . . hell for ourselves."[88] Quirks was probably also responding to labor unions, such as the Chicago Federation of Labor, which refused common cause with precariously employed men in the 1910, announcing, "An itinerant toiler must go his own way."[89] Pamphleteer Roger Payne instructed the provisionally employed to make their work reflect their grievances by working one day each week and then "living" the other six — to embrace "our true inheritance of dignity and leisure."[90]

The claims of social scientists, reformers, and journalists who assembled structures of poverty were all wrong, the *News,* the college, and the provisionally employed announced; it was work that degraded, not its absence. In the process, they rejected the taxonomy of poverty that itemized and criminalized practices associated with joblessness, indigence, and mobility. It was with these same claims that they rejected the liberty-of-contract doctrine that only appeared to deepen and substantiate their inequality — expressed most succinctly through their failure to work steadily and maintain a home.

COURT AND COMMISSION

When the Municipal Court of Chicago opened in 1906, poor and migrant men and women would discover an institution animated by the structures of poverty developed by reformers, social scientist, and journalists. With the new court, Chicago police chief John Collins envisioned a new "way to imprison or drive from the city the hoards [*sic*] of disreputables against whom no specific charge can be evidenced by police." They "may not be doing much harm to the community," Chief Collins acknowledged in 1905, but he added that they are "certainly doing no good."[91] Chief Justice Harry Olson envisioned the criminal poor — "scum" and loafers — working out their terms on the rock pile.[92] The *Tribune*, which agitated for more intervention through vagrancy law, brooded when a new law went into effect and the poor did not instantly flee.[93] Police Chief Leroy Steward, who succeeded Collins, pledged to "sweep the city streets" of vagrants and to "strengthen the methods of former crusades." He would propose that police track the movement and habits of jobless men through "vag" reports — encouraging the same formal oversight of male dependency as the Chicago City Council Committee on Crime would a few years later.[94] In fact, the pressure on formal authority could be intense. But as judges struggled to square compulsory autonomy with the conditions of precarity the jobless experienced, they found it difficult to articulate a legal justification that stressed individual responsibility for the conditions of the labor market. Annoyed, journalists responded by accusing judges of being "unduly tender in the administration of vagrancy law."[95]

Vagrancy prosecutions, which the court standardized into a checklist, would also reveal variability in the court's prosecution of the poor. Municipal court judges processing vagrancy cases used the Vagabond Information by Individual form. The form itemized the twelve components of the city's existing vagrancy law that punished joblessness, outdoor lodging, idleness, drunkenness, and lounging, among other things. The components also neatly resembled distinctions expressed by social scientists, reformers, and journalists. The court's twelve-item checklist:

Vagabond Information by Individual
(1)   Was an idle and dissolute person and went about begging
(2)   Used juggling and other unlawful games and toys

(3) Was a runaway

(4) Was a pilferer

(5) Was a confidence man

(6) Was a common drunkard

(7) Was a common night walker

(8) Was a lewd, wonton and lascivious person in speech and behavior

(9) Was a common brawler

(10) Was habitually neglectful of his employment and calling and did not lawfully provide for himself and for the support of his family

(11) Was an idle and dissolute person and neglected all lawful business and habitually misspent his time by frequenting houses of ill fame, gaming houses and tippling shops

(12) Lodges in and was found in the nighttime in (a) an outhouse; (b) open air without giving a good assessment of himself.[96]

Checklist item 10 — "habitually neglectful of his employment and calling and did not lawfully provide for himself and for the support of his family" — operated as a catchall category for compulsory work. It also marked local commitments to the liberty-of-contract doctrine that stressed compulsion over choice. Theodore Ryanovsky, Henry Geloss, and Edward McNamara felt this compulsion intimately; each was arrested for vagrancy in the mid-1910s because he did not have a job. Court records also reveal that John Williams and G. Reed (full name not listed) were arrested around the same time; in their cases, each was without a stable home. Although the vagrancy charges were facially equivalent in each instance, they would generate sentences that differed widely. Seventeen-year-old Theodore Ryanovski was arrested previously for larceny and sentenced to serve six months.[97] Henry Geloss, an unemployed eighteen-year-old, was sentenced to thirty days.[98] Edward McNamara waived his right to a jury, pled not guilty, and had his case dismissed.[99] Williams and Reed, who were arrested together for homelessness in April 1914 — accused of sleeping in a "barn and not homes during the night" — were tried separately. For reasons the transcripts do not reveal, Williams was sentenced to six months, and Reed

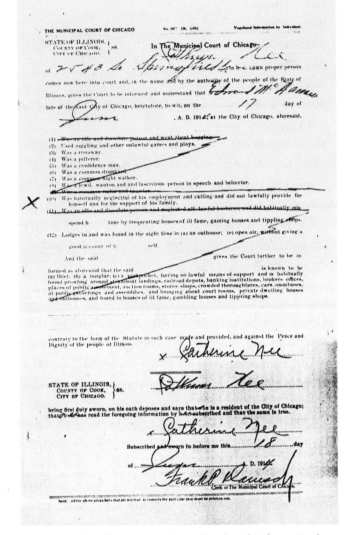

Figure 2.2. Edward McNamara's 1914 Vagabond Information by Individual form reveals how the municipal court standardized vagrancy law by itemizing its twelve separate parts. According to this form, McNamara violated line item 10, being "habitually neglectful of his employment and calling and . . . not lawfully provid[ing] for himself and for the support of his family." Municipal Court of Chicago, Vagabond Information by Individual, Clerk of the Circuit Court of Cook County Archives.

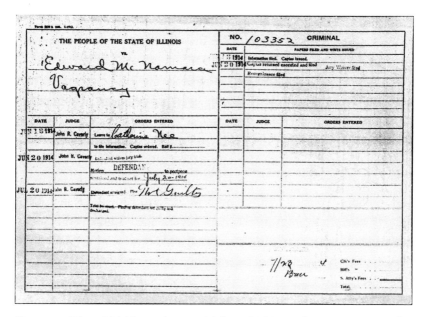

Figure 2.3. Edward McNamara's 1914 trial form. McNamara's sparse case record
lists the dates of his arrests, the charge, the presiding judge, and the verdict.
Municipal Court of Chicago, Case Number 103352, *People of the State of Illinois v.
Edward McNamara*, Clerk of the Circuit Court of Cook County Archives.

was sentenced to three months.[100] The variable sentences handed Ryanovski, Geloss, and McNamara for joblessness and Williams and Reed
for homelessness testify to variability — rather than uniformity — in the
legal punishment of men who failed to become autonomous through
work; in allotting culpability, judges would conflate culpability with
status regardless of guilt.

Court records also suggest that municipal court judges who con-
flated "idleness" with "dissolution" — each a key concept of vagrancy
law — also struggled to distinguish between the two. John Covey, who
was "shown by the evidence to be a gambler" — suggesting he was more
"dissolute" than "idle," perhaps — challenged his March 1913 municipal
court vagrancy conviction. The Illinois Court of Appeals found that
because Covey was not "idle" — he owned property, supported his family, and paid his bills — it was impossible for him to also be a vagrant.[101]

At the same time, Chicago pickpocket William O'Keefe also engaged in a practice that was perhaps more "dissolute" than "idle"; he appealed his March 1913 vagrancy conviction. In the case, the Illinois Court of Appeals clarified its rule on vagrancy, declaring it "incumbent on [the accused] to show, if he c[an], that he ha[s] lawful means of support."[102] According to this revision, O'Keefe's sin was not his swift sleights of hand but his joblessness. In 1915, David Miller and Ed Brown were each arrested for vagrancy. Afterward, William Callahan — who is identified in the court's records as a "business agent" worth a substantial ten thousand dollars — posted bail for both Miller and Brown. Despite their shared surety and joint arrest, they experienced different outcomes. Miller pled "not guilty," and charges against him were dismissed. Ed Brown pled "not guilty," but he was fined and sentenced to thirty days. The lower court's sparse trial records offer no explanation for the different trial outcomes.[103] But the unpredictable sentencing experienced by Miller and Brown was not unusual. Simon K. Ohzut, who listed his personal wealth at a considerable twenty thousand dollars, bailed out Harry Morris and Harry Jacobs after they were arrested for sleeping in a privy.[104] Both men were found "not guilty" of vagrancy. However, in the trials of Morris and Jacobs and of Miller and Brown, records suggest that judges overlooked the role of wealthy sureties: men who pledged enormous sums to resolve modest crimes and who may have employed the accused in an illicit capacity. Navigating the complicated terrain of low-level crime, municipal court judges struggled to encase poverty in legal language restricted to work and housing. Instead, the court would criminalize and punish all expressions of male dependency — regardless of its relationship to wage work — with short jail terms, small fines, and swift prosecutions. In effect, according to liberty-of-contract doctrine — which also defined men as economic agents — the compulsion to autonomy that inspired reformers, social scientists, and journalists played an important role in the prosecution of lower-level crime.

A mass trial of impoverished men in 1922 exemplifies this economic thrust — detailed in the taxonomy of poverty — and the modest judicial outcome it generated. Sociologist Nels Anderson recorded one occasion describing a visit to a Chicago courtroom in the summer of 1922. "Bring 'em all in," Anderson recorded Judge Joseph LaBuy instructing his bailiff on a late-August morning: "Empty the hull pen. Let's get this thing over with." According to Anderson, the "down and outs of West Madison" Street — men squalid, raw, and exhausted from their night penned in a putrid, crowded cell — spilled into the courtroom. LaBuy swore them in collectively and then asked, "How many of you are working men?" When nobody responded, he rephrased the question, "Is there anyone here that's not a working man?" A defendant of Polish descent, whom Anderson thought might have misunderstood the question, raised his hand. LaBuy "dismissed [him] with a warning." He then asked, "How many of you men will go to work?" Noting that the first guy got to leave, after the second question "every hand went up." LaBuy dismissed all the anonymous men with orders to find steady work. Jail, he added, awaited them the next time they entered his courtroom.[105] LaBuy's cavalier, anonymous justice — which points to the ease with which judges punished the poor and the ease with which the poor eventually escaped — serialized the legal commitment to compulsory labor. This rodeo justice, which cost untold numbers of men their freedom, if only for one night, premised detention on an unquestioned compulsion, which the court and its judges had drunk in fully.

As municipal court judges discovered, it was easier than punishing men who failed to provide for their dependent wives and children. In a court where some men had their cases processed by bailiff (and future Chicago mayor) Anton J. Cermak, figures such as thirty-seven-year-old George Bowing, who was a painter for Marshall Field's Department Store, and twenty-five-year-old Charles Matter, a teamster and foreman who no longer lived with his wife and two children, were charged on separate occasions with contributing to the dependency of their respective wives and children.[106] At the Court of Domestic Relations of the municipal court, men like Bowing and Matter were typically put on probation — Illinois passed an adult probation law in 1911 — and ordered to make weekly maintenance payments if they wanted to stay out of jail.[107] This was the case for Fred Schultz, a thirty-nine-year-old unemployed paper cutter, and Nicholas Wagner, a thirty-seven-year-old tinsmith. Both were arrested in separate incidents, convicted of "knowingly and willfully abiding, abetting, and contributing to a state of dependency of certain children," and given probation with weekly mandatory maintenance payments.[108] But in some cases not even probation could compel autonomy. Five months after he was given probation and ordered to make regular maintenance payments in August 1914, Nicholas Wagner was still without work. At the same time, his fourteen-year-old son, Leo, was living in a boys' workhouse, and his sixteen-year-old daughter, Catherine, was living in the House of the Good Shepherd — a private Catholic charity that sheltered young sex workers.[109] The court, Judge Goodnow admitted, had "failed to [make Nicholas] do anything for his children."[110]

Along with the municipal court, the 1915 *Report of the City Council Committee on Crime* ratified structures of poverty, adopting into a major report the informal views developed by social scientists, reformers, and journalists. Chaired by University of Chicago political scientist and city alderman Charles Merriam, the committee on crime physically bridged formal and informal expressions of authority. Assembled in response to a perceived crime spike, the report represented a deep faith in the capacity of city leaders to resolve issues stemming from rapid urbanization, such as crime, joblessness, and homelessness.[111]

The report's foremost finding — that "professional criminals" were dangerous and pervasive — led it to endorse a popular distinction between criminal and noncriminal classes and then to insist that criminals be punished. In the process, it reinforced reformers', social scientists', and journalists' claims that the problem with the poor was that they failed to be autonomous.[112] The report promoted the expanded use of vagrancy law. In fact, its second "Principle Recommendation" was that officials use vagrancy law more often to "arrest and convict" professional criminals and break the "crime trust": "There is no doubt," the report boasted, that "practically the entire body of criminals who now *infest* the city would be driven out."[113] In addition, it equated the jobless with crime and proposed that the provisionally employed be removed from Chicago immediately. Because criminals refused to work — or "engage in steady industry" — the committee reasoned, a law compelling work "would be the most effective way of ridding the town of the habitual criminals who commit 90% of the crime."[114] Once again, steady work empowered officials to oversee the practices of others. It was in this vein that the report supported a passbook scheme, similar to that promoted by Chicago journalists a few years earlier and by sociologist J. J. McCook a generation earlier, in which officials maintain a "card system" to track and record "all the suspicious characters."[115] The consequence was to regulate the movement of classes deemed suspicious.

The report, which singled out vagrancy, joblessness, and mobility — each a potent but also abstract and ill-defined category in its own right — argued that the poor were overcriminalized and "more liable" to arrest and conviction because they did not have access to money or attorneys.[116] Although this analysis ratified the report's principal finding that Chicago was overrun by "professional" criminals, the conception of poverty it identified also reflected criticism printed in the *"Hobo" News,* debated at the Hobo College, and summarized by journalists Samuel Leavitt in the 1880s and Walter Wyckoff in the 1890s that economic precarity is structural: "Unsanitary housing and working conditions, unemployment, wages inadequate to maintain a human standard of living, inevitably produce the crushed or distorted bodies and minds from which the army of crime is recruited. The crime problem is not merely a question of police and courts, it leads to the broader problems of public sanitation education, home care, a living wage, and industrial democracy."[117] However, while the jobless and homeless men moderated ground-level debates over scarcity, the *News* and the Hobo College failed to articulate a meaningful solution to the economic conditions menial workers encountered. Although their court files are incomplete, the ordeals of "sureties" who may have been pimps, of homeless vagrants sleeping in privies who may have been prostitutes, and of the jobless who may have been experiencing breaks in the labor market point to a deeper set of shared understandings.

Joblessness, crime, dependency, and homelessness do not exist in isolation from each other but together as structures, as part of a comprehensive system that the impoverished experienced intensely. Impoverished men — or tramps — recognized this. Meanwhile, our persistent desire to view poverty as an individual flaw — as discrete rather than structural — reflects our continued refusal to come to terms with the ways that structures unite and divide people and the ways the impoverished experienced them: not as a liberty but as a compulsion that courts were willing to enforce.

CONCLUSION

Early twentieth-century juvenile dime novels depicted the perils of criminal joblessness, indigence, and mobility as reformers, social scientists, and journalists described them. Mass produced and widely consumed, Ray Livingston's popular "A No. 1" series epitomized this form. It cast tramps amid the pastoral and bucolic vistas of rural America — as bygone figures roaming bygone landscapes. The series — which adhered to autobiography, "tale-telling," or novel formats — presented folksy wanderers affecting a "smattering of hobo lingo" and platitudes and describing mishaps experienced while camping along roads or in railroad hubs.[118] For instance, *Hobo Camp Fire Tales,* published in 1911, narrates encounters with tramps on trains, in "jungles," and around campfires in brief thematic chapters, such as "How Pacific Jimmy Held up the Sheriff" and "The Tramp and the Owl."[119] But the series would also do more than imagine hobo places. By marketing hobo obsolescence to a mass audience, dime novels went beyond plain description to reinforce the message that even the most charming tramp is really just a criminal.[120] According to Livingston, the "best of tramps" suffer a "miserable" existence, "constantly hounded by the minions of the law."[121] In this way, the tramp becomes a cautionary tale, a model for how *not* to exist in an industrial economy. Unlike Livingston's fictional tramp, the taxonomy of poverty that reformers, social scientists, and journalists developed in post-Fire Chicago was anchored in the flesh and blood of individuals. Despite the apparent coherence of this taxonomy, however, Chicago's lower-court judges would struggle to square social statement with formal law. In their criminalization of poverty, they would endorse individual compulsions and overlook the structures they experienced and the liberties their inequality—their difference—prevented them from enjoying. The liberty-of-contract doctrine would only reinforce and replicate their status as failed economic actors.

The compulsory autonomy that criminalized joblessness would also compel women to be virtuous. When Mary Lewis took her husband, John Lewis, a forty-four-year-old mail driver, to court in 1914 to have him tried for his failure to support his family, John was put on probation and formally required to make weekly maintenance payments if he wanted to stay out of jail.[122] However, in upholding John's duty to provide for his dependent wife, the lower court announced that Mary was not expected to become self-sufficient through the labors *she* performed. According to this logic, the same order that compelled men—such as John—to autonomy also compelled women—such as Mary—to live virtuously, as dependents. As women flocked to Chicago in the late nineteenth century, where many pieced together tentative work and housing scenarios, they would encounter this compulsion to virtue. Their ordeals and the administration of their poverty through virtue are the subject of the next chapter.

3. Virtue: Trading in Sex and Wages

Society possesses a conventional standard whereby it judges all things. All men should be good, all women virtuous. Wherefore, villain, hast thou failed?

— Theodore Dreiser[1]

Mary Henning had been begging door to door in a Michigan Avenue neighborhood for three years before the reformers at the Chicago Bureau of Charities had her arrested in April 1900. Police charged her with vagrancy. In court, attorney Kate Kane, a well-known defender of the poor and among Chicago's most recognizable attorneys, represented Henning. Kane opted for a jury trial after the presiding judge, James Martin, rejected her argument that Henning could not be a vagrant because a "woman was not made to work." Alarmed, the judge cited examples of women who brought in washing to help support their households. His appeal, which contradicted Kane's claim, was futile. Kane instead explained to a jury that neither "history, custom, [nor] tradition" provided "one instance in which a woman was regarded as a being who had been created to work." She quoted lyrics from a popular song — "woman, woman, lovely woman" — and asked, "How could a 'lovely woman' be supposed to handle mortar on a cold day?"[2] She argued that women's wage work was unnatural — that it existed only because of man's "inability to provide for her." "Tradition showed that woman" was a not a laborer, Kane elaborated, but "a doll to be petted."[3]

Kane's legal strategy worked. The all-male jury of Mary Henning's putative peers agreed — a woman cannot be a vagrant because "she was not made to work" — and dismissed the vagrancy charge against her.[4] Astonishingly, in a case that involved the initiative of a destitute woman and the skill of a veteran female attorney, a jury accepted that dependency was women's true lot in life.[5] After the trial, Chicago attorney Catherine McCulloch accused Kane of single-handedly setting back the cause of equality of the sexes by spreading an argument Mc-

Culloch considered to be degrading, baseless, and "anti-suffrage."[6] But Kane was hardly a proponent of women's inequality.[7] Rather, by skillfully exploiting views about women's dependency in court — to free Henning and win her case — Kane exposed the distortions that were used to interpret women a century ago.

In the trial of Mary Henning, Kate Kane also revealed that the compulsion we use to interpret white women — virtue — are deepened and enhanced by the compulsions we use to interpret white men — autonomy. And as novelist Theodore Dreiser points out, together these compulsions identified subversions — or "villains" — that typically marked the impoverished when they failed to comply. From the perspective of women who worked for wages and traded in sex, these compulsions come together to form an order that shaped how they experienced life in the city.

Historians and legal scholars tend to describe Gilded Age and Progressive Era workingwomen as agents of urban life rather than victims of its penury and prostitution. This chapter builds on this view. In the process, it ratifies claims that employers and lawmakers used domestic obligations and duties to restrict workingwomen's rights, to degrade their status, and to confine their wage to a family economy.[8] It endorses assertions that marginal women regularly made economic and legal decisions and then acted on them.[9] Finally, it confirms depictions of young migrating women "adrift," acting like "delinquent daughters," or communing as members of a "sisterhood."[10] At the same time, these accounts also tend to isolate workingwomen from the structures of poverty described in this book. This chapter argues that virtue — which coordinated workingwomen's unpaid domestic work and justified their exclusion from wage earning — was the focal point of a larger order that these workers perceived and that managed the practices of all women who worked for wages outside the home. In this regard, virtue was not just about shuttering the Levee Vice District in 1912 — scattering vice geographies that at one time connected sex workers to clients, reformers, and lawmakers. It was not just about criminalizing the practices of women acting independently. And it was not just about policing bodies in the municipal court's Morals Court or empowering women to police men's practices in the Court of Domestic Relations. It was about all of these things. Virtue, as endorsed by reformers, social sciences, and journalists, had another important impact: it would ensure that the labors of female launderers, seamstresses, department store clerks, domestic workers, and factory employees — women who made up a growing segment of Chicago's workforce — remained cheap. In this way, gender distinctions — like virtue — might be understood to serve business interests, making high-minded morality into cover for low-wage enterprise.

Structures of poverty in Chicago developed on the backs of workingwomen and sex workers after the Great Fire would evolve to shape women's moral bearing in the early twentieth century. Although her use of the term "lovely lady" may have been subterfuge, in Kane's hands it also played into a larger conviction — that workingwomen should be virtuous. Theodore Dreiser's novel *Sister Carrie*, published the same year that Kane defended Henning in a Chicago courtroom, elaborates on the impact of virtue on city life. The novel catalogs Caroline Meeber's rise to fame — from low-wage toiler to celebrated actress — coordinated by contingencies: chance encounters, fortune, and serendipity. Just as literary depictions of the tramp figure corroborated the view that the jobless were degraded, Meeber's story might be understood to confirm the claims of workingwomen that virtue was not a condition of the workforce but rather of reformers', social scientists', and journalists' attempts to manage it. From the perspectives of the real-life Mary Henning and the fictitious Carrie Meeber, virtue ratified an order that stigmatizes women by connecting work outside the home to sexual "ruin" within it.[11] As this chapter shows, the correlation between wage work and "ruin" transcended fictitious and nonfictitious work sites and leisure sites to influence local law. As they did with jobless men, municipal court judges struggled to reconcile moral crimes with formal law, to fashion a stable, legal justification for virtue. Instead, they would endorse the blanket criminalization of "immoral" practices that jeopardized women's capacity to be virtuous. But they would also encourage wage work and hold out the promise of virtue for women who abandoned vice. This concession was too much for the reformers on the Committee of Fifteen, social workers in the Friendly Visitors program, and advocates for mothers' pensions, who complained about judicial leniency; they demanded more robust commitments to virtue. In the process, they revealed how authority shifted between formal and informal sites, from the claims of reformers, social scientists, and journalists to courts and commissions and then back again. They would also demonstrate — as Dreiser demonstrated, as tramps demonstrated — that virtue and the structures that it upheld were never inherent but always manufactured and in need of constant reinforcement and maintenance.

THE TAXONOMY OF RUIN

Sex defined workingwomen in the city. Sociologist J. J. McCook recorded jobless men describing prostitution as "God's arrangement" — a thing that "a man can't get along without."[12] According to "Boxcar Bertha" Thompson, the self-fashioned female hobo, sex was women's principal and most consequential labor.[13] Activists Elizabeth Gurley Flynn and Emma Goldman viewed sex as the basis of women's exploitation in the industrial economy.[14] White slave crusader Clifford Roe argued that immigrants were dangerous because they threatened women sexually.[15] The Catholics at House of the Good Shepherd, or "Magdalene Asylum," and the Protestants at the Erring Women's Refuge equated sex work with spiritual "ruin" and offered sanctuary to women who had "fallen."[16] The reformers at the Protective Agency for Women and Children who cared for workingwomen's physical well-being also emphasized their "ruin": "for the self-dependent girl to announce her shame is to weigh her hands and feet with lead, to take hope out of her heart, and to close the doors of homes to her all over the land."[17] The reformers of the Women's Christian Temperance Union argued that all vice, including sex work, was linked in the "the sacrifice of women's purity" and in the generation of "tempted and betrayed" women.[18] The imperiled bodies and souls of workingwomen justified a taxonomy of ruin distinguished from that imposed on tramps by its almost total focus on women's sexual conduct.

Depictions of ravaged virtue enticed journalists to stress the economic dimensions of workingwomen's "ruin." The reform-oriented newspaper *Chicago Inter Ocean* launched a series in the summer of 1887 titled the "Woes of Working Girls." "The road of a working girl is exceedingly slippery," the newspaper cautioned, explaining that young workingwomen "toil for a mere pittance day after day, and wear their lives out."[19] These front-page stories, which described women's work in moral terms, enlisted three "ruin" tropes. In the first scenario, workingwomen were prey. The paper describes a "young girl just over 16 years of age" who worked for a man who "flattered the girl." He kept her at work late one night, and "when she left she was ruined."[20] In the second scenario, workingwomen were dependent. The paper describes life outside the family economy as perilous, offering the experience of an anonymous young worker living away from home as evidence; unable to earn enough from her wages, she turned to sex work, which led to her "ultimate destruction."[21] In the third scenario, workingwomen were unsuccessful wives and mothers. This scenario is confirmed by the story of "a young woman" who left her jobless husband and began working for wages. She ultimately loses custody of her child after her husband convinces a judge that she is "employed in a store in which it was well known no woman who [i]s virtuous could work."[22] In the hands of reform-oriented journalists, these scenarios endorsed claims that wage work endangered women.

Workers Julia Burnhardt and Lyda Stinger deepened the *Inter Ocean*'s claims about the "woes of working girls." The *Inter Ocean* told the tragic story of thirteen-year-old Julia, who filled in for her father at a shop when he became ill. According to the daily, Julia's boss, Frank Mumford, a married man in his forties, began a sexual relationship with the child and took her on dates to museums; he was arrested only after a police officer spotted the two enter a "disreputable resort" together.[23] Despite compelling evidence of Mumford's predations, Chicago's courts were powerless to punish him; the law raising the age of consent from ten to fourteen was awaiting the governor's signature, and Julia's testimony that she "went along willingly" precluded an abduction charge. "There is no statute in the state of Illinois to punish a crime of this class," the *Tribune* lamented.[24] A second story, involving seventeen-year-old Lyda Stinger, came to light a year later, immediately after her body was retrieved from Lake Michigan. With no one to "watch over her and protect her," an *Inter Ocean* journalist explained, Lyda got pregnant with the child of Louis Michael, who subsequently abandoned her to "bear the consequence of their mutual shame alone." Sensing "disgrace and darkness ahead," the *Inter Ocean* reported, Lyda crept down to the lake.[25]

Like journalists, reformers also argued that moral "ruin" awaited women at work. As women flocked to jobs in late nineteenth-century Chicago, reformers' alarm ripened into a focus on working conditions and work's impact on women's moral and sexual bearing.[26] Social reformers imagined in the late 1890s that widespread unemployment was "driving helpless women into that vortex," toward a "worse fate than starvation," where they might be required to sell "sexual services on occasional nights for gifts or extra money." The most spectacular of these types of depictions had unemployed young women participating in the "nightly orgies of the maddened and dissolute," where they risked becoming "heartless, hardened, [and] irreclaimable wretch[es]" and not wives and mothers.[27] Even seemingly measured observers harbored these fears. Describing women's work as "honest and virtuous," federal labor commissioner C. D. Wright argued that despite a workingwoman's low status, it should "not be possible to classify her as the forgotten woman."[28] In the early twentieth century, Hull House founder Jane Addams interpreted work as an impediment to virtue that kept women from marriage, wrecked their health, weakened their charm, and diminished their desirability — making them more likely to "fall."[29] Addams lamented the case of an anonymous garment maker — perhaps not unlike Dreiser's Caroline Meeber — who, in the throes of desperation, "sold out for a new pair of shoes." Sex work, Addams avowed, was the "crowning disgrace of our civilization."[30]

In their studies, social scientists confirmed these accounts of "ruin." For instance, Chicago school sociologist Edith Abbott argued that historically women never became autonomous through work — instead it was a temporary station before marriage and the unpaid labors of child-rearing and housework.[31] In fact, social scientists would develop this point and elaborate on the relationship between virtue and needlework, domestic work, and department store work. Needlework, which employed roughly one-fifth of workingwomen in early twentieth-century Chicago, epitomized the moral hazard of paid employment, according to reformers, because it paid so little.[32] Its poverty wages, irregular hours, and terrible conditions prompted reformers such as Bertha Palmer, the wife of hotelier Potter Palmer, to independently fund a relief initiative in 1894 through Chicago's Emergency Relief Association. The association vowed to filter out "worthy women in want" — virtuous and moral workingwomen — and to provide them with an income. Palmer and the association also invited other prosperous Chicagoans to act, to "employ some of these [women] at low wages and have the patience to teach them housework," explaining that patronage "would do a grand thing for them" by giving "virtuous" and "worthy" women the skills they need to be successful mothers and wives.[33] Ultimately Palmer's charity sought to insulate the virtue of women deemed "worthy" but doomed by inadequate wages.

Domestic work — characterized by low pay, abuse, and isolation — anchored narratives of sexual ruin. At the turn of the twentieth century, girls as young as twelve were kept in private homes where they were employed in domestic labor at poverty wages. They reported conditions that were long and difficult. One worker told a state senate vice committee, "You are like a machine, wound up in the morning you work until all hours."[34] Because it was practiced in the spaces of private homes, domestic work was prone to abuse that was difficult to detect and even more difficult to penalize. As with needlework, efforts to insulate domestic workers from "ruin" focused largely on the practices of young women rather than those of their employers. Sociologist Sophonisba Breckinridge recognized that domestics were "exposed to temptation, separated from their families," and lived with "no protection." But as with social worker Mary Conyngton, who argued that many young women "fell" during stints in domestic service, she attributed "falling" to those who were "least likely to resist" rather than to those who were overpowered and physically unable to resist.[35] The spaces of domestic service, typically private homes, were largely out of the physical reach of social reformers. However, as with needlework and department store work, these spaces were shaped by the structures of poverty, defined by the presence — or absence — of virtue.

In contrast to the closed world of domestic work, the gaping, open, unpredictable spaces of department stores appeared to put "ruin" on public display. Sophonisba Breckinridge indicted department store employment as "responsible for a very large number of cases of delinquency among girls." William Stead, the famed English reformer who visited the Columbian Exposition and then stayed on in Chicago to write his famous reform tract *If Christ Came to Chicago*, accused department store managers of paying women "at a rate which assumed that they would be supplemented by the allowance of a 'friend.'"[36] Jane Addams cautioned that department stores exposed young women to the fabrics and jewels they coveted but could not afford and warned of sexual predators lurking in the aisles and at the counters of department stores, where they tempted young women with gifts in exchange for dates.[37] *Harper's Bazaar* published editorials that described department stores beyond Chicago and that declared that within them many "upright, honest, and faithful" women found "chances for advancement." But Boston retailer and philanthropist Edward Filene did not entirely agree. He acknowledged that "underpay, the strain of work, and, for some, [the] instability of work" endangered virtue.[38] In fact, moral concerns about women who worked outside the home were so pervasive that they even framed the demands of labor organizers: "Can

a half starved, poorly clothed woman clerk give your business the energy — physical and mental — the clearness of thought, the cleverness
of work, the care for detail which means trade and income to you?"[39]

Women who worked for wages pushed back against this taxonomy
of ruin and described their experiences navigating the world of work
and relationships on their own. Department store employee Gerty was
eighteen years old in 1913 and earned six dollars a week, which was not
enough to survive on. She explained to investigators from the Illinois
Senate Vice Committee that she met with two "steady fellows" each
week at a "room downtown," collecting two dollars from each. Rosie,
who faced similar hardships, was employed as a dressmaker. She visited dance halls "because if she [stayed] at home she would be sewing,
and when she worked by gas light her eyes hurt." At one dance hall, she
told the vice committee, she finally went out with a fellow who offered
her five dollars — roughly a week's wages — for sex. When she "saw she
should make money so easily, she made up her mind it was better than
ruining her eyes and her health by sewing." Likewise, twenty-two-year-
old Paulette earned six dollars a week. She explained to the senate vice
committee: "It was impossible to make a living where I was. And, even
while I was in the store I made money on the side. I was in the habit of
taking men to hotels, one, two, or three times a week when I wasn't too
tired. After I had been working two months I left."[40] Twenty-one-year-
old Mag, who traveled to Chicago from Kentucky to find work, "could
not make enough money waiting on tables." She met up with a "fellow
who took her out, bought her some clothes, gave her money and not
long afterward they took a room together." Nineteen-year-old Lizzie
earned five dollars a week in a department store — a wage that would
require she live at home. Unlike Gerty and Rosie, Lizzie explained that
she was wary of the pitfalls of sex work; she "will go out for a 'good
time,' but will not take any money. Her friend gave her a bracelet last
week. He is a clerk in the same store."[41]

Although even the severest critics of virtue would have been hard-
pressed to promote sex work, according to women toiling in clerk,
seamstress, and service work, it "beat the department store game to

hell."[42] Their individual anecdotes cast vice not as "ruin" but as a labor strategy, a tool they used to navigate the contingencies of urban life — and to confront the employers, regulators, and reformers preoccupied with virtue and with their involvement in the labor market. By working, boarding, migrating, consuming, and interacting, many workingwomen rejected the narrow view of virtue incorporated by reformers, social scientists, and journalists into a taxonomy of ruin. Stressing casual employment, provisional housing, and endemic poverty, they sought to bring the legal administration of their virtue in line with conditions of their everyday lives — to confront an order based on acclamations virtue. The forces of formal authority, operating from a very different perspective, sought to do the same thing.

COURTS AND COMMISSIONS

As it turned out, the sexual dimension of women's work also captivated judges. Their opinions, which built on and formalized the claims of reformers, social scientists, and journalists about virtue, point to efforts to define virtue in legal terms. Although sex work was never legal in Chicago, in the last quarter of the nineteenth century it was not entirely illegal either. And to the dismay of prostitution's critics, efforts to prosecute sex work produced few "righteous verdicts."[43] To make their point, critics of sex work — peddling generic chronicles of urban workingwomen — generated rousing accounts of "ruin." These accounts clustered the dissolute — from "the prostitute, the thug, and the 'masher'" to the "painted prostitutes" and the "15 year old strumpets newly started upon the town" — and defined them as a threat to "law abiding citizens," to "decent people" and their "rights," all of which, the *Chicago Tribune* insisted, "prostitutes ought to be compelled to respect."[44] When Mayor Carter Harrison proposed the licensing of houses of prostitution at the end of the 1870s, a group that called itself the Ladies' Social Evil Association "objected vigorously" to the plan in local newspapers and helped to kill the legislation.[45] The result of reformers' intransigence was an "unofficial policy" of containment. It would lead, eventually, to criminalization.[46] Informal ideas developed and expressed by reformers, social scientists, and journalists would propel this criminalization as they reinforced the structures of poverty that venerated virtue.

In the decade after the Chicago Fire, judges appeared unwilling to use law to regulate moral conduct. Sex worker Laura Raymond appealed her conviction to the Illinois State Court of Appeals in 1881. She had been found guilty of "patronizing a house of ill-fame by being an inmate" in Alexander County, located in the southern tip of the state, and fined fifty dollars and court costs. However, the appellate court overruled Raymond's conviction when it ruled that laws targeting houses of prostitution — the spaces prostitutes worked — did not also target their physical bodies.[47] However, ten years after Raymond successfully challenged the Illinois law, judges appeared to be making larger accommodations for moral regulation. In the words of the *Inter Ocean* daily, "the notorious Molly Monroe receive[d] her just desserts" in Chicago. Charged with keeping Mary Hamlin, a girl under eighteen, in her "dive on Fourth Avenue," Monroe was convicted in Circuit Court and handed eighteen months in the penitentiary. She was a recidivist previously charged with "the same crime or even more heinous ones," and her case fit precisely the language of the vice statute, targeting those who "shall suffer or permit any unmarried female under the age of 18 to live, board, or room in such houses."[48] In Monroe's case, the youth of the sex worker, rather than the performance of sex work, was the basis of her conviction. In both cases, the bodies of sex workers were not connected — legally — to the physical act of sex work.

In late nineteenth-century Chicago, moral regulation was most firmly emplaced in disorderly and nuisance statutes. The Lake Street police used their oversized logs to inventory sexual misconduct, which they uncovered through irregular blitzes on "houses of ill-fame" in the 1880s.[49] For instance, on June 27, 1885, police launched three raids, which produced more than a dozen disorderly charges and a host of modest fines, typically around two dollars.[50] This crackdown, the larg-

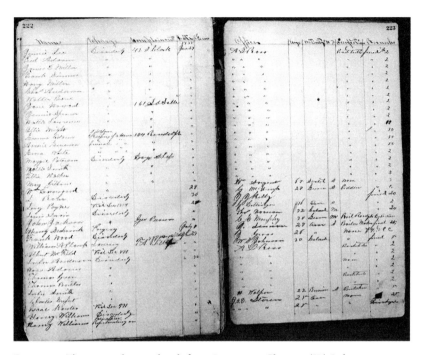

Figure 3.1. The original arrest book from June 1885. Chicago (IL) Police Department, Chicago Police Department Collection [Manuscript], 1866–1969, Chicago History Museum.

est registered in the Lake Street police rolls in the first six months of 1885, points to the ways that disorderly law, like other vice statutes, was principally about containments — about keeping disorder and nuisance from spreading throughout the city.[51] At the same time, Chicago's nuisance ordinances were presented in ways that minimized their moral dimension. For instance, in 1881, the *Inter Ocean* printed Amendment 1662 to the Chicago City Code — "declaring houses of prostitution a nuisance" — between announcements that regulated the uses of the street: "wagons shall not be washed in the street or alley," and "ash gatherers shall not gather up the ash from the street between the hours of 8 A.M. and 6 P.M."[52] The posting neutralized sex work by classifying it alongside other, familiar urban enterprises. In the 1880s, the moral outrage over the physical spaces and bodies of sex work were largely absent from Chicago's urban legal administration.

This began to change in the 1890s, when the city ordinance was revised, expanding the authority of local police and making the "maintenance and support" of a "House of ill-fame" grounds for arrest. The new statute signaled a departure from the Laura Raymond case, which separated women's bodies out from the spaces of sex work; the new statute made the bodies and spaces of sex work the same.[53] The 1890 statute focused on conspicuous vice-spaces; journalists dressed the new approach as a statutory ban on the "gilded dens of infamy" and the "polluting presence of abandoned women." However, these assessments were less concerned with districts where vice was already concentrated, such as the Levee Vice District.[54] Despite this new statutory kick, vice remained a quasi-legal but thoroughly quarantined activity — protected where it was concentrated, criminalized where it was absent.

As the Chicago statutes that were used to prosecute sex work evolved in the early twentieth century, they registered a transition from nuisance and disorderly to criminal misconduct — issuing a new formal status to accompany the claims of reformers, social scientists, and journalists. The Chicago Revised Code of 1905 transformed legal regulation by granting police the authority to make arrests for "fornication" and "lewdness" in houses of assignation and also "on the streets, alleyways or public places of the city."[55] While the 1905 ordinance created new legal space for the prosecution of women's sex work where none previously existed, the transformation in the policing of sex work — from containment to nuisance and from nuisance to criminalization — in previously protected zones represented an increased willingness to use lower-level law to regulate women in public spaces. For instance, civic leaders in Chicago sought to criminalize wine rooms, partitioned compartments in saloons "once legitimately used to sample wine or drink privately," which increasingly provided cover for sexual exchange. The criminalization of wine rooms indicates two important features of early twentieth-century vice law. First, it located virtue at the center of statutes regulating women's participation in public urban life.[56] Second, because it was quickly and widely ignored, it suggests that, at the least, Chicagoans were divided over the criminalization of sex work.[57] The new law also criminalized status rather than conduct — an innovation that men described as vagrants likely already recognized. Legal libertarians noticed too. According to the University of Chicago's Ernst Freund, the problem with punishing sex workers is that "the disposition which justifies the original detention would also justify its continuance."[58] The law regulating vice, Freund complained, punished an individual's status as a sex worker rather than the specific act of sex work; in this scenario, remediation involved abandoning a status. As legal libertarians also noted, local law was beginning to reflect the intensifying compulsion that white women be virtuous.

When it was formed, the Chicago Vice Commission was the first municipal commission set up to study vice — or sex work — in a major American city.[59] Convened by Mayor Fred Busse in March 1910, the commission included Chicago's leading lights, from municipal court chief justice Harry Olson to Sears president Julius Rosenwald and Chicago Commons Settlement House founder Graham Taylor. Their final report, *The Social Evil in Chicago*, demanded the abolition of vice districts and "all practices which are physically and morally debasing and degrading" of women.[60] The report also suggested that low wages and prostitution were linked, and it identified poverty as a leading threat to the "chastity of our women" and the "sanctity of our homes" — poverty being the "the principal cause, direct and indirect, of prostitution."[61] According to the report, the problem was that sex workers "could not live on the wage paid them."[62] However, rather than further exploring the conditions of women's work, commissioners instead injected a new figure into debates over virtue and work: the *casual* sex worker. She did not "reside in houses of prostitution but solicited on the street two or three times a week."[63] The casual sex worker, commissioners argued, had "discovered that luxuries and ease come to them when they sell their bodies, rather than work with their hands." This figure — who was white — signaled a departure from the vice-virtue binary by describing women who traded in sex occasionally as amenable to reform.[64]

The Illinois Senate Vice Committee, which published its finding in

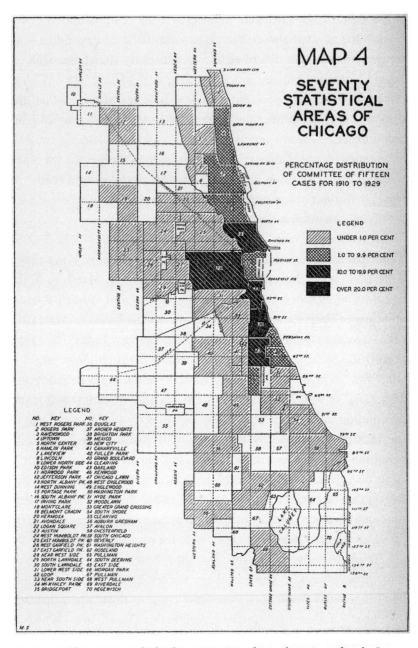

MAP 4

SEVENTY
STATISTICAL
AREAS OF
CHICAGO

PERCENTAGE DISTRIBUTION
OF COMMITTEE OF FIFTEEN
CASES FOR 1910 TO 1929

LEGEND
UNDER 1.0 PER CENT
1.0 TO 9.9 PER CENT
10.0 TO 19.9 PER CENT
OVER 20.0 PER CENT

LEGEND
NO. KEY   NO. KEY
 1 WEST ROGERS PARK   36 DOUGLAS
 2 ROGERS PARK   37 ARCHER HEIGHTS
 3 RAVENSWOOD   38 BRIGHTON PARK
 4 UPTOWN   39 MEXICO
 5 NORTH CENTER   40 NEW CITY
 6 HAMLIN PARK   41 CANARYVILLE
 7 LAKEVIEW   42 FULLER PARK
 8 LINCOLN   43 GRAND BOULEVARD
 9 LOWER NORTH SIDE   44 CLEARING
10 EDISON PARK   45 OAKLAND
11 NORWOOD PARK   46 KENWOOD
12 JEFFERSON PARK   47 CHICAGO LAWN
13 NORTH ALBANY PK.   48 WEST ENGLEWOOD
14 WEST DUNNING   49 ENGLEWOOD
15 PORTAGE PARK   50 WASHINGTON PARK
16 SOUTH ALBANY PARK   51 HYDE PARK
17 IRVING PARK   52 WOODLAWN
18 MONTCLARE   53 GREATER GRAND CROSSING
19 BELMONT CRAGIN   54 SOUTH SHORE
20 HERMOSA   55 CLEARING
21 AVONDALE   56 AUBURN GRESHAM
22 LOGAN SQUARE   57 AVALON
23 AUSTIN   58 CHESTERFIELD
24 WEST HUMBOLDT PK.   59 SOUTH CHICAGO
25 EAST HUMBOLDT PK.   60 BEVERLY
26 WEST GARFIELD PK.   61 WASHINGTON HEIGHTS
27 EAST GARFIELD PK.   62 ROSELAND
28 NEAR WEST SIDE   63 PULLMAN
29 NORTH LAWNDALE   64 SOUTH DEERING
30 SOUTH LAWNDALE   65 EAST SIDE
31 LOWER WEST SIDE   66 MORGAN PARK
32 LOOP   67 PULLMAN
33 NEAR SOUTH SIDE   68 WEST PULLMAN
34 MCKINLEY PARK   69 RIVERDALE
35 BRIDGEPORT   70 HEGEWISCH

M.S.

Figure 3.2. This map reveals the disaggregation of sexual services after the Levee Vice District was closed. Information in this map was collected by the vigilantes at the Committee of Fifteen. Reprinted from Reckless, *Vice in Chicago*.

1916 based on data collected two years after the Chicago commission published its study in 1911, was more forceful about the correlation between poverty and vice. Building on a legacy of cruel labor practices — such as fining — the state senate focused directly on wages.[65] Thirty-one-year-old Illinois lieutenant governor Barratt O'Hara chaired a state senate vice investigation. In early March 1913, O'Hara interviewed Sears president — and Chicago vice commissioner — Julius Rosenwald in the gilded surrounds of Chicago's glamorous Palmer House about the gap between the wages that were paid to female employees and their actual cost of living. Rosenwald explained that the young women he employed at Sears were paid low wages because they were members of a family economy and were not expected to be individually self-sufficient.[66] The exchange became heated after O'Hara accused Rosenwald of contributing to vice, asking him if he thought that "low wages has anything to do at all with the immorality of women and girls." Aggravated, Rosenwald responded, "I think the question of wages and prostitution has no practical connection. I think there is no connection between the two." Rosenwald explained that, in his opinion, employers had "no moral responsibility for [a girl's] down fall," and he added that making employers responsible and instituting a minimum wage for workingwomen "would cripple any business" and "put Illinois in a position where it could not compete with other states."[67] By arguing that women's low pay underwrote corporate prosperity in Illinois, and by asserting that managers had no stake in the well-being of those employees, Rosenwald would put himself at odds with an investigation that was increasingly interested in protecting poor, workingwomen from "ruin." But by arguing that the women should be moral, he aligned himself neatly with reformers, socials scientists, and journalists in their commitment to virtue — a compulsion that degraded women through the labors they performed in the workplace.

Sears employees Eleanor Benson and Emily Houck, who were subsequently interviewed by O'Hara from the Illinois Vice Commission, disputed Rosenwald's assertion that wages and prostitution had "no practical connection." Their scathing testimonies denounced Rosenwald—and employers like him—and the conditions they fostered. Benson, a four-year Sears employee, testified that women worked hard at the department store, and she recalled "drivers," or "office scolders," who pushed young women to produce when "they didn't get as much work out of [them]."[68] Houck, also a Sears employee, testified that "working girls" were treated severely when they did not work fast enough, explaining, "I never heard any parent speak to any girl the way that forelady spoke to some of the girls."[69] Both Benson and Houck estimated that only half of the young women who earned less than eight dollars per week—which the Senate Vice Committee identified as a poverty-level wage—were members of a family economy, living at home. When pressed about the turn some women and girls took to sex work, Emily Houck would also differ in her response from Rosenwald: "I wouldn't excuse the girl, but I think her employer would be most to blame."[70] According to Houck and Benson, rapacious, cost-saving, profit-driven employers—and not wage work alone—imperiled virtue in Chicago.

In fact, the encounter between O'Hara and Rosenwald resonated in a national debate where it exposed divisions between journalists. The *Chicago News* defended Rosenwald when it editorialized that "good girls" will "go right under any circumstance." The paper even questioned the accuracy of Benson's estimation of the number of "immoral girls" working at Sears—as though it was a numbers problem and that fewer women driven to penury was acceptable. The *Dallas Morning News* quoted Rosenwald's complaint "I don't think the purpose of this Committee is sincere" before he withdrew his support for the investigation; this Texas editorial would also claim that the real issue was the low wages paid men, suggesting that maybe women should not be working at all. The *Philadelphia Public Ledger* and the *Grand Rapids (MI) News* instead argued that individual workers were most to blame and rejected the efforts of government and "notoriety seeking politicians" to regulate business.[71] On the Pacific coast, the tone was different. The *San Francisco Examiner* advocated for worker protections and criticized Rosenwald as "anti-democratic," describing him as an impediment that "stands between the great majority of our decent citizens and the enactment of humane laws." The ripples from this exchange over workingwomen's virtue — its implications and consequences — washed over readers nationally.

The figure of the casual sex worker would ultimately frame, but not resolve, debates over women's "ruin" at work. In Chicago, Jane Addams, who relied on patronage from men such as Julius Rosenwald, walked a fine line between workingwomen's practices and employers' responsibilities. In 1914, she criticized O'Hara for equating "the wages paid workingwomen with girls' morality," criticized workingwomen for using low wages to justify not being "chaste," and defended the right of employers to pay what they could.[72] However, in the process, she appeared to have abandoned her observation, made the year before O'Hara and Rosenwald clashed in the Palmer House, that "certainly employers are growing ashamed to use the worn out, hypocritical pretense of employing only the girl 'protected by home influences' as a device for reducing wages."[73] Addams's pragmatism not only reveals the vulnerability of private charity to private donors but also suggests that virtue was understood to cheapen women through their labors.

As municipal court judges convened to manage workingwomen, they struggled to enshrine virtue as a legal principle. The Morals Court was created at the behest of the Chicago Vice Commission as a branch of the municipal court to formalize its claims about virtue and the effects of wage work.[74] But local judges on the Morals Court and the Court of Domestic Relations struggled to articulate a formal legal justification for virtue that they might apply to the experiences of workingwomen. Instead they would encourage workingwomen to use law to express their grievances. For instance, judges encouraged women to swear out warrants and make out charges against cruel or absent husbands and sometimes against pimps. By making women into legal actors, by suggesting that not all women were responsible for their "fall," and by embracing the figure of the casual sex worker, judges sought to actively separate out wage workers from sex workers. This would also lead them to overlook the ways the two were often connected in everyday life, as Rosie, Mag, Lizzie, and Gerty could attest.

Municipal court judges distinguished between types of sex workers, branding some as "casual offenders," who "in other respects [are] law abiding citizens," and others as "professional prostitutes." According to the court, the latter group merited vigorous prosecution.[75] In their hierarchy of vice, "casual" sex workers were least culpable, whereas professional prostitutes, panderers, keepers, or "parasites" were "shown no quarter."[76] The case of an indigent prostitute, which inaugurated the Morals Court, however, would reveal that conditions on the ground were less clear-cut; it was seldom clear who was "casual" and who was "professional." This case involved a "woman of 35 living in Washington Boulevard" who was "charged with soliciting." "Did you ever work?" Judge Jacob Hopkins asked the defendant. "Yes, at a power machine in [a] factory. They paid me $3.50 a week, and I couldn't live on it, much less support my parents. Then I worked," she continued, "in a cigar factory and later tried running a rooming house. But I couldn't make them go." Ignoring the futility of the defendant's work history, Hopkins asked, "Will you work if a job is secured for you?"[77] Convinced that fines and jail terms encouraged the "wrong" type of work, Judge Hopkins proposed that, in general, sex workers be reformed through occupational training — "cooking, sewing, laundry work and other methods of earning a living wage" — that closely resembled domestic work.[78] Judge Harry Fisher, who replaced Hopkins after his one-year term on the Morals Court, continued the project of enforcing virtue through law, despite recognizing that workingwomen continued to trade in sex because of the "financial advantage the life offered."[79] In the Morals Court, virtue was a barometer of right conduct and a counter to economic self-sufficiency.

Virtue guided judges in a court that was swamped with litigants. For instance, in its first three years, the municipal court processed from 1,846 to 2,254 streetwalking cases annually.[80] For instance, for Mary Carter, a maid; Rose Murphy, a housekeeper; and Pearl Lucas, a stenographer — each arrested in separate prostitution raids in April 1917 — the failure to be virtuous carried the threat of criminal prosecution. Despite the fact that Arnold Prowess, a wealthy barber, paid the bail of each, thus suggesting they were enlisted in the same enterprise, Rose was found not guilty, whereas Mary and Pearl were convicted and fined five dollars each. Meanwhile, Marcie Murphy, a housekeeper, and Ethel Smith, a clerk — each arrested on separate days — were convicted of prostitution in May 1917 and assessed similarly low fines.[81] As with jobless men, judges' strict adherence to an abstraction — virtue, in this case — led them to overlook everyday, on-the-ground conditions that fostered the scarcities and the sense of despair that many workers experienced and that connected them to different types of work.

Legally compelled virtue also extended to men. Here the fines were larger and the recriminations crisper. Theodore Venos received a one-year sentence and three-hundred-dollar fine for pandering his seventeen-year-old wife, Charlotte Venos, who had only recently moved to Chicago. His conviction allowed her to return to her family home in La Porte, Indiana.[82] After Edith Connors charged her husband, William Connors, with pandering in August 1910 — before the Morals Court opened — he was ordered to meet his domestic obligation and "take care of his wife and support her." William "promised he would."[83] Pandering cases, which championed women's use of law to mitigate their sexual exploitation, also stressed their dependency. One month after Connors's case, Irene Bowering charged Claude Powers with pandering, claiming he put her "in the family way" and then tried to prostitute her. Powers pled guilty to bastardy and was fined $550, though the pandering charge was dropped "on the grounds that Irene could not locate the house of ill-fame"; because she was a "poor girl [who] needed the money toward the support of her bastard child," police treated her claims with suspicion.[84] Edith Scott used the pandering law to stay out of jail after she was arrested for sexual solicitation. Court records do not explain whether Scott was an "occasional" or "regular" sex worker or define her relationship to C. W. Scott (whom she did not claim as a family relation). At trial, she was not charged, but C. W. Scott was. His pandering conviction, one-thousand-dollar fine, and eighteen-month sentence suggest he was her full-time pimp.[85] George Wine was convicted of confining twenty-one-year-old Sophie Smith to a small room and then forcing her to "hustle between River and Chicago Avenues and take her clients to the Hotel Mayer." He was fined three hundred dollars and sentenced to one year in jail. Meanwhile, Smith was taken to the Coulter House, a "private refuge that regularly received young women on referral from the Morals branch."[86] For C. W. Scott and George Wine, virtue also structured legal commitments to pandering.

Like virtue, pandering cases reinforced the idea that women encountered danger outside the home. Notorious Chicago panderer Adam Lewicky met twenty-year-old waitress Stella O'Connor while she dined at a chop suey restaurant off Monroe Street in late May 1911. He offered to buy her dinner. It was a ploy. When she refused to accompany him in a taxicab afterward, he had a nearby police officer arrest her for the theft of fifteen dollars. After a night in jail, O'Connor appeared the next morning before Judge Hugh Stewart in the Desplaines Street municipal court. But in a twist suggesting he recognized the ploy, Stewart reversed O'Connor's and Lewicky's roles; Lewicky became the defendant and O'Connor the plaintiff after Judge Stewart dismissed the case against her and ordered her to swear out a pandering warrant against Lewicky. O'Connor, Stewart recognized, had become ensnarled in a recruitment gambit. Nineteen-year-old Anna Turren, O'Connor's coworker, and Helen Blewski, Lewicky's "housekeeper," later corroborated this account.[87] In the end, Lewicky served nine months for attempting to make Stella O'Connor a prostitute. O'Connor's ordeal, which ratified claims that women encountered danger when they worked for wages outside the home, also appeared to suggest that with help from judges they could protect themselves from "ruin." In this way, pandering cases appeared to reinforce the lower court's commitment to virtue policing, even if it led judges to overlook the social and economic perils that many women encountered in their everyday work lives — low wages, intermittent work, and poor living conditions.

Chicago's lower courts and commissions recall an important sequence of state and national legal decision-making linking women's work to virtue. The Supreme Court's ruling in *Muller v. Oregon*, a 1908 opinion about the constitutionality of an Oregon law limiting women employed in laundries to ten-hour workdays, is often presented as an outlier opinion of sorts — a sexual regulation positioned against a rising tide of liberty-of-contract rights championed by a divided United States Supreme Court in 1905 in *Lochner v. New York*.[88] But the *Muller* opinion represents an important confluence. *Bradwell v. Illinois* (1873) and *Ritchie v. People* (1895) are both based in Chicago, and both stress the role of virtue in the regulation of women's work. After passing the Illinois bar, Myra Bradwell was infamously denied a law license by the Illinois Supreme Court because she was married. Her appeal — on Fourteenth Amendment (Privileges and Immunities Clause) grounds — met with an unsympathetic US Supreme Court, which was convinced that paid work interfered with the unpaid duties of mothers and wives and that those duties were more important.[89] In *Ritchie v. People* twenty years later, the Illinois Supreme Court rejected an 1893 state law limiting the working hours of female garment workers in Chicago tenements to eight-hour days and forty-eight-hour weeks — purportedly to allow them to act as wives and mothers. Finding "no injury to her physique" and "no reasonable ground . . . for fixing upon eight hours," the state's high court appeared to contradict the US Supreme Court in *Bradwell* when it ruled that women should be permitted to contract their labor unobstructed by regulations.[90] But this focus on liberty-of-contract doctrine may not be the only way to look at the opinion, as *Muller* corroborated and formalized reformers', social scientists', and journalists' analyses of women and work. In *Ritchie*, workingwomen's virtue was ignored or was not perceived to be endangered by wage work in the same way.[91] We might understand *Muller* as combining *Bradwell*'s maternal duty with the modest labor regulation at issue in *Ritchie*.

The Brandeis Brief, a pioneering social-scientific legal brief that supported the majority opinion in *Muller*, scrapbooked studies documenting the relationship between work and virtue and would deepen the compulsion described by reformers, social scientists, and journalists. In the brief, Louis Brandeis and his sister-in-law, Josephine Goldmark, assembled snippets from policy, welfare, and medical studies that they hoped would encourage the court to uphold protective labor legislation for workingwomen. The brief asserts that women are not physically as strong as men and that their bodies break down more quickly when they work long hours for wages outside the home. When their bodies break down, the brief explains, workingwomen develop habits that jeopardize their virtue.[92] By stressing connections between steady, paid work and "laxity of moral fiber," "degeneracy," "low standards," and a "general decline in morality," the brief endorsed the influence of structures of poverty.[93] This commitment to virtue had immediate implications for workingwomen. For instance, during World War I, the federal government would issue strict "safeguards" for workingwomen, which it described as a "social measure." These measures stipulated the terms of women's labor: an eight-hour workday, a minimum wage, and regular ten-minute breaks; they also included prohibitions on women's exposure to heavy lifting, extreme temperatures, and toxins or poisons.[94] By World War I, virtue was a centerpiece in the federal regulation of women's work.

The link between virtue and women's work, spotlighted by the US Supreme Court in *Muller*, was folded back into Chicago and Illinois law in 1909 when that state adopted, verbatim, the opinion in *Muller* that because women might become mothers, they needed to be protected at work. Sophonisba Breckinridge responded for a delighted cast of social scientists: she heralded the law as a measure to confront inequalities between workers and employers and to strengthen the connection between "the health of women workers and the public health."[95] However, the law's enforcement, which fell under the jurisdiction of factory inspectors — the same state officials in charge of regulating the labor of children under sixteen — also appeared to reduce women through paid work to the status of children.[96] At the same time, while they welcomed the new law, reformers, social scientists, and journalists in Chicago pointed to it and demanded a more emphatic criminalization of the failure to be virtuous. In the 1910s, they set out those demands.

COMMITTEE OF FIFTEEN

In response to court decisions and commissions that they perceived as weak and vacillating, reformers, social scientists, and journalists devised and implemented campaigns in surveillance, policing, "visiting," and pensioning to engender virtue in women at home, at leisure, and at work — to enhance an order based on virtue. Their efforts would reveal the continued capacity of structures of poverty, often expressed locally, to shape virtue and to define the status of workingwomen.

Chicago's Committee of Fifteen — a private organization originally formed in 1909 to combat "white slavery" but "increasingly interested in [combating] all vice" — endorsed virtue.[97] Committee investigators were known to replicate police methods. They roamed Chicago's streets in pairs, inspecting saloons, stores, dance halls, and homes in relentless and single-minded pursuit of the names and addresses of pimps and prostitutes; they recorded their encounters with sex workers in "police-report fashion."[98] They imagined that the information they assembled from raids would be used in future investigations, arrests, and trials. But their reports, which were created to record the activities of sex workers, also reveal important changes in sex work in the era of vice prohibition: as surveillance intensified, services got more expensive, and "innkeepers grew more suspicious." One supposed madam reportedly told an undercover committee investigator that "she had to be very careful with whom she did business because of being watched by the Committee of Fifteen." Sex workers responded with technological innovation: "call flats" disaggregated the spaces of vice by allowing workers to prearrange price and preselect a location anywhere in the city in advance over the phone.[99] But not all vice was concealed. Committee investigators would also describe being hounded by solicitations on sidewalks and streets, in parks, on the quasi-public grounds of cafés and saloons, and the ostensibly private domains of houses and hotel rooms.[100] Finally, committee members' reports replicated a central finding of the vice commission: that sex work appealed because it paid better than wage work. "Bobby Morton" earned "$25/night" when "they have tricks coming up at all hours," while "Ruth," whom investigators encountered at the "Perfecto Bar," claimed she made "between $20 and $30 on a Saturday, 'but worked until 7am.'"[101] Through their patrols and interventions, committee members profiled women: they observed them based on their sexual identity and then assumed they were guilty of a crime.

City officials deepened their surveillance and, in the process, they formalized claims about virtue. In the summer of 1913, the City of Chicago hired ten new policewomen to supervise and regulate working-women's leisure spaces, where they would use virtue to gauge women's practices. Policewomen were not entirely new—police stations had employed matrons since at least the 1880s.[102] But the new hires in 1913 were about more than insulating male attendants from charges of sexual impropriety in police stations and jails; they reflected a new, vigorous commitment to the protection of workingwomen outside the home.[103] Hull House benefactor Louise deKoven Bowen, a talented architect of moral explanations of workingwomen's "ruin," produced several influential pamphlets in the 1910s detailing the hazards of dance halls and department store, hotel, and restaurant work.[104] While overseeing the hiring and training of policewomen, Bowen distinguished between policewomen and policemen: "She could not do the same work that a policeman does at all"; instead, the "skirted Police Guardians" would "look after the girls" and "possibly follow girls that were going away with young men."[105] Astonishingly, Chicago mayor Carter Harrison endorsed this policing of "dance halls, bathing beaches, and small parks and playgrounds," while journalists Mabel Daggett and social reformer Jane Addams applauded the protection of young women "speeded up by industry" who "go so far as to appear indecent in the street." The hiring of policewomen to confront "things [that] go on in amusement

Figure 3.3. Ten newly appointed Chicago policewomen photographed by the *Chicago Daily News* on August 5, 1913. *Left to right*: Mrs. Anna Loucks (*partially visible*), Miss Clara Olsen, Miss Fannie Willsey, Miss Margaret Wilson, Mrs. L. C. Parks, Mrs. Margaret Butler, Mrs. Alice Clement, Mrs. Emma F. Neukon, Mrs. T. D. Meder (supervisor), and Mrs. Gertrude Howe Britton (supervisor). Bain News Service Photograph Collection, Library of Congress, Prints and Photographs Division, LC-DIG-ggbain-14109.

parks, which should not," to "improve our street morals," and to cover "bloomer bathing costumes" at the city's beaches, implied — like the Committee of Fifteen — that workingwomen also needed to be protected outside the workplace.[106] In fact, the Chicago Women's Aid Society would tout its protection of a "seventeen-year-old girl" from a "small town in Wisconsin" and a "Michigan woman [who] answered an advertisement in a local paper" for "immoral" employment at a "questionable location" to validate the efforts of the members of Travelers Aid Societies who greeted women at railroad depots and other ports of entry to ensure their "moral and physical protection."[107] In the 1910s, reformers, socials scientists, and journalists endorsed the expansion of the compulsion to virtue beyond the confines of the workplace.

Reformers' commitments to virtue also brought them inside the private homes of the poor. The Friendly Visitors program promoted a "normal home life" in working-class homes and stressed the domestic virtues of mothers and wives.[108] "Visiting" was the product of Progressive Era urban life and made an initial appearance in Chicago in the late nineteenth century, when Jane Addams described it as a "moving spirit" in poverty reform.[109] Despite Addams's backing, these type of programs did not take hold until the early twentieth century when the University of Chicago's School of Civics and Philanthropy began to train social workers to refashion the practices of working-class homes around healthy eating and thrifty consumption and to encourage the maintenance of "clean, well lighted and ventilated [homes kept], in good repair." Rather than spurning the poor as de facto homeless, as Robert Hunter did a decade earlier, "visitors" — essentially social workers — sought to reconstitute the meaning of "home" around women's virtue.[110]

Visitors also tied women's virtue to male breadwinning. While they learned to earn the "confidence and good will" of wives and mothers, Friendly Visitors textbook author Amelia Sears instructed program trainees that husbands were the "most significant member of the family" because "society holds him responsible for the support of his wife and family."[111] Visitors' commitment to male breadwinning — widely endorsed by reformers and lawmakers — prohibited family economies in which women earned. In fact, the Illinois state government backed this claim by supporting mothers' pensions, which subsidized families without a male breadwinner by paying women to stay home.[112] Opponents of these pensions criticized the use of tax dollars to prop up the homes of the poor, and they complained that pensions supported "immoral," divorced, unmarried, deserted, and foreign women. Lawmakers immediately made each constituency ineligible for the benefit.[113] Supporters argued that pensioning was "cheaper" than the cost of institutionalizing needy and dependent children. And, tellingly, neither supporters nor opponents appeared to complain that the pensions, which did not cover all living expenses, required that mothers also work for wages to support households.[114] In effect, the pension — which appeared to subsidize homes — indirectly subsidized business by allowing employers to continue paying women a lower wage as members of a "family" economy in which the state was breadwinner, or head of household.

Along with the Committee of Fifteen, initiatives in policewomen, the Friendly Visiting program, and Travelers Aid, advocates for mothers' pensions endorsed virtue as the defining feature of women who worked at home and of women who worked for wages. In response to courts and commissions where judges and civic leaders encountered the complexities of poverty and wage work, social scientists, reformers, and journalists — alongside city officials — endorsed virtue as the central feature of an order. In the process, they would reveal how foreign the concept was to women who worked for wages and how frequently — and continuously — structures of poverty upholding virtue needed to be maintained.

CONCLUSION

In the early 1920s, an anonymous woman placed herself "up for sale" in the *"Hobo" News*. Her heartbreaking advertisement read:

> Personal: For Sale — Woman. Have walked the streets looking for decent employment until my money is gone. My shoes are worn out and my feet are so tired. I have a beautiful gift of god five years old. There seems to be no place for us to earn a living. Will offer myself to the highest bidder in order to support my angel.[115]

Like the story of Mary Henning, which appears at the beginning of this chapter, this anonymous posting speaks to the condition that many workingwomen encountered. She and her child were deserted and homeless — conditions their virtue was engineered to guard against but had not. The compulsion to virtue would complement the compulsory autonomy foisted on white men and lead agents of virtue to overlook the everyday ordeals that shaped workingwomen's lives. When judges and courts failed to reinstate women to the stations of wives and mothers, vigilantes and reformers intervened and attempted to do so. Their interventions point to carefully crafted, extralegal efforts to endorse an order in which women's virtue was continuously made contingent on their supervision. In an era of mass urbanization and exploding workplace involvement, virtue kept women's wages low and their bodies tethered to the home.

African American women who migrated to Chicago in search of work would encounter enormous obstacles to steady work and stable housing. Their labors were confined principally to meat packing, domestic service, and laundry work; by and large, they earned less than their white counterparts, and they quickly became overrepresented among the city's sex workers — "led into immoral habits," sociologist Frances Kellor explained, by "questionable employment agencies."[116] The Great Migration — which for so long has been a story of economic and social opportunity and uplift, would be manifested for many as a story of isolation. Unlike poor white men and women — who to some extent could cast aside their exclusions or hope to escape them — African Americans migrants faced systematic isolation. The next chapter describes that isolation.

4. Isolation: Quarantine and the Legacy of Migration

What causes the eruptions, the riots, the revolts — whatever you want to
call them — is the despair of being in a static position, absolutely static, of
watching your father, your brother, your uncle, or your cousin — no matter
how old the black cat is or how young — who has no future.

— James Baldwin[1]

Nannie Ambler was desperate. In February 1914, the twenty-two-year-
old African American was arrested for solicitation only three weeks
after giving birth to her daughter and less than one week after being
expelled from a county hospital. Alone, penniless, burdened by a disease that made her "a frightful menace to her community," she stood
before Judge Joseph Uhlir of the Municipal Court of Chicago's Court of
Domestic Relations to face charges of contributing to the delinquency
of her infant. Observing Ambler's tragic state, Judge Uhlir insisted that
"something be done for her." But he encountered a wall of resistance.
Ambler's poor health prevented her from performing washing or
cleaning work — traditional provinces of African American women's
labor.[2] Meanwhile, civic institutions that might have offered support
refused "to take her on and treat her" because of her race. Ultimately,
Uhlir would negotiate Ambler's "treatment" in a local jail, where she
would be incarcerated without commitment.

In the process of adjudicating the delinquency charge against Ambler — but finding room for her only among populations of convicted
criminals — Judge Uhlir realized what a generation of African American migrants would soon discover: in Chicago, reformers, social scientists, and journalists used race to sanction physical, social, economic,
and legal isolation.[3] This chapter builds on what James Baldwin described in 1968 in the chapter's epigraph as the despair of being "absolutely static" to explain how isolation emerged alongside compulsory

autonomy and virtue to shape structures of poverty that defined life for African Americans migrating to Chicago in the early twentieth century.

Ambler's devastating experience, buried on the fourth page of Chicago's leading African American newspaper, the *Chicago Defender*, deepens our understanding of Black life in the industrial, urban North. By inviting us to look back from 1914, her ordeal reflects how legal landmarks of late nineteenth-century race relations — the *Civil Rights Cases, Plessy v. Ferguson*, and *Williams v. Mississippi* — not only degraded the protections outlined in the post–Civil War constitutional amendments but also shaped struggles for survival in the North in at least three ways. First, and most broadly, Ambler's incarceration points to the ways that racial discrimination was at the center of the post–Civil War legal order.[4] "The public becomes accustomed to a scheme," Howard University's Kelly Miller explained in 1906, in "which the Negro is excluded and soon comes to look upon [that exclusion] as a fixed, natural order."[5] Second, Ambler's incarceration recalls the private right to discriminate, preserving what the great dissenting jurist John Harlan called the "badge of slavery."[6] Third, Ambler's incarceration invites us to view liberty of contract in an alternative light, not as a legal system of contracted labor relations but as a doctrine that presumes a broad social and political equality for African Americans that *never* existed. It was this structural inequality that undercut Black Americans' access to the very industrial jobs that attracted them northward during the Great Migration, an event triggered by the outbreak of World War I in Europe in 1914.[7] Together these facets of northern life — which systematized exclusion, endorsed private discriminations, and deepened inequality within the existing system of labor law — helped to secure patterns of racial isolation in the North on the eve of the Great Migration.

Ambler's ordeal also invites us to look forward from 1914, to view the Great Migration — an episode that puzzled W. E. B. Du Bois as simultaneously vast, grassroots, and leaderless — as one part of a larger story about poverty and social and legal regulation.[8] In this vein, this chapter borrows the term "quarantine" from sociologists St. Clair Drake and Horace R. Cayton's landmark 1945 study of Black life in Chicago, where they used it to describe the separation and intensification of racial difference that African Americans experienced in the urban North.[9] Better housing, good jobs, and fairer treatment constituted a *heroic* view of the Great Migration, which tends to overlook or minimize the fear, loneliness, and isolation migrants encountered.[10] This chapter seeks to recover some of this sense of isolation, of what historian Khalil Gibran Muhammad describes as the criminalization of "Blackness," which emerged as a concrete feature of African American urban life in the early twentieth century.[11] Interrogating these dimensions of racial isolation, this chapter identifies the Great Migration as facilitating structures of poverty, coordinated by reformers, social scientists, and journalists who promoted racial isolation as a solution to the challenges confronting migrants in the city. This intervention requires a shift in focus that takes us away from the migration's upbeat beginning to focus instead on its dreary ends. In the process, it invites us to view the Great Migration as a story about endings — about stalled momentums, lousy jobs, and crumbling homes — which for many migrants existed alongside, and even overrode, aspirations of opportunity, fair treatment, and heroic mobility.[12]

The Great Migration deepened racial isolation in Chicago. This chapter's focus on the first five years of the migration, from Ambler's incarceration to the racial violence culminating in a riot in the summer of 1919, tracks the development of isolation in housing, strikebreaking, migration, service, uplift, and law — as an alternative to the heroic narrative stressing opportunity. The official report on the riot, *The Negro in Chicago*, which offers a summary of events and opinions, would also formalize reformers', social scientists', and journalists' claims about the relationship between race, vice, and class. The quarantine, which preceded the migration and intensified with it, orients us to one of the great, devastating stories of twentieth-century city life: the racialization of urban poverty. The riot — which stemmed from the murder of an African American youth who had floated across an artificial racial boundary at a public beach — might be understood as an attempt to reimpose quarantine.[13] It was with the legacy of this violent isolation that social critic Baldwin wrestled when he described men in the 1960s in "a static position" without a future.[14] This chapter turns its attention to the origins of this legacy, when the isolation at the center of the Great Migration did more than announce the conditions of work, housing, and fair treatment. Alongside compulsory autonomy and virtues, isolation would amplify the structures of a social and legal order that engendered Black urban poverty.

A RIGHT TO DISCRIMINATE

In an era noted for its enthusiastic devotion to racial discrimination, late nineteenth-century race relations in Chicago were relatively stable. Alongside its large numbers of domestic and casual workers, the city boasted a small but prominent professional class of African Americans who famously dismantled Illinois's Black Codes and school segregation policies.[15] Among this class of activists, Tennessee-born migrant Ferdinand Barnett stood out. He graduated from Northwestern University with a law degree in 1878 and established the short-lived but influential newspaper the *Chicago Conservator.*[16] In Chicago the African American community's growth was stable too, supplemented by a steady influx from states in the upper South.[17] Furthermore, in an era of declining civil rights nationally, this community also benefited from civil rights protections that were spelled out locally, in Illinois law. Legal historian Elizabeth Dale describes the ordeal of Josephine Curry, who sued under the Civil Rights Act — and won — after she was relegated to the second-floor balcony of Chicago's People's Theater.[18] After the Curry trial, dailies continued to register instances of the Civil Rights Act's enforcement, noting, for example, that in the spring of 1888, the Brevoort House restaurant was fined twenty-five dollars after it overcharged a Black customer.[19] In fact, when the Illinois Supreme Court struck down the Civil Rights Act in the 1890s, state legislators responded swiftly, reinstating an expanded version that also prohibited discrimination at soda fountains, saloons, public restrooms, skating rinks, concerts, and cafés, as well as on elevated trains, buses, and railroads.[20] In late nineteenth-century Chicago, state law announced itself as an agent of racial equality.

That began to change in early twentieth-century Chicago, when declarations of social equality between the races were countered by new adherences to racial separation and racial difference. Hull House founder and social reformer Jane Addams — noted for innovations in child care, labor reform, and civic participation — announced that Black Americans lacked "responsibility" and "control," and she accused them of possessing a "primitive instinct."[21] According to social scientist and reformer Richard R. Wright, African Americans were incapable of "estimating the value of work and its relation to wages."[22] His views that Blacks were not prepared for the free enterprise system in the industrial North were reinforced by the explanation by Tuskegee Institute president Booker T. Washington at Quinn Chapel that "ours is only a child race" and by the extraordinary claim of social scientist Carl Kelsey that "the lessons begun in slavery must be fully mastered" — as though work had ever made anyone "free."[23] Together, Addams, Wright, Washington, and Kelsey reveal that efforts to bring African Americans into the city — and into the twentieth century — would hinge on practices of racial separation that often generated unevenness and exclusion rather than equality and inclusion. Together they also make a larger point about Jim Crow in the industrial North: sometimes legal authority originates from private quarters.

As Addams, Wright, Washington, and Kelsey — among others — framed pervasive, ground-level commitments to racial isolation, African American leaders in the city pushed back. In 1916, Oscar De Priest, Chicago's first Black alderman, proposed a city ordinance that would strip businesses of their licenses if they excluded African Americans.[24] The ordinance never materialized, but it did register stiff opposition; proponents of racial exclusion embraced the private right to discriminate that was enshrined in the *Civil Right Cases*.[25] Such a law upholding social equality, the *Chicago Tribune* editorialized in response to the De Priest ordinance, was not "enforceable and will not be in this generation," calling it a "fiction" that the "Negro has full civil, meaning full social, rights anywhere in any American community."[26] Perhaps more than anything, the ordinance pointed to a racial boundary. Veteran Chicago attorney George W. Ellis, an African American, described the private right to discriminate as "an old southern trick, adopted to secure in peace in the North what the South had lost in war," namely its capacity to exclude Blacks from a "theater, hotel or other public place."[27] In the decade before the Great Migration, the pace of racial equality slowed dramatically and was brought to a standstill by formal legislation.

STRIKEBREAKING

African American E. Raglan arrived in Chicago from Kansas City in July 1904. Exiting the train at Forty-Third Street, Raglan reportedly heard a man yell, "There goes a strikebreaker." Within minutes, hundreds of white stockyard strikers were in pursuit. He ran down the street, through a yard, up a tree; police would rescue him from a reported crowd of two thousand people. During the ordeal, Raglan declared repeatedly that he was not a strikebreaker. But his skin color and his proximity to the stockyard strikers of 1904 announced to many that he was.[28] Social scientist Alma Herbst has described the stockyards, which would emerge as the largest single employer of African Americans in the early twentieth century, as a "rite of passage" for newcomers to the city.[29] But Herbst's "gateway" explanation conceals the violence, divisions, and conflicts embedded in the putrid industrial conditions at the stockyards, which would do as much to advance as to halt Black momentum in the era of the migration.

Strikebreaking — as practiced in the decades before the migration — speaks directly to this isolation, which restricted African American participation in the industrial workplace. In 1894, Chicago employers intentionally "fired [up] racial animosities" when they hired African Americans to break the slaughterhouse workers' strike.[30] In 1902, eighty Black strikebreakers at a University of Chicago construction project were dismissed after they broke a strike.[31] Sensitive to exploitation, some Black workers also resisted being used by their employers as pawns. For instance, at Latrobe Steel in 1901, steelworkers imported from Birmingham, Alabama, reportedly refused to work jobs that were not theirs. Strikebreakings were strategic but also violent. A few years later, journalists reported incidents from the stockyard and Teamsters strikes in 1904 and 1905 — which saw Raglan treed — that were particularly gruesome: William Hoyle, an African American porter in a local barbershop, was "dragged from his streetcar, beaten," and "left for dead" by white union sympathizers; a mob of five hundred attacked a single Black worker and his teenage son; furious white strikers elsewhere stabbed both eyes out of a Black strikebreaker.[32] Strikebreakers retaliated. White union men "wearing union buttons" were severely beaten after they unknowingly boarded a bus full of "Negro strike breakers."[33] In fact, despite the presence of large numbers of Italian and multiethnic workers marshaled by exploitative padrone labor agents throughout the American West, it was these confrontations between white workers and Black strikebreakers — and not the padrones — that consumed national attention and cast African Americans, in the public perception, as dangerous strikebreakers and not as free laborers.[34]

Journalists also pointed to the ways that strikebreaking appeared to jeopardize the respectability of all African Americans. The *Broad Ax*, a Black-owned newspaper, blamed strikebreakers — "the lowest and toughest elements of the race" — for making it "much more difficult for the respectable colored people in this community to get along" by assisting "such Negro-hating concerns as Marshall Fields and Company."[35] The conservative Black Ashland Avenue Business Men's Association argued that strikebreaking only deepened racial exclusion; this association envisioned an even greater threat, in which jobless migrants became a "menace" as "future paupers."[36] The *Tribune* welcomed the opportunity to stigmatize all Black workers, describing strikebreakers' boarding facilities as "scab hatcheries" and providing lurid accounts of sex, craps games, and brawls. In their descriptions of "less than deplorable" and "licentious" conditions, journalists from the *Broad Ax* and the *Tribune* did find some common territory when they expressed their opposition to strikebreaking in moral, rather than racial or economic, terms.[37] For many Chicago journalists, the violence of the strikebreakings was a moral problem that justified racial quarantine.

As a result, strikebreaking became synonymous with antiunion sentiment, which was widespread among African Americans.[38] "Unions ain't no good for a colored man," an anonymous Black migrant announced in 1916, while another declared, "I've seen way too much of what they don't do for [Black men]," adding, "I can't understand why they strike and keep men out of work."[39] National figures such as Howard University's Kelly Miller, educator Anna Julia Cooper, and Booker T. Washington echoed this view,[40] as did the *Chicago Defender*, which characterized unions as among the Black worker's "worst enemies for they deny him an opportunity to earn an honest living."[41] But as Chicago attorney S. Laing Williams pointed out, strikebreaking posed risks, namely by isolating African American workers in their jobs apart from industry: "The men who must toil with their hands," he vowed, "shall not be allowed to drift and become the victims of organized labor's contempt, or the easy tool of selfish and soulless capital."[42] As Williams suggested, union exclusion would emerge as a leading cause of the 1919 Chicago race riot. University of Chicago sociologist Charles S. Johnson, who oversaw the assembling of *The Negro in Chicago*, seized on the words of American Federation of Labor organizer William Foster to explain the labor movement's failure to engage with Black workers: "The more we tried to help the colored worker the more intense the opposition was. There was a force working against us," he explained, "and we could not help but feel it." "Race prejudice has everything to do with it," Foster added. "It lies at the bottom" and cuts straight through the workplace.[43] According to Foster, unionization only intensified the discrimination it was meant to alleviate. "The problem of labor is fundamental," added Robert Park, a sociologist and one-time secretary to Booker T. Washington. Echoing Foster, he added, "Most other problems, whether of national morale or social welfare, are intimately bound up with it."[44] Strikebreaking and its violence, typically experienced at stockyards but also elsewhere — as E. Raglan's experience testifies — facilitated the structural isolation African Americans experienced in the era of the Great Migration.

KENWOOD–HYDE PARK

Reformers, social scientists, and journalists also used race to police housing — to enforce boundaries created to keep African Americans out of white neighborhoods. In Chicago, migrants were quarantined in dilapidated housing located in the "Black Belt" — the derisive term describing the thirty-block strip of land running south from the warehouse, industrial, and vice districts abutting the southern edge of Chicago's downtown Loop.[45] Civil rights leader Walter White described the badly overcrowded district contemptuously as trying to put "ten gallons of water in a five-gallon pail."[46] Visiting journalists published detailed accounts of crumbling housing without plumbing or running water, with "rickety staircases without handrails, gaping rents in the plaster, leaky roofs [and] wet basements."[47] The degraded facilities reflected migrants' degraded status, a place where they found themselves — antilynching activist Ida B. Wells would explain — hemmed in by prejudice. It was in this vein that Wells reproached residential hotels, such as the YMCA's and the Salvation Army's, for their refusal to "give a Negro a bed to sleep in or permit him to use their reading rooms and gymnasiums."[48] Surgeon George Hall, also a leading light of Chicago's African American community, sided with Wells when he called housing "the greatest cause for demoralization among colored people."[49] Together, they agreed that derelict, overcrowded housing physically restrained migrants from realizing the benefits of migration, arrested them in their pursuit of economic opportunity and fairer treatment, and grounded their lives in the spaces of physical decay.

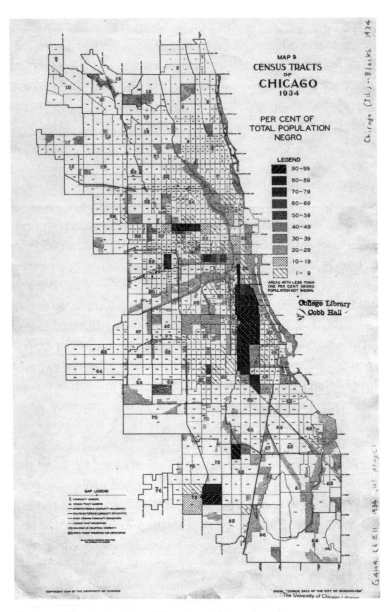

Figure 4.1. During the Great Migration, African Americans were
concentrated in districts on Chicago's South Side and West Side. As the
census tracts of Chicago reveal, by the 1930s, population concentrations
of African Americans were highly visible. Social Science Research
Committee, University of Chicago, 1934.

The isolation found in housing also expressed itself in neighborhood units, which sociologist Robert Park described in his 1925 book as the "simplest and most elementary form of association."[50] In May 1915, the *Tribune* told the story of African American Charles H. Davis, who hired a white proxy to purchase a house in the northwestern part of the white Kenwood–Hyde Park district. When his white neighbors realized that Davis was about to move in, the local homeowners' association promptly raised five thousand dollars to buy the house back.[51] "It was all settled," the *Tribune* reported, after Davis agreed not to move in. However, after realizing he would lose money on the transaction, Davis changed his mind and again announced his intentions to move in. This time, the homeowners' association escalated its response: it was "not looking for trouble" but was ready for it.[52] Davis, once again, agreed not to move in, but he added that this time he also wanted an apology. Wallace Clark, a representative of the local white property owners, obliged him: "I could tell the minute I saw him that Davis was an honorable man," Clark said, explaining that "the residents on the block never had any hard feeling against him personally . . . [but] feared the presence of Negroes on the block would lower real estate values." The exercise was "unfortunate" and rare, the *Tribune* soft-pedaled — but entirely legitimate, it also suggested.[53]

A few years later, activist Walter White of the National Association for the Advancement of Colored People (NAACP), who frequently "passed" as white, investigated the same Kenwood–Hyde Park homeowners' association and discovered that Davis's expulsion was far from rare; rather, it was planned, systematic, and anticipated. After attending a meeting of the association undercover, he reported white homeowners discussing strategies designed to "keep Negroes in their part of town," including buying and closing Black mortgages and having employers fire Black workers. As White pointed out, the exclusions orchestrated by the association were not entirely unlike the rash of residential bombings targeting "colored homes and houses occupied by Negroes outside the Black Belt" in the spring of 1919 — both were about racial separation and isolation.[54] In fact, the legitimacy these

groups — from vigilante vice inspectors to the homeowners' association — perceived in racial quarantining as a form of self-protection was
self-perpetuating: it would continually justify the structures of poverty
that permitted — provided cover for — bad acts.

The Social Evil in Chicago, the landmark municipal study of vice in
Chicago published in 1911, further bolstered the association of Black
neighborhoods with vice and did so only a couple of years before the
Great Migration. The social scientists, reformers, and journalists who
made up the Chicago Vice Commission would also link vice to Black
women at the precise moment that sex work was indicted as a threat
to white women, white families, and white homes. The closing of the
Levee Vice District in 1911 — the commission's number-one recommendation — was "more spectacular than complete," according to historian Cynthia Blair, as it scattered "prostitutes, thugs and cadets" into
"the so-called colored residential sections" of the city.[55] The aesthetics
of conspicuous dilapidation the commission ascribed to vice had an
equally enduring legacy, as it served to further racialize degradation,
disrepair, and undesirability. In fact, the equation of migrants with vice
might be understood to replicate the all-too-familiar conditions of a
Jim Crow railcar but outside the railcar; their mobility was confined
to the smoke, ash, and filth of "separate" spaces that whites were invited to pass through.[56] It was in this vein that, two decades later, E.
Franklin Frazier, the leading sociologist of Black family life in Chicago, would describe an anonymous stenographer living in the Black
Belt. She recalls that in her neighborhood "the white people were all
prostitutes" but that "it wasn't so among the colored people. They were
decent people who attended Quinn Chapel" — where Booker T. Washington spoke in 1905. In this account from Frazier's enduring study of
the African American family, the anonymous girl knows that her white
neighbor, Sophie, ran a brothel — with "men coming in and going out
all day and night" — because occasionally they "knock[ed] at our gate
thinking it was the place." This — she complained — was why she was
"never permitted to sit out back" alone.[57]

As reformers, social scientists, and journalists operating under the cover of Jim Crow would explain — and as Frazier's anonymous stenographer could attest — in the early years of the Great Migration racial quarantine would transform African Americans, and African American women in particular, from individuals relegated to the smoking car of a Jim Crow train into metaphorical smokers in that car, into purveyors of vice — whether they were or not.[58] Their experiences — justifying the residential exclusion, crumbling tenements, and vice that made up their environments — would amplify the isolation that governed Black life in Chicago in the era of migration.

"FAREWELL DIXIE-LAND"[59]

In the summer of 1917, Hudmon Carr, an African American well digger from Monroe County, Alabama, informed his employer of his plan to quit his job to move north. Furious, his violent employer brandished a pistol and a threat: "if he dared leave he would be severely thrashed." The *Chicago Defender* reported that instead of capitulating, Carr struck his employer, took his pistol, and ran, eventually boarding a passing train that took him to Chicago. A nastily worded arrest warrant followed Carr north, instructing the Chicago police to "pick up a big black nigger buck that is dirtier than a skunk and meaner than a rattlesnake. He is charged with the larceny of a pistol valued at $10." At Carr's trial, municipal court judge Joseph Uhlir — who had been unable to help Nannie Ambler three years earlier — threw out the case, which local journalists had equated with the antebellum Fugitive Slave Act — a devastating federal law that empowered enslavers to track and seize human property. "The second bow of slavery," the *Defender* crowed after the ruling, "will never be welcome so long as the North is widening its doors to race members."[60] In fact, the *Chicago Defender*, one of the nation's leading African American newspapers, acted as an ambassador to the migration, deploying columns, features, and promotions to entice southerners north.[61] Stories in the *Defender* reminded its southern readers of the brutal, systematic mistreatment they encountered daily in the South — on streets, in factories, and in fields. "You see they are not lifting their laws to help you. Are they?" the *Defender* asked. "Have they stopped their Jim Crow cars?" it added rhetorically.[62] But as many migrants would discover, abuse in the South did not mean fair treatment in the North — and many encountered widespread racial hostility in Chicago. "Black Man, Stay South," a *Chicago Tribune* headline advised in the early summer of 1917. "They have come north. It was a huge mistake. They are disliked," the *Tribune* editorialized.[63] In response to mean-spirited police warrants and vitriolic editorials, proponents of a heroic narrative of migration sought to amplify the benefits of migration and to tell a story based on an aspiration rather than reality. The world Hudmon Carr would inhabit was guided by this aspiration but grounded in isolation.

Established in 1916, the Chicago Urban League cooperated with the *Defender*'s heroic view of the migration as it sought to break the quarantine of racial separation.[64] It stationed greeters at ports, "upon [migrants'] entrance into the city." It networked with local government and promoted itself through cards and pamphlets that offered to "handle difficulties" when they flared up "among the new people."[65] Chicago municipal court judge Daniel P. Trude recalled dispensing these cards, which he imagined were particularly helpful for "boys [who] would jump freights from down south and come up here and be picked up and brought into Court and be left in jail." He "made it a practice to give every one of them a card" so "they would know where to go and get advice on any difficulty."[66] At the same time, the league depended on a coterie of white businessmen for money, but this group, however public spirited, was "reluctant to experiment with these workers" on a full-time basis — a reluctance that imposed white limitations on migrants' opportunities.[67] The Chicago Urban League was led by sociologist Robert Park, who promoted racial assimilation but on white terms; his view was not entirely different from that held by W. E. B. Du Bois, editor of the NAACP's magazine the *Crisis*, who conditioned Black equality on whites "who wanted to associate with" them, insisting that migrants demonstrate "the moral, mental and physical fitness

to associate with one's fellow man."[68] According to these league officials, isolation and aspiration — for better jobs and homes and fairer
treatment — were in constant tension.

African American attorney Richard Westbrooks, himself a migrant
from Texas who had attended law school in Chicago, sought to aid
migrants by increasing their knowledge of law through his innovative
"Legal Helps" column — published weekly in the *Defender* from 1914 to
1917. The letters to the column would reveal an astonishing lack of legal
understanding among migrants. For instance, one anonymous reader
wrote to ask if the Mann Act — a federal law prohibiting the transpor-
tation of young women across state lines for sexual purposes — also
applied to African Americans.[69] Westbrooks fielded questions about
insurance-claim denials, the dangers of recording false information, and
the benefits of receipt keeping, of resolving disputes over beneficiaries
and wills, and of avoiding delay tactics. In response to a question about
fraud, Westbrooks advised potential victims to read policies carefully,
to hand-deliver payment, and, if necessary, to hire an attorney.[70] He
would devote an entire column to the law regulating tenement lighting
and invite readers to report code violations.[71] For readers who were
concerned about the operation of local courts, he described the role of
witnesses in court, the purposes of a citation, the costs of subpoenas,
and the organization of hearings and appeals.[72] And he implored readers to stand up to racial discrimination: with police, "take the name and
number of such an officer"; in the case of a stationmaster who ordered
African American passengers to leave the Polk Street train station, sue
under the Civil Rights Act.[73] His column, which invited readers to view
themselves as members of the Chicago community and to put "petty"
officers in their "proper place," was directed at breaking down the barriers and distinctions that isolated migrants.[74] Perhaps unintentionally
it would also detail the vastness of those barriers.

According to journalists and reformers, military service held out
the same promise: the opportunity to break out of racial isolation. The
Defender linked the "fight at home" with the fight "abroad."[75] "Close
ranks," W. E. B. Du Bois ordered readers of the *Crisis*, and "forget our

special grievances" — as though forgetting would also erase, or diminish, the memories of white prejudice.[76] *Defender* editor Robert Abbott
instructed migrants to translate service into new opportunities to enter
"gainful occupations which he was denied a couple years ago."[77] White
leaders, no doubt desperate for troops, actively promoted Black mobi-
lization.[78] "There is no color in patriotism," Colonel Franklin A. Deni-
son, leader of the "Fighting Eighth" — Illinois's celebrated all-Black
regiment — announced at a rally in Grant Park.[79] In Chicago, Mayor
"Big Bill" Thompson appeared to endorse African Americans' military
service when he vowed, "Justice and equality of citizenship shall [be] a
living truth."[80] Black soldiers were feted with medals for their service.
And proud South Side merchants posted photographs brought back
from the front of African American servicemen, alongside helmets,
rifles, and canteens.[81] War service appeared to promise to breach racial
isolation.

Migrants' fragmented, intermittent, and incomplete encounters
with Chicago's courts would diminish the heroic pledges printed in
the *Defender*, embraced by the Chicago Urban League, and promised
by the US armed forces. Reformers who described these discrepan-
cies also point to overlap in views held by judges and social scientists.
Hull House benefactor and social reformer Louise deKoven Bowen
depicted the arrests of African Americans on "excuses too flimsy to
hold a White man," describing convictions attained on "evidence upon
which a White man would be discharged."[82] At the court's Morals
Court, which was created to punish vice and to reform sex workers,
judges were known to assign Black women larger fines and to circumvent jury trials in their case, and — along with bailiffs and clerks — they
"appeared to think colored persons have no rights."[83] By the late 1920s,
sociologist Walter Reckless noted that African American women ac-
counted for roughly 70 percent of the caseload at the Morals Court; exclusion from jobs and quarantining in "disorganized" neighborhoods
had increased the likelihood of their arrest, he explained.[84]

At the municipal court's Court of Domestic Relations — which was
set up to adjudicate domestic obligations — judges appeared to overlook

Figure 4.2. Edward Pryor of the all-Black Eighth Illinois Regiment with daughter, Elizabeth, in Chicago, 1917. Military service held out the promise of a better future for many African American families in the era of World War I—and confirmed a heroic view of migration. Chicago History Museum, *Chicago Daily News* negatives collection, DN-0069075.

the turbulence that migrants experienced in their everyday life. For example, according to court records, George Mason, an unskilled laborer, married Ida in 1919, but they separated in March 1923 when George was fifty, Ida was forty-four, and their baby, Josephine, was six months. By 1926, the charges Ida originally brought in the Court of Domestic Relations were dismissed for want of prosecution; most likely Ida stopped pursuing the case.[85] Also in 1926, Ike Holiday faced charges in the same court for nonsupport of his daughter, Grace Holiday. His interaction with the branch was also incomplete; his case was similarly dismissed for want of prosecution.[86] Meanwhile, the high-profile divorce trial of renowned jazz musician Louis Armstrong and the equally high-profile election of African American Albert Bailey George to a judgeship on the municipal court in 1924 appeared to enhance racial inclusion in local law.[87] But the *Defender*'s claims that the new judicial appointment was "epoch making" and represented "the new birth of tolerance" only confirmed a fact that migrants already knew: symbolic gestures seldom attenuated actual ordeals.[88] The racial inclusion promoted by the league, the *Defender*, and Richard Westbrooks — who clearly recognized the forces behind racial isolation — was countered by Louise deKoven Bowen's and Walter Reckless's observations that local law, like federal law, endorsed racial isolation. Perhaps more disturbingly, the fragmented, intermittent, and incomplete transactions migrants experienced through the courts were rooted in their isolation from law and from courts, which was intensified by — rather than abated by — the heroic narrative of migration.

THE NEGRO IN CHICAGO

Early on the morning of July 31, 1919, white rioter Joseph Carka smashed African American William Dozier with a hammer outside the stockyards. Startled, Dozier bolted down Exchange Avenue and was eventually cornered in a sheep pen on Morgan Street. When the pursuing members of the white mob caught up, they beat him to death with brooms, shovels, and rocks.[89] Dozier's violent murder testifies to the brutality of the 1919 Chicago race riot: days of racial, urban violence that spanned late July and early August and spread from the Twenty-Ninth Street beach, where it began, throughout the city's South Side, where it crested.[90] When it ended in early August, officials counted more than thirty-eight dead and five hundred injured.[91] The devastating conflict, which appeared to have eviscerated the heroic view of the Great Migration, in fact represented a culmination of the violence that preceded it, peaking in Chicago in the first half of 1919.[92] *The Negro in Chicago* — the formal study of that violence — sought to curate color blindness and racial progress as emblems of migration; its immediate effect was to ratify and reinforce — to formalize — the structural isolation that reformers, social scientists, and journalists had endorsed for years in Chicago.

For migrants, 1919 was a terrible year. Police responded sluggishly to an estimated twenty-seven separate bombings in the months before the race riot; they made just two arrests.[93] Records of these encounters survive in the pages of the *Chicago Defender*, which preserves an account of a mini race riot that erupted after Alfred Thomas, a Black student, was accosted in June 1919 by a group of white students who demanded his belongings. Escaping this assault, Thomas continued making his way home from school when a white crowd at a baseball game pelted him with bricks and stones.[94] As summer wore on and temperatures rose in Chicago, violence targeting migrants also intensified: Joseph Robinson, a forty-seven-year-old father of six, was shot in the stomach, twenty-seven-year-old World War I veteran Charles Mitchell was beaten and "severely cut," and groups of anonymous whites paraded through the South Side promising to "kill all the blacks."[95] When Illinois governor Frank Lowden empaneled a commission to "get the facts and interpret them and to find a way out," he was probably also thinking of this devastating racial violence and instability that preceded the riot, which had already diminished the city's reputation nationally and abroad.[96]

Lowden's report, *The Negro in Chicago*, ratified structures of poverty that reformers, social scientists, and journalists identified and endorsed, sustaining racial isolation in housing, work, and law. In fact, the report's lead author, African American sociologist Charles Johnson, would argue that the riot itself exemplified racial isolation, explaining that African Americans in Chicago "live and think in a state of isolation which is almost complete," which "no one group understands . . . or can fully understand." Not only did Johnson use the word "isolation" in the same way that sociologists St. Clair Drake and Horace R. Cayton would use the word "quarantine" in *Black Metropolis*, he would also argue that "the riot of 1919 is an example of the effects of this isolation."[97]

The Negro in Chicago embroidered its analysis with the views of social scientists, reformers, and journalists. The report, which boasted "plenty of jobs" for white and Black workers, also acknowledged that strikebreaking was a feature of Black, industrial urban life and an impediment to racial equality.[98] The report wove discussion of packing-houses into a narratives of mobility, citing an anonymous grocer from Memphis who became a day laborer after a lard-making stint in the stockyards and the preacher from Tennessee who "established" his church on the city's South Side while packing at Swift.[99] Although the report hailed the jobs to be found in packing and slaughterhouse work, it also acknowledged roadblocks to promotion — especially when the promotion involved the supervision of white workers — along with exclusion from overtime, frequent changes of tasks, limited assistance, and exposure to racist foremen, which together strengthened the quarantining of migrants.[100] Finally, the report detailed Black workers' "unresponsiveness to organizing" and described antipathy among white unionized employees toward Black workers, who — they felt — did not support the union but benefited from it.[101]

The report echoed claims about strikebreaking, packing, and unionization made by social scientists such as Alma Herbst and by reformers such as Jane Addams; both described the benefits of racial isolation.[102] Meanwhile, migrants' high rate of mobility between jobs appeared to reaffirm their isolation in unskilled work — a condition validated by social scientists such as Carl Kelsey, who argued that "the lessons begun in slavery must be fully mastered" — and that menial work was one part of that mastering.[103] The report endorsed this view when it reprinted a white trade union's claim that "Negroes were inherently unable to perform tasks that white men did as a matter if course."[104] The authors of *The Negro in Chicago* canvassed Illinois Steel, packers Swift, Armour, and Morris, and mail-order house Montgomery Ward — each a major employer of African American migrants — to ask open-ended questions that invited criticism of migrants' labors, such as "What are the merits of your Negro workmen?" and "What are their failings?"[105] They also asked employers to explain why they hired Black workers, to describe the duration of their employment, and to assess their adaptability, skill, and output.[106] These questions, which presumed the newness of industrial work for migrants, identified novelty — and not race — as the basis of their exclusion. For instance, Montgomery Ward manager B. A. Patterson cited the "competitive spirit" of the Black women who worked in his office, explaining that it made up for their lack of business training.[107] As Herbst points out, these types of responses, stressing migrants' *eventual* fitness for industrial work, blindly overlooked employers' direct reliance on "twenty thousand starved negroes" as potential strikebreakers.[108] Instead, the report enlisted banal criteria in which profligacy, irregular attendance, and the "need for supervision" endangered gains secured by their loyalty, endurance, and willingness to work.[109] This arithmetic amounted to a much darker point, that migrants were to blame for the problems they encountered — that their inadequate labors reproduced the isolation in which they found themselves.

The report mirrored the claim of reformers, social socialists, and journalists about housing, that migrants lived in desultory districts because they were not ready to live in nicer neighborhoods. In fact, race riot commissioners even went back to the Kenwood–Hyde Park neighborhood — where the *Tribune* described the homeowners' association's expulsion of Charles H. Davis in 1915 and where Walter White visited a couple of years later — to describe that community's investment in "streets sprinkled and clean," along with "better lighting" and "improve[d] civic conditions." In their report, these improvements served as a justification for racial exclusion.[110] Along with the Grand Boulevard homeowners' association, the Kenwood–Hyde Park association circulated a flyer promoting the benefits of racial exclusion in October 1918:

> Every White person Property Owner in Hyde Park come to this meeting. Protect your property. Shall we sacrifice our property for a third of its value and run like rats from a sinking ship, or shall we put up a united front and keep Hyde Park desirable for ourselves? It's not too late.[111]

While fears of declining property values appeared to present a justification for white "unfriendliness," the report pointed out that white objections to migrants varied from "studied aloofness, taunts, warnings, slurs, threats, or even the bombing of their homes" but found common cover — as they would before the report — in claims that the neighborhood was not ready for migrants.[112] According to political activist Arthur Waskow, the homeowners' associations may have actually spearheaded the bombing campaigns — among the most violent expressions of compulsory isolation — that intensified in the spring of 1919.[113]

The majority of migrants were forced away from Kenwood–Hyde Park, banished to Chicago's least desirable, least improved districts. In the report, the concentration of migrants in the Black Belt invigorated a classification system long used by social scientists such as English social worker Charles Booth, sociologist W. E. B. Du Bois, and Chicago reformer Alice Solenberger. Each employed a ranking system, from Type A to Type D, to document migrants' statuses.[114] According to *The Negro in Chicago*, Type D was the lowest grade of housing: "Most of these dwellings were frail, flimsy, tottering, unkempt, and some of them literally falling apart. Little repairing is done from year to year. Consequently, their state grows progressively worse, and they are now even less habitable than when the surveys quoted at the beginning of this section were made." In addition to the dilapidated interior of these structures — where Black migrants were forced to live — the report also described the "surroundings of these localities" and their "extreme neglect" and disregard for "the laws of sanitation: Streets, alleys, and vacant lots contained garbage, rubbish and litter of all kinds. It is difficult to enforce health regulations."[115] Graded housing and neighborhoods replicated the racial hierarchies devised by reformers, social scientists, and journalists in the official reports on the 1919 Chicago race riots. In fact, this same type of ranking system would again be visible a decade later in the Federal Housing Administration's use of "redlines" to exclude African American neighborhoods from contention for federally backed home loans.[116]

According to *The Social Evil in Chicago*, "the lodger evil" persisted inside these neglected spaces. Published to rave reviews on the eve of the Great Migration, the report largely ignored the racialization of vice that it helped to substantiate: instances where vice districts "have been created within or near" Black communities or migrants moved in "just ahead of the prostitutes."[117] One of the principal grand jury recommendations recorded in the report was that vice, "rampant in the 'Black Belt,'" was a factor contributing to the 1919 riot and that "cleaning up that district" was "absolutely essential."[118] If vice outside the home was associated with African American communities, so were lodgers inside the home — the result, principally, of the "lack of hotels and lodging houses" and of the exorbitant rents that forced many migrants to take on lodgers.[119] The report described "hundreds of unattached men and women [who] could be seen on the streets as late as one or two o'clock in the morning, seeking rooms shortly" in private homes upon their arrival in Chicago.[120] As a result, these migrants who were already isolated in neighborhoods by vice were further isolated within their homes by anonymous lodgers. The story of "Mr. J.," his wife, and daughter recounted in the report summarized this predicament: "The Family stayed in a rooming-house on East Thirtieth Street. This place catered to such an undesirable element that the wife remained in her room with their daughter all day. . . . She was so lonesome that she cried daily and begged her husband to put her in three rooms of their own or go back home."[121] The report used the experiences of this anonymous migrant to intensify existing claims made by reformers, social scientists, and journalists that vice entrenched racial isolation.

The report echoed Richard Westbrooks's and Louise deKoven Bowen's arguments that local law and local courts were not available to migrants in Chicago in the same ways that they were available to whites. Judge Kickham Scalan's view that "juries will convict a colored man with less hesitation than they will convict a White man on the same kind of evidence," Judge George Kersten's contention that "colored persons" are convicted more easily in municipal court than whites, and Judge Hugo Pam's view, "I don't think that Negroes have as able lawyers as whites," facilitated this tenting—or separation—of migrants in law.[122] One anonymous municipal court judge even complained that because "Negroes look alike," it was "more difficult off-hand to place them than it is to identify a White criminal," offering evidence of the criminalization of race already imbedded within the legal system.[123] Systems of surveillance, implemented to track the accused, would further codify these discriminations. According to the report, the "Bureau of Identification," assembled to collect the photographs and fingerprints of criminal suspects, disproportionately impacted African Americans suspects, who had "fewer resources and less influence." Migrants had their information recorded at a rate twice that of whites—typically because, unlike whites, they were kept in jail because they could not afford bail.[124] As with the jobless men described by J. J. McCook, *The Negro in Chicago* acknowledged procedures by which migrants might be surveilled—criminalized because of their status.[125]

Critics attacked the report for overlooking the structures it reinforced. For instance, in an article for the *Crisis*, journalist Augustus Hill was incredulous about the nature of opportunity in the industrial North. Claims about "decent housing" and about a "decent living" are unrealized, he explained; in neither "of those fields have the Negroes as a whole been given anything like a decent chance."[126] According to Arthur Waskow, the report "stopped short of looking at the power structure"—at the ways that migrants experienced an order that systematically structured their isolation.[127] By accepting white prejudice, tying migrants' ordeals to their lack of industrial preparedness, and overlooking structures of poverty, the report justified — rather than repelled — claims made by reformers, social scientists, and journalists that reinforced the deep isolation at the center of the Great Migration.

CONCLUSION

Accounts of the city's efforts to manage racial violence, vice, and crime endeared Chicago to its progressive documenters. And the commissioners who assembled *The Negro in Chicago* — where they replicated the views of Chicago's most prominent, influential, and wealthy — were no exception. "I got into piecework and my wages have steadily gone up," "C. W." explained to the Chicago Commission on Race Relations. "There is more of a chance here to learn a trade than in the South," he added. "I live better, can save more, and I feel like more of a man."[128] Anonymous migrants corroborated C. W.'s claim. "I had better be out of work in Chicago than out of work in Mississippi," one migrant explained,[129] and a teacher from Mississippi appreciated that Chicago still represented a "part of the country where people at least made a pretense at being civilized."[130] These claims — some anonymous, some attributed — which acknowledged that Chicago was somewhat less racist than the sharecropper South, would replicate structures of poverty that anchored the migrants' experience in isolation.

This heroic view of the Great Migration, which has long framed our approach to the mass exodus of African Americans from the South in terms of economic opportunity, distorts our understanding of the migration and — especially — of its legacy. Sixty-five thousand African Americans migrated from the South to Chicago from 1916 to 1918.[131] In Chicago they were part of an order that grew out of reformers, social scientists, and journalists claims and built up around the labors of impoverished white women who worked for wages and impoverished white men who did not. As these structures of poverty make clear, the false incarceration of Nannie Ambler, the brutalization of William Dozier, and the frenzied rioters encountered by E. Raglan are not unrelated but rather are events connected by a larger urban order that shaped the conditions of Black life in the industrial North a century ago. Whether we call it "quarantine," "isolation," or "absolutely static" — as James Baldwin does — scholars, activists, journalists, social scientists, and courts need to come to terms with an order that continually — and artificially — separates out and isolates Black Americans from opportunity.

This book's final chapter explores the decline of the structures of poverty in the 1920s and 1930s, as the claims of reformers, social scientists, and journalists splintered and fragmented into new configurations of "tramps" as gangsters, of workingwomen as self-sufficient, and of "Negroes" as "New." In the process, it would point to a new legacy for this thinking about poverty — as structural rather than individual — in the 1930s and beyond, as its influence on governance, and within government, strengthened.

5. Fall: "Gangster Tramps," Contracting Women, and the "New Negro"

There is no device whatever to be invented for securing happiness without industry, economy, and virtue.

— William Graham Sumner[1]

These unhappy times call for the building of plans that rest upon the forgotten, the unorganized but the indispensable units of economic power . . . that put their faith once more in the forgotten man at the bottom of the economic pyramid.

— Franklin D. Roosevelt[2]

In late 1934, Chicagoan Carl Kolins was unemployed and homeless. The former steam-shovel operator had been out of work since the market crashed four years earlier. Although he may not have known it, he was living through one of the greatest economic depressions in American history. Kolins's outlook, which he shared with a University of Chicago researcher, was bleak. With unemployment rates soaring and consumption rates plummeting, he bemoaned the abundance of commission sales jobs and the dearth of wage and salary jobs. Commissioned sales work was particularly discouraging in the middle of a downturn, he explained, because no one was buying. In fact, Kolins felt that this type of work illustrated a feature that was common to all physical labor — it "burned [workers] out" and threw them away "like a dirty rag." Kolins had discovered that work in Great Depression America was not able to make men autonomous. Instead — echoing the grievances of Progressive Era "tramps" — he viewed it as a mechanism of inequality and subordination, designed to "keep us on the bum."[3] Kolins's grievances, registered in a case study and preserved in the papers of renowned Chicago school sociologist Ernest Burgess, described the failure of manual labor — a tenet of compulsory autonomy stretching back to the Great Fire — to stem the tide of poverty in early 1930s Chicago.

An army of Chicago's unemployed ratified Kolins's view of work. In November 1930, journalists reported that homeless men in Chicago had formed "colonies" of temporary shelters, such as the one located at the foot of Randolph Street near Grant Park, in the "shadow of Michigan Avenue." Like the "hobo jungles" of old, these makeshift camps had sprung up in cities across the nation after October 1929 — the month the stock market crashed — and they were given the name "Hoovervilles" in mock tribute to a president widely believed to have disregarded the suffering brought on by the economic collapse. Despite this shared contempt for federal intransigence, Hoovervilles varied by governance structure, building materials, and location. On Randolph Street, Mike Donovan, a disabled and unemployed brakeman and miner, "ruled by common assent" as "mayor." Shelters were jerry-built, rudimentary; Donovan assembled his with discarded brick, wood, and sheet iron. His shelter, like others, was located along "faintly defined" passageways — streets — that were named to mark the nation's passage from abundance to scarcity: "Prosperity Road," "Easy Street," and "Hard Times Avenue." Journalists described passing motorists who furnished Hooverville tenants with building scraps, blankets, cigarettes, and sandwiches. They also reported that jobless men procured food from local hotels and, in some cases, through efforts to "beat the garbage man to anything that's edible."[4] In the early 1930s, Carl Kolins and Mike Donovan were just two among millions of men cast out by the economic collapse. Collectively their ordeals point to a breakdown in reformers', socials scientists', and journalists' shared conceptions of poverty. They point to the failure of a labor theory — liberty of contract — to define people as economic units. And they point to the inability of either the labor theory or conception poverty to structure a legal order through compulsion to autonomy, virtue, and isolation.

Figure 5.1. A man pushes a wheelbarrow in a Hooverville located at Harrison and Canal Streets, Chicago, in 1932. Chicago History Museum, *Chicago Daily News* negatives collection, DN-0097663.

As primary accounts attest, Americans struggled to grasp the vastness of the poverty generated by the Great Depression. Journalists readily furnished American readers with grim accounts of distraught men. The *New Republic* described the jobless made "unemployable" by the Depression, "sapped [of] moral and physical strength." Some of these figures, the magazine added, sought only seclusion: "Half of them are ashamed to be like they are and they just want to be left alone until there's jobs again."[5] But while some workers retreated into solitude, others burst forward, armed with demands. In Chicago; Springfield, Illinois; and Washington, DC, the jobless marched for food. Although an alarmist Secret Service investigation reinforced claims made by President Herbert Hoover's administration when it dismissed the protesters as "a gigantic communist joyride," marchers' aims did not waiver; they sought direct aid from their local governments.[6] In Chicago, marchers insisted on immediate assistance with housing, heating, and groceries.[7] In other marches, jobless Chicagoans sought a fifteen-dollar weekly dole and the immediate "opening of all vacant buildings and apartments for shelter."[8] Like the men and women burned out by the Chicago Fire more than half a century earlier, marchers demanded aid. Unlike the burned out, they sought it from a government agency, which in the year before Americans embraced a New Deal would struggle to structure status through work.

In the epigraphs to this chapter, William Graham Sumner encourages greater industry, economy, and virtue, while President Franklin Delano Roosevelt — who reinvented national policy fifteen years later — bemoans our collective failure to reward industry, economy, and virtue. In a sense, both men were debating the structures of poverty described in this book as originating in individual or structural conditions; their assessments might also be understood to bookend its decline. Together their claims point to the ways those structures underwent change after World War I. Before Roosevelt's New Deal programs sought to restore the nation's economic activity, Sumner's prescription for "happiness" — based on individual compulsion — had largely broken down. In the period between their statements — the 1920s — structures of poverty were contested by men and women who felt that autonomy was unattainable, by white women who felt that virtue was an impediment to equality, and by African Americans who observed that racial isolation curbed opportunity. These grievances, reflecting long-standing claims made by jobless men, sex workers, and migrants, were spearheaded in the 1920s most visibly by the figure of the "gangster tramp," the "contracting" workingwoman, and the "New Negro." They would reveal that autonomy, virtue, and isolation distorted actual lived conditions. Taken together, their grievances help bridge an era typically partitioned by the stock market crash between the Roaring Twenties and the Great Depression, to stress continuity, rather than change, in the decline of an order assembled to facilitate authority by defining and ratifying structures of poverty.[9]

THE GANGSTER TRAMP

On November 4, 1930, Harry Olson ended twenty-five years at the helm of the Municipal Court of Chicago. Although he complained of "gross fraud" in his election defeat, the court would continue under the leadership of John J. Sonsteby much as it had: committed to "efficient" justice and "good business methods," principles that had justified the court for the past quarter century.[10] Despite this institutional continuity, the figure of the vagrant that anchored shared meanings of poverty in Chicago since the Great Fire of 1871 had begun to change. Most strikingly, in the Prohibition era, officials used vagrancy law to punish bootleggers rather than the jobless — to pursue and apprehend the classes of rumrunners and gangsters that federal Prohibition had created. The genesis of this change was in the 1920s, when new configurations of work, leisure, and violence displaced shared meanings of poverty.

In early 1920s Chicago, social scientists remained committed to combatting the "evils" of criminal dependency and joblessness. They would argue that joblessness was a consequence of increased competition from foreign workers — mostly from Mexico and the Philippines — and of increased mechanization, which decreased the need for manual labor.[11] They observed the genesis of "tramp families" — entire domestic units that took to the road in private automobiles. Here, their "disorganization" and provisional homelessness was not an expression of leisure but a consequence of the mobility mandated by wage work.[12] "Disorganization" undermined the stability that work was intended to provide.

Among social scientists, shared conceptions of poverty gave way to disagreement. The nature of the American frontier would provide an example. Sociologist Robert Park recalibrated Frederick Jackson Turner's "frontier thesis" — originally presented in 1893 at Chicago's Columbian Exposition — to describe the tramp as a "belated frontiersman," living in a "time and in a place when the frontier is passing or no longer exists."[13] Nels Anderson, Park's student, agreed in part. He argued that the tramp was not a frontiersman but constituted a physical frontier that "moved westward two decades or so behind the first," composed of men willing to "go anywhere to take a job."[14] In both cases, the figure of the tramp was made obsolete by the progress of modern, industrial America, which they suggest had washed over the country, moving from east to west. Harvey Zorbaugh, also trained in Park's Sociology Department at the University of Chicago, agreed that rootless and jobless men were a counterpoint to progress. But progress meant something different for him as well. In his 1929 study *The Gold Coast and Slum*, he contrasted the tramp's "shabbiness" with the "march of the city" and his "careless dress" with the "smart shops of North Michigan," and he argued that his disorganization threatened order, while his slums haunted the appointed mansions of the Gold Coast. However, if Park and Anderson were correct that a frontier had passed, Zorbaugh pointed out that it had missed hundreds of thousands of men living transitory lives on North Clark and West Madison, bunked in residential hotels such as the Eureka, and scattered throughout Grant Park and in the myriad "jungles" strewn in and around Chicago.[15]

Journalists echoed social scientists' concerns about the inability of autonomy to speak for a collective experience. As a result, they tended to overstate the dangers presented by the impoverished. Physician W. A. Evans argued in the *Chicago Tribune* that the jobless made themselves sick because they "neglect their colds, [and] live in badly ventilated spaces." He explained that they were not in need of protection, but that society was in need of protection from them.[16] The *Tribune* also warned its readers that picking up hitchhikers could "involve a risk of infection." But the paper added — acknowledging a wrinkle in its own argument about poverty — that it was difficult to distinguish "tramps, vagrants, hold up men, indigent unemployed, moochers" — the criminally dependent — from "law abiding citizens exercising their privilege to walk on a public right of way."[17] This problem, distinguishing the unlucky from the criminal, points to factors in the structures of poverty — in reformers', social scientists', and journalists' attempts to distinguish between categories of poor people — that began to announce themselves in the 1920s. These factors were exacerbated by a new emphasis on leisure and rum-running — neither of which had anything to do with autonomy.

In the 1920s, "entrepreneurs of leisure" celebrated tramps as cultural symbols of nonproduction — as men who were not supposed to work.[18] College students Arthur Smith and Robert Crawford made national headlines in the summer of 1921 when they "tramped" from Washington State to Chicago to compete for a fraternity prize of one hundred dollars; the newspaper reported that they had made the journey in just over a week living as "tramps," and it boasted that they had survived on a meager $1.80 each.[19] In the summer of 1925, when journalist Samuel Blythe "confessed" — slyly — in the *Saturday Evening Post* that he was addicted to overwork and called for a greater commitment to leisure activities, he replicated advice that was common in early twentieth-century "hobo" advice manuals: to work less and rest more.[20] That same year, journalist F. C. Kelly announced that Americans needed better ways to waste time, and he held out the figure of the "idler, who is capable of wasting days and weeks" while convincing others "that he is usefully engaged." "Cease to be ashamed of various pursuits," Kelly boasted sardonically, "merely because they are futile."[21] According to the *Literary Digest*, life on the road filtered by "jungles," dimly "lighted restaurants," and "hobo" clichés was "not so bad."[22] Actor Charlie Chaplin exemplified "civilized leisure" before a mass audience in his cinematic interpretations of a tramp's life.[23] Illustrator Norman Rockwell — another connoisseur of everyday life — depicted the leisurely idler in his painting *The Tramp* — which graced the cover of the *Saturday Evening Post* in 1924.[24] This tramp figure, which depicted poverty, was not about autonomy — or its absence — but leisure.

Rumrunners also appropriated vagrancy law in the era of Prohibition. In the *"Hobo" News* in the early 1920s, complaints about job shortages and low wages were overshadowed by Chicago mayor William Dover's plans to "squeeze illicit beer and booze out of Chicago and drive beer and rum running gangsters out of the city or into jail."[25] When vagrancy law was used to describe this new criminal class, the term's meaning expanded. In the early 1920s, police chief Morgan Collins suggested that "gangsters without guns" could be tried in local courts as vagrants.[26] This use of vagrancy law caught on. By the decade's end, Chicago detective William O'Connor used it to prosecute the city's "most celebrated and infamous hoodlums."[27] Statistics helped to capture this growth. Vagrancy prosecutions in the municipal court increased from 220 in 1922 to 1,300 five years later.[28] The bootlegger, the *Tribune* explained to its readers in the summer of 1930, "like the old fashioned vagabond, is a parasite, contributing nothing to orderly society, but exploiting it."[29] During Prohibition, the gangster — a product of federal law — competed with the figure of the tramp — defined locally — to disrupt the shared meanings and shared compulsions that underwrote reformers', social scientists', and journalists' claims about the impoverished.

In addition to Prohibition, judges would stretch vagrancy law to cover acts of public violence, sometimes in response to public pressure. The daytime murder of veteran *Tribune* columnist Alfred "Jake" Lingle in a tunnel under Michigan Avenue leading to the Illinois Central train station below at Randolph Street in June 1930 was one of these instances; it shocked Chicagoans. It also helped to solidify the gangster tramp as a figure of popular imagination.[30] After months passed without a major development in the case, police — under intense public pressure — arrested Israel Alderman, a known "alky peddler," and Joseph Condi, only recently released from Leavenworth Penitentiary, in early September. But rather than charging each with manslaughter or murder — which might be expected in a murder investigation — municipal court Judge John Lyle presided over their vagrancy charges and sentenced each man to six months of hard labor, with the brazen warning: "When your six months is done and you are released, take this advice from me: get out of Chicago. If you don't, you'll be in for another dose."[31] Alderman and Condi's legal saga, which lasted several months, also saw municipal court judges use the threat of a vagrancy charge to pressure suspects, to acquire information, or to cancel bonds — each having little or no connection to steady work and stable homes — to making men autonomous.[32]

Even apart from the high-profile Lingle murder, the figure of the gangster tramp divided Chicago's local lawmakers, much as joblessness had in previous decades. Some authorities preferred this new application of vagrancy law. For instance, in January 1930, Chicago deputy police commissioner John Stege responded to a perceived "increase in the number of petty robberies within the last week" with a massive campaign "to drive 'floaters' out of the city."[33] The following spring, in 1931, acting police commissioner John Alcock boasted that his pursuit of bootleggers had spearheaded 105 new vagrancy charges and produced thirty-seven vagrancy convictions resulting in jail terms and fines. Frank Davis, Samuel Wilson, and John Peterson were each listed in the *Tribune* as vagrants — their names presented publicly, testaments to the new strategy's success.[34] Opponents of a diffuse vagrancy law argued that it created more problems than it solved. Municipal court judge Justin McCarthy complained in early 1931 that overuse of vagrancy law clogged courts and distracted judges. "We must expedite justice," McCarthy explained, "by clearing away the chicken feed and getting to the serious business" — vagrants, he implied, were by definition not "serious business."[35] McCarthy was not alone in this view. "You cannot fight lawlessness with lawlessness," municipal court judge Harry Fisher explained in 1930, concerned that by stretching vagrancy to fit new suspects and scenarios, judges and police were distorting law. The "temporary relief" it provides, he explained, will "rise up and plague us, and far from serving the community," Fisher predicted, it would endanger community.[36] Journalists also appeared to reject diffuse uses of vagrancy law. One *Tribune* editorial deemed vagrancy law "about as [much] nonsense as the Eighteenth Amendment" — another widely unpopular law in the early 1930s — and equated punishing men for not working with "trying to get milk from a dry cow."[37] The figure of the gangster vagrant, which appeared to frustrate and divide officials, was abandoned shortly after Prohibition ended when the Illinois Supreme Court struck down sweeping applications of vagrancy law in 1934.[38]

Amid deepening disagreement over the figure of the tramps and mounting evidence of wage work's futility, Chicago's jobless men retreated into makeshift shelters — spaces where the expectation of autonomy was cynical. In August 1930, *Tribune* journalist Virginia Gardner visited some of these men and described the new environment they had created. In the Hooverville at Polk and Canal Streets, a few blocks from the Loop, she described the fruits—and vegetables—of men's labors. "Frank's" extensive gardens boasted "zinnias, Shasta daisies and sunflowers, along with beans, carrots, corn, tomatoes, turnips and a bird bath."[39] The following year she hinted at breakdown in structures of poverty when she described one hundred men building shelters, sewing, cleaning, maintaining homes, and cooking at Harrison and Des Plaines Streets "as proud of themselves, these jobless men who have so much time on their hands and so little money in their pockets."[40] Abandoned alongside the scraps they used to shelter themselves, these men endured as testaments to the breakdown in local officials' authority to compel autonomy. These labors of everyday life, journalists pointed out, failed to make anyone autonomous. When he ordered the demolition of the Hooverville that housed "Frank's" gardens in 1930, Chicago collector of customs Anthony Czarnecki made the opposite claim—that "bands of hoboes" were "distinct from the bands of unemployed men walking the street," who he presumed could become autonomous—implying that aid may be made contingent on autonomy.[41] As poverty overwhelmed greater numbers of Americans, the ordeals of the poor would testify that the structures of poverty assembled by reformers, social scientists, and journalists no longer meaningfully organized city life. The liberty-of-contract doctrine that guided labor relations up to the 1930s no longer made sense in an era when men were not reducible to economic units.

CONTRACTING WORKINGWOMEN

In 1923, four years after the Nineteenth Amendment guaranteed women political equality, the United States Supreme Court tossed out a 1918 minimum-wage law for women—authorized by a World War I–era wage board—and appeared to endorse women's full economic equality with men.[42] *Adkins v. Children's Hospital* rejected—in substance, if not law — the court's previous ruling in *Muller v. Oregon* that long workdays imperiled women's health and virtue.[43] *Adkins* touched on issues of doctrine when it announced that workingwomen possessed a liberty to contract equal to men's and invited women to define and contract the terms of their employment unimpeded by government regulation. Claiming to bring differences of the sexes to the "vanishing point," the court in *Adkins* heralded women's "emancipation from the old doctrine that she must be given special protection."[44] However, the nonlegal benefits of this emancipation were not immediately apparent. For instance, women's wages did not grow in the 1920s; instead, they declined — steadily — to average only 50 percent of men's by decade's end.[45] In fact, avowals of economic liberty and political equality in the 1920s would destabilize rather than dissolve declarations of virtue made by the reformers, social scientists, and journalists over the preceding half century. As with migrants, liberty of contract described a set of circumstances that many workingwomen would not experience.

In the 1920s, debates over the meaning of equality of the sexes engrossed journalists. Some, such as Eunice Fuller Barnard, argued that men and women were the same. She described students at Vassar and Smith Colleges who competed successfully with men at academies and also managed to keep their "health, [their] looks, and [their] much discussed femininity." Barnard thought that these women might use their talents to reorganize the home, explaining, "For women of intelligence cannot as a class be freed from it, or genuinely immersed in it until they reorganize it."[46] Other journalists, such as Dorothy Blake, whose syndicated advice column appeared in the *Tribune*, cautioned against competition with men and advised women to focus exclusively on domestic life, explaining that "ambition often ruins happiness." Blake's column steered readers through the "lonely" and "isolated" world of wage work with dubious-sounding headlines such as "How to Be Happy though Married."[47] She urged job hunters to be "of good appearance," suggesting that success at work and in the home were somehow connected: a "girl must be reasonably slender, graceful and well groomed," and "there must be that engaging sparkle of hair, complexion, hands, teeth, that just speak out efficiency in personal management."[48] Mrs. L. H.

Figure 5.2. "This decision affirms your constitutional right to starve" is a 1923 political cartoon by Rollin Kirby in response to the decision in *Adkins v. Children's Hospital*, which overruled the minimum wage for workingwomen. The cartoon appeared on a brochure for a nationwide conference on the minimum-wage decision called by the National Consumers' League. Used by permission of the estate of Rollin Kirby.

Walker of the Illinois Free Employment Office appeared to endorse Blake's claim when she argued that wage work and domestic life were linked: "The Loop is the best marriage mart," she announced. "The contacts formed in business are now the greatest source of matrimonial alliance."[49] For women, virtue was not entirely severed from work in the 1920s.

But the connection between the two was becoming tenuous, as local courts found its meaning muddled. For instance, in 1924, Nellie Meckling divorced her husband and moved in with her father, a wealthy hotelier who controlled the Great Northern Hotel in Chicago. At the divorce hearing, the presiding Cook County Superior Court judge decided to share his personal interpretation of sexual equality: "When women claim the rights of men, to vote, to smoke, and to enter business, they should also be required to take upon themselves a responsibility commensurate with men's." "Commensurate," in this case, was alimony. "I cannot force it upon you," the judge told Mr. Meckling, "but if you wish it I will grant you a proper sum of alimony." According to this judge, suffrage — and alimony — heralded "women's entry into an era of economic independence."[50] The interpretation expanded beyond Nellie Meckling's personal privilege to reach women of modest means. By the late 1920s, journalists described female tramps — "lady vagabonds" or "lady hoboes" — taking to the road in search of work and living independent lives in "jungles" where they replicated the existence of figures castigated for their failure to be autonomous.[51] Alongside advice columnists and journalists, "lady vagabonds" and "a proper sum of alimony" provocatively recast the terms of virtue vivified by claims to economic and political equality.

While claims to full equality of the sexes fell short of formal recognition, they challenged the compulsion to virtue. Alice Paul, head of the National Women's Party, petitioned Congress for a permanent equal rights amendment between 1921 and 1923 that would commit lawmakers to equality of the sexes. Paul referenced the legal opinion in *Adkins*, which she understood to announce blanket equality for women.[52] But other activists found the amendment to be misguided.

Progressive Wisconsin senator Robert La Follette, for instance, criticized the *Adkins* opinion as a violation of the "sanctity of human rights" because it denied workingwomen a minimum wage.[53] Chicago attorney Catherine McCulloch — who had accused Kate Kane of being "anti-suffrage" after her defense of Mary Henning in 1900 — would argue in the early 1920s that it was not "best to have all laws treat men and women alike."[54] In fact, McCulloch welcomed hours laws, mothers' pensions, and legislation that restricted women from working in mines and in the military. "Blanket equality bills," she explained, "cover more than is wanted in some cases and less than is desirable in others."[55] Journalist Valeska Bari agreed. She argued in the *Nation* that political equality did not diminish other forms of inequality and that removing protective legislation "would not change the physical handicap of those functions or its importance to society but," she added, directly referencing the issue raised in *Adkins*, "would only grant the doubtful benefit of an eighteenth-century liberty [of contract] to engage in twentieth-century industry."[56] The liberty enshrined in the right to enter contracts appeared to overshadow other expressions of inequality identified by La Follette, McCulloch, and Bari.

Equality of the sexes found formal recognition at the Supreme Court. In *Adkins*, Justice George Sutherland rejected the link between vice and wages, echoing Julius Rosenwald in his interview with Barratt O'Hara in the Palmer House a decade earlier. "The relation between earnings and morals is not capable of standardization," Justice Sutherland explained in *Adkins*. "It cannot be shown that well-paid women safeguard their morals more carefully than those who are poorly paid."[57] Sutherland's claim — that "fallen" women were not the same as wageworkers — also validated the views of journalists such as John Kelly, who demanded that wayward women be punished and who repudiated lenient judges for issuing "small fine[s]." Kelly commanded wayward women to accept invasive tests designed to detect "contagious" diseases and then to "leave the city or walk the straight and narrow path" within it.[58] Sociologist Walter Reckless corroborated Kelly's claims with statistical evidence that sex workers were not *worth* helping because they had committed moral sins. Because "only a few have ever been reached and saved by welfare agencies," Reckless speculated — without explaining "reached and saved" — it should be left to sex workers "to assist themselves in getting out of their profession." Their salvation, he added, was not in better jobs; rather, it was in "marriage with men willing to overlook their past." Reform, he declared, had "not been as effective as it could be."[59]

Lawmakers in Chicago echoed Sutherland's claim. Kate Adams, the namesake of the 1915 law that jailed women convicted of prostitution, would argue in the late 1920s — like Reckless — that sex workers were beyond reform. Sex workers had not been transformed into wives and mothers, Adams complained, but into "repeaters, hardened in their hopeless lives." She cited the case of M. L., an anonymous woman she described as "young, attractive and well dressed . . . one of the 'flappers' who has appeared in the Morals Court as elsewhere." "M. L." had been arrested 113 times from 1924 to 1928. Adams explained that she had not been successfully "reformed" by morals laws and that in five years she had cost the city a reported $3,950 in court and policing costs.[60] Illinois judges hearing the appeal of prostitute Sophie Hassil would also embrace Sutherland's interpretation of sex work. After she was convicted, fined, and sentenced for pandering in December 1928, Hassil appealed her Chicago municipal court conviction on a technicality.[61] In rejecting her petition, the appellate court distinguished between wage work, which it considered "free," and sex work, which it considered criminal. Only wage earners, the court explained, could become "free" by performing labor — and Hassil was not a wageworker.[62] As Sutherland, Kelley, Reckless, and Adams asserted, women who traded in sex were incapable of virtue.

As a result, virtue became an anomaly. The sexual equality and liberty to contract outlined in the *Adkins* opinion would most closely resemble practices associated with sex work and not wage work. The records of the Committee of Fifteen, which describe sex workers as resilient and innovative — bolster this view. Investigators observed sex workers conduct their business in houses, apartments, and hotels across the city, acquiring clients through direct solicitation or informal networks — such as those coordinated by bellboys and taxi drivers.[63] Committee investigators reported that despite official prohibition, sex workers continuously negotiated, entered, and abandoned contracts *at will*—in restaurants, in parks, from windows, and openly on the street.[64] Committee files detail personal interactions with sex workers. According to these files, Leslie Austin solicited investigators on the street in mid-April 1922 and unwittingly invited committee investigators to take her to the Atlantic Hotel, where she told them "she was not charity" but a worker who "made her living by sexual intercourse with men."[65] In another file, investigators were greeted by a man at the Cairo Hotel in early March 1926 who explained, "The girls were not there during the daytime" — possibly because they had day jobs — "but if we returned at night he would have some good lookers for us." Later that month, at a house on South Wabash, investigators were told to return "in the evening when she had two good ones."[66] Records also suggest that sex workers frequently negotiated their rates with potential clients. Dot, who provided massages and sexual services at 112 East Oak Street for ten dollars, offered to reduce her price when the investigator complained that "it was higher than usual and couldn't she just leave out the massage and charge $5 for the other." According to his notes, "she laughed again and said alright."[67] Files also describe competition for customers. For instance, at 4600 Calumet Street in March 1926, investigators asked for Suzie, only to be told by a young woman that "Suzie herself was working, but she herself would jazz me for $3."[68] Finally, the files register annoyance with the investigators themselves. A Mrs. Falvin referred to the Committee of Fifteen as a "dirty bunch of grafters."[69] When Mary, working at 803 Sunnyside Avenue, set her rate at seventy-five dollars, she probably was not expecting the recipient to hire her.[70] And when an investigator downed four beers at a saloon at 115th and Sixty-Fourth Streets and later complained, "I was absolutely unconscious. I believe the beer had ether in it," he was probably right.[71]

Beginning in the 1920s, the structures of poverty upholding women's virtue were overwhelmed by national suffrage and political equality and by arguments that workingwomen held a liberty to contract employment.[72] But the economic activity outlined in the *Adkins* opinion — and among Chicago's reformers, socials scientists, and lawmakers — appeared to sever vice from low wages and to endorse the economic practices associated with sex workers; this type of endorsement is likely the opposite of the impact the opinion was meant to have. Perhaps most alarmingly, in an era of political equality and liberty of contract, the compulsion to virtue ceased to coordinate women's wage work as coherently as it had. In fact, as the conditions of economic depression deepened after 1929, Illinois governor Henry Horner vowed, astonishingly, that women "must be able to sustain themselves by their own efforts."[73] As with white men, structures of poverty assembled to regulate workingwomen — compulsory virtue — no longer reflected conditions as they existed.

THE "NEW NEGRO"

The "New Negro" — a figure elaborated upon by African American Harvard graduate and Rhodes Scholar Alain LeRoy Locke twice in the mid-1920s — demanded immediate social, economic, and political equality for African Americans less than three years after the publication of *The Negro in Chicago*, a document that announced that racial equality did not exist. The New Negro projected, in an essay by Locke, "a new vision of opportunity, of social and economic freedom, of a new spirit to seize" and affirmed migrants' creative, industrial, and intellectual capacities.[74] The genesis of the New Negro lay in African Americans' — and America's — cultural renaissance in the 1920s. But its spirit also pervaded migrants' ambitions, where it reflected the failure of the heroic view of the migration to manage Black mobility and facilitate economic opportunity and settlement. Among Chicago's poor — men and women cast out of work sites and neighborhoods — the New Negro was a profound, symbolic statement that promised to disrupt entrenched commitments to isolation — to structures of poverty — that had long made migrants ineligible for the presumptive equality of the liberty-of-contract doctrine.

Chicago Urban League records revealed that, outside the packing, steel, and iron industries, Black men found employment "practically closed" in the 1920s. In the face of these exclusions, the league continued to promote thrift, cleanliness, health, and "general good behavior," despite evidence that migrants were concentrated in industries where "the health of the worker is impaired."[75] After two thousand Black women in Chicago hired as clerks and typists in early 1920 were laid off, the Chicago Urban League turned on the workingwomen — rather than their employers — citing *their* failure to make "suitable progress."[76] The idea that Black women were somehow out of synch with wage work inspired reformers' condescending exhortation — "Give her time. Guide her." — and extended the racial isolation of Black workers into the 1920s.[77] Amid these admonitions, the New Negro would provide an important counter to the isolation — the quarantine — that St. Clair Drake and Horace R. Cayton described as an overriding feature of migration designed to keep migrants "in their place."[78] As with the gangster tramp and the contracting workingwoman, the New Negro destabilized structures of poverty described by reformers, social scientists, and journalists who interpreted and championed racial isolation.

Black workers fought to break the quarantine from without. Strikebreaking was a quintessential outsiders' revolt, with which migrants had a lengthy history in Chicago. Describing strikebreaking as the "medium through which advancement is accomplished," the Chicago Urban League's William Evans implored white workers to "realize that their security is tied to the acceptance on equal terms of the colored workman."[79] The appeal of strikebreaking was widespread. For instance, the *Chicago Defender* endorsed the break of a Chicago transit strike in 1922 as a way of seizing "the privileges accorded [white] American citizens to earn a livelihood." Like Evans, the *Defender* blamed the white union for denying "economic rights to any man."[80] As the daily explained, if white workers kept African American workers out, it was only "natural that they accept, when the union men are ousted, the positions vacated by them."[81] In this way, strikebreaking exposed migrants' vulnerability by reinforcing their status as provisional, auxiliary workers: Black strikebreakers were often the last hired and first fired, and during strikebreakings they were physically quarantined in separate rooms "as if they were diseased"; they also experienced devastating violence.[82] The *Tribune* reported that James Brooks, a Black strikebreaker outside Oklahoma City, was kidnapped from his home and found hanged "three miles south of town" in early 1922.[83] Later that year, the *Defender* reported that twenty Black strikebreakers were killed when violence erupted at a mine in Herrin, Illinois. The *Defender* attributed this, and other violence, to exclusion from "work that should be ours under union protection, but which is denied us on account of our color."[84] Despite its enduring appeal, strikebreaking largely reinforced, rather than contested, migrants' isolation.

In contrast to strikebreaking, welfare capitalism and union organizing represented attempts to break the quarantine from within. The decline of the labor movement in the 1920s, marked by the loss of one million union memberships over the decade, left employers' authority in the workplace largely uncontested, ushering in one of the great eras of welfare capitalism — a term denoting employer-controlled unions, grievance policies, and benefits packages.[85] Although these programs varied, at Chicago's slaughterhouses they typically involved employee representation in business operations, bonuses, health insurance, vacation pay, and company-sponsored social activities, such as picnics. Unlike strikebreaking, company unions modeled racial inclusion and familiarized workers with pensions, vacation pay, grievance procedures, and health-care benefits; in the process, it deepened their involvement in the workplace.[86] If welfare capitalism inadvertently fostered a greater voice for African Americans in the workplace, A. Phillip Randolph's Brotherhood of Sleeping Car Porters (BSCP) — which would become the nation's largest union of African American workers — intentionally sought to strengthen the voices of all Black workers. Although the BSCP would not become the Pullman porters' official bargaining agent until 1935, it had an immediate impact after it was formed in 1925. Randolph's campaign to organize the porters at the Pullman Company — which operated the cars and was the largest single employer of African American workers in the United States at the time — elicited enormous resistance from proponents of delayed equality and of isolation in Black churches and businesses, including *Defender* editor Robert Abbott.[87] In fact, individual porters risked censure and even firing for openly supporting the BSCP. Welfare capitalism and unionization — both collective-action strategies — broke with strikebreaking and promised to break with the isolation it fostered.[88]

Despite these strategies, isolation continued to dog migrants throughout the 1920s. "Not in recent years," National Urban League director T. Arnold Hill announced in frustration at the end of 1927, "has there been exerted so much effort to find jobs for our people with so little success."[89] The next year journalists described a "constitutional" right to work "if we ever expect to reach the economic independence to which we have been aspiring."[90] "The place which the Negro has secured in the industrial life of Chicago is indicative of the Negro's future in industry," sociologist E. Franklin Frazier predicted darkly in the National Urban League's journal *Opportunity*.[91] The problem faced by Black workers, labor economist Abram Harris explained, was that they remained excluded from unions, "undisciplined in collective bargaining, ignorant of trade union traditions, [and] distrustful of white workers especially when organized."[92] NAACP activist Walter White argued in late 1931 that "unemployment and suffering are most acute among Negroes," who faced joblessness at a rate four times higher than whites. As migrants' suffering deepened, White noted "the almost chronic American indifference to the Negro's plight," and he begged northern employers, "Give them jobs." Racial isolation, White concluded in the era of economic collapse after 1929, is economically rooted.[93]

Chicago's African American migrants pushed back against "their subordinate position in the economic system" through campaigns that, like welfare capitalism and unionization, stressed the economic dimensions of isolation and embraced the figure of the New Negro.[94] They embarked on "Spend Your Money Where You Can Work" campaigns, which flourished on Chicago's South Side in the summer of 1930. By withdrawing support from white businesses that refused to hire Black employees, these campaigns signaled a shift away from Black workers' traditional allegiance to white employers. Chicago Urban League secretary T. Arnold Hill also began to pressure employers for a new approach, explaining, "Before any great improvement can come in the occupational status of Negroes, there must first come a change in [businesses'] attitude towards work."[95]

Migrants also pushed back against a legacy of isolation through housing. For instance, when the municipal court ordered the eviction of seventy-two-year-old African American Diana Gross from her home in the summer of 1931, neighbors responded. The *Defender* described a mob "like Coxey's army"— the legion that famously marched to the White House to protest the lack of federal support for jobs during the Panic of 1893 — that gathered at her home at 5016 South Dearborn Street and carried back inside the furniture and personal belongings that police and bailiffs had moved outside. In the ensuing skirmish, three African American demonstrators were killed. Business and civic leaders quickly blamed "red agitation among unemployed men and women" for the deaths — overlooking a history in which African American migrants had been regulated through housing.[96] Meanwhile, in August 1931, the *Tribune* attributed "rent strikes in the negro district" to the recruitments efforts of the Communist Party, which was in the process of defending the Scottsboro Boys, nine Black youths accused of sexually assaulting two white women aboard a moving train in rural Alabama in March 1931. The trial had become a national event. Astonishingly, the *Tribune* even blamed Viola Montgomery, mother of Scottsboro defendant Olen Montgomery, for "disturbances" after she described his ordeal in a Chicago speech within hours of Diana Gross's eviction.[97] These women and their supporters would encounter enormous resistance in their efforts to destabilize and erode isolation.

Despite these challenges, isolation would remain a feature of Black life. In late 1935, white University of Chicago students Margaret Haywood and Virginia Miller were arrested alongside African Ameri-

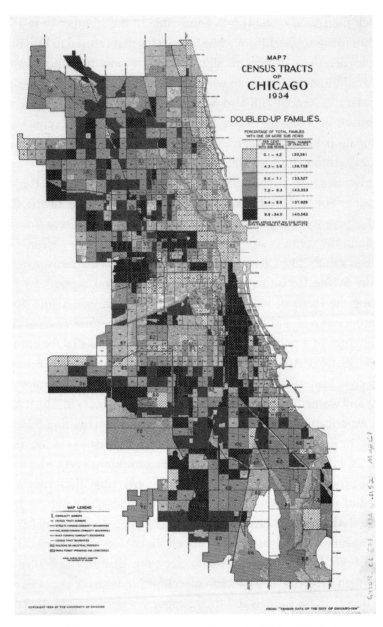

Figure 5.3. Hoovervilles were not the only strategy for families living on the economic margins in the 1930s. According to social scientists, families also "doubled up" in shared housing, as shown in this 1934 census map. Social Science Research Committee, University of Chicago, 1934.

cans Tony Morton, Luther Watson, William Dixon, and George Jones
for picketing the closure of a transient relief shelter at 4949 Indiana
Avenue. While they were all charged with disorderly conduct, these
officials were principally interested in policing racial and sexual divisions. Despite giving aliases and false addresses, however, the young
white women were promptly released from police custody after they
promised to "have nothing more to do with the communists and labor defense people." By contrast, the "four colored men" were kept in
jail, where their experiences — once again — affirmed and normalized
physical separation and isolation.[98] Migrants on Chicago's South Side
attempted to destabilize the isolation that bound them in the urban
North. But two decades after the first trickles northward anticipated
the Great Migration, they continued to experience the effects of racial isolation in Chicago. Alongside new iterations of crime stressing
rumrunning and work stressing sexual equality, African Americans in
the urban North continued to endure structures that facilitated their
isolation.

CONCLUSION

"Chicago has a dependable population of homeless men larger than
any other in the United States," the Council of Social Agencies announced in January 1933 — only a couple of months before Franklin
Roosevelt moved into the White House. The council had been formed
twenty years earlier to coordinate the efforts of local lawmakers, business leaders, and reformers to manage poverty in the city. But its task
had changed by the early 1930s as the council began to look past local
authorities to seek aid from the federal government.[99] It was clear that
in the 1920s, work no longer structured poverty as comprehensively
and coherently as it had in the past — or as clearly as William Graham
Sumner suggested in this chapter's epigraph. Reformers', social scientists', and journalists' views of the poor were inundated by new practices attributable to bootlegging and by demands for equal rights for

the sexes and racial equality. In fact, criminal joblessness, virtue, and isolation — however fractured — would remain structures, obstacles to the obligatory equality at the center of the liberty-of-contract theory of labor exchange. As a result, labor relationships would continue to structure differences in the social world, even in an era when Prohibition, an equal rights amendment, and labor organizing promised their reorganization.

The municipal court, which at one point had galvanized — formalized — the claims of reformers, social scientists, and journalists, was fractured by internal disputes over fees and salaries and decimated by government cuts in the early 1930s. In May 1933, municipal court judges' pay was cut for the second time in two years.[100] In addition, the creation of additional jury and filing costs, Judge Edgar Jonas complained, threatened its ability to operate as "a poor man's court" because the "poor man won't be able to afford it."[101] Some of the new work the municipal court performed was visible in its reorientation from local to state and federal relief efforts. For instance, in late 1933, Chief Justice Sonsteby would dedicate an entire downtown branch to relief fraud cases "growing out of the drive against relief cheaters."[102] At this new branch, thirty-nine-year-old John Jakubik was sentenced to nine months and ordered to pay eight hundred dollars to the Illinois Emergency Relief Commission because his wife had worked steadily from 1932 to 1935 — years when he had collected relief money.[103] Roy Leach also got in trouble for misusing aid. His wife, Jean Leach, testified before Judge Abraham Edelman that Roy squandered his fifty-five-dollar monthly stipend from the Works Progress Administration "in a tavern on other women." Judge Edelman ordered Roy Leach to support his wife or face six months in jail and a two-hundred-dollar fine.[104] Meanwhile, John Sandilands was convicted of accepting more than six hundred dollars in federal relief money in 1934 and 1935 while earning more than one thousand dollars annually as a plumber. Sandilands would have his conviction stayed after his wife complained to the judge that he would be unable to support her and their two young children from jail.[105] In each case, men were not punished for being dependent but for misusing aid.

Mired in relief violations, riven by internal discord, and desperate for a path forward, the municipal court looked to its own past for inspiration. In the early 1930s, Judge Sonsteby hired municipal court founder Hiram Gilbert — now in his mideighties — to do what he had done three decades earlier when he created the court: collect and organize its procedures, rules, and policies and strengthen its voice in the community. Although Gilbert's work "eliminated the need for a number of other books on rules and practices," his presence failed to revive a court that had built its authority by formalizing shared meanings of poverty described by reformers, social scientists, and journalists.[106] By the mid-1930s, federal policies had supplanted their views and recast the impoverished as "forgotten" or "down and out" — not individually responsible for the status of the economy. Although Gilbert's municipal court would never reclaim its central place in urban poverty administration, the autonomies, virtues, and isolations that it identified would justify federal authority through the New Deal and through other policies deep into the twentieth century to make poverty — the ordeals and obstacles faced by the impoverished — into the keystone of local and federal authority.

Epilogue: The New Deal's Social Origins

There is hardly a person listening in who does not know of an intimate friend, people whom you have known all your life, fine hard-working, upstanding men and women who have gone overboard and been caught up in this relief structure of ours. They are . . . the finest people in America.

— Harry Hopkins[1]

For University of Chicago sociology student Paul Oien, out collecting case studies in 1934, sex worker Ruth Johnson was a godsend — salty, salacious, and shrewd. And superstitious. The twenty-seven-year-old forbade hats on beds, always kept two clocks, and thought that "one whore [should never] see the pussy of another." She was pragmatic. Johnson explained that she survived the Great Depression by "turning tricks" and by forging intimacies with women such as Julia, whom she knew to be "queer on broads," and with men such as "Jim," a junk peddler who was also hooked on her. She was independent. Johnson navigated spaces outside domestic life, where she associated with "chippies" and "fat hustlers turning a trick for a buck." She was mobile too and described "camps," "joints," and apartments she occupied temporarily across Chicago.[2] For our purposes, Johnson breathes life into structures of poverty and reveals that the racial and sexual hierarchies constructed by reformers, social scientists, and journalists after the Great Fire would live on in New Deal programs, where white men were restored to work, white women to homes, and African Americans to isolation. At once mobile but isolated, independent but attached, Ruth Johnson spoke to the ways the structures of poverty survived — bifurcated and disorganized — into the 1930s.

But while President Franklin Roosevelt's New Deal programs revived the structures of poverty, they would reflect the concerns of the impoverished — principally white men — that autonomy was unattainable.[3] As president, Roosevelt promised Americans at Chicago's 1933

A Century of Progress International Exposition that a "century of even greater progress" lay ahead that would "release all peoples from the outworn processes and policies that have brought about such a commercial and industrial depression."[4] In a 1934 fireside chat — a device he used to address millions of Americans directly and instantaneously over the radio — Roosevelt vowed to speak for "a community of people that cannot do so for themselves in their separate and individual capacities." In this particular address, he endorsed a new interpretation of liberty of contract — a concept that had defined work in the first three decades of the twentieth century as individualistic, contracted, and unregulated. "I am not for a return to that definition of liberty," Roosevelt explained, "under which for many years a free people were being gradually regimented into the services of the privileged few." Instead, he called for "a broader definition of liberty" providing "greater security for the average man."[5] New Deal czar and presidential adviser Harry Hopkins idealized the "average man" in a radio address on October 12, 1933: "Who are these fellow-citizens? Are they tramps? Are they hoboes and ne'er-do wells? Are they unemployables? Are they people who are no good and who are incompetent? Take a look at them, if you have not, and see who they are."[6] The impoverished were not outliers, Hopkins claimed, but ordinary, everyday Americans.

New Deal programs resurrected structures of poverty through work. They pledged to renew white male autonomy. In this vein, the short-lived Civil Works Administration (CWA) would employ millions of previously unemployed men at paid, manual labor, while the Civilian Conservation Corps paid the families of young men to work in remote public locations and the Works Progress Administration catered to male heads of households by restoring unemployed men to steady work.[7] Meanwhile, despite women's prevalence as heads of households and breadwinners in the 1930s, as workers they were largely excluded from New Deal programs, relegated — as they had been by the Chicago Relief and Aid Society — to helper status and domestic duty.[8] The work they performed for money was often tied to a minimum wage, which, far from liberating them, further inured them to low-paying service work as clerks, maids, and waitresses.[9] Finally, the New Deal only emboldened Jim Crow: outside of a tiny Black elite, most African Americans were vigorously, systematically excluded from its programs.[10] Chicago's Black industrial workers, for instance, were steadily pushed out of steel and stockyard jobs in the 1930s; by the end of 1932, nearly half of Chicago's Black workforce was unemployed, a number roughly double the unemployment rate experienced by white workers. It was this isolation that spurred E. Franklin Frazier to study the African American family and St. Clair Drake and Horace Cayton to study the conditions of Black life in Chicago.[11] Ultimately New Deal programs would seek to revive the racial and sexual hierarchies initially assembled by reformers, social scientists, and journalists after the city was decimated in the fall of 1871.

In the mid-1930s, the Supreme Court embraced these hierarchies as it turned away from the liberty-of-contract doctrine and began to uphold New Deal programs.[12] Repudiating government nonintervention and asserting that government should help the common "man," Justice Charles Evans Hughes asked in his majority opinion in *West Coast Hotel Co. v. Parrish* (1937) — a case about a minimum wage for women — "What is this freedom? The Constitution does not speak of freedom of contract." Using workers' "unparalleled demands for relief which arose during the recent period of depression" as the basis of his legal argument, Hughes maintained that in times of economic crisis the government had a duty to intervene, to prevent the "exploitation of a class of workers who are in an unequal position," and to ensure that "the bare cost of living must be met."[13] The government's regulation of the economy through a minimum wage, Hughes argued, stemmed from its authority to intervene in the ordeals of the impoverished. Two weeks after *West Coast Hotel Co.*, the same court upheld the National Labor Relations Act in an opinion in which it describes workers' right to combine and negotiate collectively for better hours and wages. Justice Hughes, writing again for the court, stressed the inequalities generated by the Great Depression. The "single employee," he explained, "was helpless in dealing with an employer." "If the employer refused to pay him the wages that he thought fair," Hughes wrote, "he was nevertheless unable to leave the employ and resist arbitrary and unfair treatment."[14] In both cases, the ordeals of the poor and the inequities of the Great Depression fostered a legal reimagining of liberty of contract. While this reimagining largely did not reach working women, African American, or seasonal and occasional workers, it acknowledged limitations to the structures of poverty that compelled autonomy, if not virtue and isolation.

The structures of poverty described in this book leave us with two overlapping legacies. The first is in Supreme Court decisions that ratify racial and sexual hierarchies and institute them in national policy. The second is in the New Deal programs' correlation of work and status. In fact, in her interview with Paul Oien, the prostitute Ruth Johnson played with these statuses as she described the ways that she worked through them — sometimes autonomous, sometimes virtuous, often mobile, and frequently isolated. Johnson's artful storytelling connects us back to the stories described in this book, of Kate Kane, who manipulated vagrancy law; of Hudmon Carr, who escaped violence; of journalists Richard Westbrooks and Dan O'Brien, who set out to educate migrants; and of Gerty, who morphed the distinctions between wage and sex work by trading in sex casually. These figures invite us to interpret governance, work, and law as they did — as the product of minutiae, contingency, and everyday interactions. In the messy sequence of interactions and observations announced by reformers, social scientists, and journalists, they observed an order that derived from social relationships but that would express itself in law and policy. They remind us that work is about more than freedom; it is also about status and compulsion, particularly for people on the margins — men and women impoverished by official policies and practices. Together, their arrests, escapes, advice, dependencies, labors, grievances, and mobility — their survival in the margins — invite scholars to better understand the orders that occupy the impoverished.

Notes

INTRODUCTION: STRUCTURES OF POVERTY

1. For the *Tribune's* reaction to the Fire, see "Fire! Destruction of Chicago," *Chicago Tribune*, October 11, 1871. For Mason's appointment of the Chicago Relief and Aid Society, see Sawislak, *Smoldering City*, 81.

2. For President Roosevelt's New Deal programs, see Leuchtenburg, *Franklin D. Roosevelt and the New Deal*. For the War on Poverty, see Johnson's 1964 State of the Union address: "Johnson's State of the Union Address," *New York Times*, January 8, 1964. The poverty program included efforts to "restore" prosperity by disrupting welfare programs accused of nurturing a "culture of poverty" in the 1980s and 1990s. President Ronald Reagan used the term "culture of poverty" in a 1986 radio address to the nation on February 15, 1986: "We're in danger of creating a permanent culture of poverty," he asserted. See Caputo, *U.S. Social Welfare Reform*, 30. The *New York Times* used the term recently; see "'Culture of Poverty' Makes a Comeback," *New York Times*, October 18, 2010.

3. According to the White House, the "promise zones" policy did not pledge new money but "aid in cutting through red tape to get access to existing resources." President Obama described promise zones in January 2014. See "Obama Announces 'Promise Zones' in 5 Poor Areas," *New York Times*, January 10, 2014.

4. Ryan's proposal paired low-income residents with "case managers"—state agents with whom they crafted "opportunity plans." These contracts were devised to coordinate and incentivize self-sufficiency. While in theory residents who met preset benchmarks could earn a bonus, those who missed targets were punished with a reduction in service. For news coverage of Paul Ryan's antipoverty plan, see "G.O.P. Congressman's Plan to Fight Poverty Shifts Efforts to States," *New York Times*, July 25, 2014. For discussion of "worth," see Chicago Relief, *Chicago Relief and Aid Society*, 3–10.

5. For Carson, see "Ben Carson Calls Poverty a 'State of Mind,' Igniting a Backlash," *New York Times*, March 25, 2017. For President Trump, cuts in aid to the impoverished are also policy, see "Trump's Budget Cuts Deeply into Medicaid and Anti-Poverty Efforts," *New York Times*, May 23, 2017. For Trump endorsing work requirements, see "The Republican Plan to Tighten Food Stamp Work Requirements Is Advancing without a Single Democratic

Vote, *Washington Post*, April 18, 2018, and "Trump Signs Order to Require Recipients of Federal Aid Programs to Work," *New York Times*, April 10, 2018. For food stamps disqualify recipients from receiving citizenship, see Torrie Hester, Mary E. Mendoza, Deirdre Moloney, and Mae Ngai, "Now the Trump Administration Is Trying to Punish Legal Immigrants for Being Poor," *Washington Post*, August 9, 2019.

6. On the occasions that I use the word "Black" instead of "African American," I capitalize it out of respect for the people I am describing.

7. Chicago Relief, *Chicago Relief and Aid Society*, 3.

8. I do not capitalize the word "white" because of the word's association, in capitalized form, with white supremacy.

9. According to Paul Spicker, "structural poverty refers to poverty that is patterned by the social or economic structure" and "attribute[s] poverty to patterns of inequality (including class, race, gender and geographical inequalities), or to the structure of power, including economic, political and elite structures." See Spicker, Leguizamón, and Gordon, *Poverty*, 195–197.

10. I use the word "vice" in this book because reformers, social scientists, and journalists used it during the time period I discuss to assemble the structures of poverty that impoverished men and women experienced. Scholars have criticized the word for degrading and disparaging marginal men and women. See, for instance, White, *Comforts of Home*, 7–8.

11. Political scientists Stephen Skowronek and Theda Skocpol have profoundly influenced contemporary state studies. See Skowronek, *Building a New American State*, and Evans, Rueschemeyer, and Skocpol, *Bringing the State Back In*. Subsequently, historian William Leuchtenburg made the case for the state in a paper he developed from his 1986 American Historical Association presidential address in Leuchtenburg, "Pertinence of Political History," 585. Fifteen years later, Brian Balogh envisioned a smaller, but still significant, role for state study among historians. See Balogh, "State of the State," 455.

12. The state figures prominently in twentieth-century studies of capitalism, culture, and citizenship. See, for instance, Moreton, *To Serve God*; Cowie, *Staying Alive*; and Canaday, *Straight State*. William Novak challenges the "myth of statelessness" in the nineteenth century. See Novak, *People's Welfare*, 3–10. Novak also spearheaded a provocative *American Historical Review* roundtable, "The Myth of the 'Weak' American State," that enlisted historian Gary Gerstle, sociologist Julia Adams, and legal scholar John Fabian Witt and demanded greater attention be paid to the evolution of the state, to its philosophical underpinnings, and to its implications for foreign policy. See Novak, "Myth of 'Weak' American State," 752–772. Gary Gerstle, Julia Adams, and

John Fabian Witt each responded in the *American Historical Review* in June 2010.

13. For popular justice, see Dale, *Rule of Justice*. For popular constitutionalism, see Kramer, *People Themselves*, and Holton, *Unruly Americans*.

14. Katz, *Progress and Poverty*; O'Connor, *Poverty Knowledge*.

15. Michel de Certeau presents everyday acts as instances of uncoordinated resistance—of agency. In his formulation, walking, talking, and reading compose a "succession of action" that contest and destabilize power, however indiscriminately. See Certeau, *Practice of Everyday Life*, 96–121, 118. Historians and political scientists have expanded on Certeau's claims about the significance of the everyday. For rights, see Lovell, *This Is Not Civil Rights*. For challenges of modernity in Brazil, see Chazkel, *Laws of Chance*. For the developments in criminal law in Mexico, see Piccato, *City of Suspects*.

16. For mixed labor regimes influenced early American capitalism see Rockman, *Scraping By*. For work—and thinking about work—influenced the development of early American law, see Tomlins, *Law, Labor, and Ideology*.

17. Abraham Lincoln is quoted in *The Collected Works of Abraham Lincoln*, vol. 3, edited by Roy P. Basler, "Address before the Wisconsin State Agricultural Society, Milwaukee, Wisconsin" (September 30, 1859), 478–479. For free labor granted little of its promise, see Foner, *Free Soil, Free Labor*. For unfree labor, see Lichtenstein, *Twice the Work*, and Mancini, *One Dies, Get Another*. For unfree labor in the West, see Peck, "Reinventing Free Labor," 850. For unfree labor along the Pacific, see Smith, *Freedom's Frontier*, 1–4. For unfree labor in the North, see Stanley, *From Bondage to Contract*.

18. Hall, *Magic Mirror*, 211–222.

19. For a definition, see Hall, 242–243.

20. According to this view, substantive and contract rights developed out of the minority opinion in the *Slaughter-House Cases* were sharpened in opinions in *Powell v. Pennsylvania* (1888) and *Allgeyer v. Louisiana* (1897) and would convene in *Lochner v. New York* (1905), a Supreme Court decision exulting liberty of contract as the primary economic theory governing labor relations. Legal accounts of this process tend to stress doctrine. For accounts stressing law's relationship with society, see Forbath, "Ambiguities of Free Labor," and Ross, "Justice Miller's Reconstruction," 649–676. For an examination of the relationship between personal experiences and legal theory, see Ross, *Justice of Shattered Dreams*. For the political implications of the *Slaughter-House* opinion—the first substantial interpretation of the Fourteenth Amendment—see Labbe and Lurie, *Slaughterhouse Cases*. For a discussion of the ways that nonlegal things such as public health can acquire a legal dimension,

see Parmet "From Slaughter-House to Lochner," 476–505. For the legacy and legal implications of the *Slaughter-House Cases*—and an argument against historical narrative—see Barnett, "Three Narratives," 295–309. For relevant legal opinions, see *Slaughter-House Cases, Powell v. Pennsylvania, Allgeyer v. Louisiana,* and *Lochner v. New York.*

21. Pound coined the term "sociological jurisprudence" to describe a legal, scientific approach to urban life. In a series of law review articles, Pound beseeched urban authorities to apply "sociological" and "scientific" insights to the legal administration of urban life. A selection of Pound's relevant law review articles would include "Administration of Justice," "Need of a Sociological Jurisprudence," "Mechanical Jurisprudence," "Liberty of Contract," and "Scope and Purpose."

22. Pound, "Liberty of Contract," 482, 487. Italics added.

23. For a history of American neoliberalism, see Harvey, *Brief History of Neoliberalism.*

24. For current criticisms of neoliberal practices, see Standing, *Precariat*; Beckett and Herbert, *Banished*; and Wacquant, *Prisons of Poverty.*

25. Scholars have often made the claim that Chicago provides a template for how we understand Progressive Era urban life. See, for instance, Willrich, *City of Courts*, preface.

26. Work structures social, economic, and legal inequality. See Tomlins, *Law, Labor, and Ideology,* and Steinfeld, *Invention of Free Labor.*

CHAPTER 1. RISE

1. Jacobs, *Death and Life,* 376.

2. In the years from 1875 to 1885, vagrancy arrests filled roughly one quarter of the Lake Street rolls and generated small fines and short sentences. Fines were typically from five to sixty dollars, and sentences were typically from fifteen to sixty days in the local jail. However, the six-month sentences that Thomas Prendergras landed for vagrancy in August 1875 and William Barkley received in July 1877 suggest that police magistrates enjoyed significant discretion in sentencing. See Chicago Police Department, *First Precinct Arrest Book.*

3. According to the story, by the time his friends had discovered the man, his sentence was almost complete; he was promptly freed. While it is impossible to verify his existence or that of Sarah McGinty, the veracity of their existence may not matter — they represented a *problem* with vagrancy law. See

"Evils in the Police Court in Chicago," *Chicago Tribune,* May 23, 1897.

4. Bessie Louise Pierce puts the vagrancy rate from two thousand to three thousand. See Pierce, *History of Chicago,* 305.

5. For fears that galvanized around vagrancy, see "City Ordinances Are Defective," *Chicago Tribune,* December 10, 1892; "Cause of Crime," *Chicago Tribune,"* December 20, 1892; and "To Make Law Effective," *Chicago Tribune,* January 12, 1893.

6. Chicago's 1890 vagrancy statute reveals how these views of poverty were expressed statutorily. It punished an array of misconducts, from the jobless "habitually neglectful of their employment" to the homeless "found in the nighttime in outhouses, sheds, barns, or unoccupied buildings, or lodging in the open air." The vagrancy law of 1890 is also representative of Chicago's vagrancy law in general. It describes as vagrants

> all persons who are idle and dissolute, and who go about begging; all persons who use juggling or other unlawful games or plays; runaways; pilferers; confidence men; common drunkards; confidence men; common night-walkers; lewd, wanton and lascivious persons, in speech or behavior; common railers or brawlers; persons who are habitually neglectful of their employment or their calling, and do not lawfully provide from themselves, or for the support of their families; and all persons who are idle or dissolute, and who neglect all lawful business, and who habitually misspend their time by frequenting houses of ill-fame, gaming houses or tippling houses; all persons lodging in or found in the night time in out-houses, sheds, barns, or unoccupied buildings, or lodging in the open air and not giving a good account of themselves; and all persons who are known to be thieves, burglars or pickpockets, either by their own confession or otherwise, or by having been convicted of larceny, or other crime against the law of the state, punishable by imprisonment in the state prison, or in a house of correction of any city, having no lawful means of support, are habitually found prowling around any steamboat landing, railroad depot, banking institution, broker's office, place of public amusement, auction room, store, shop or crowded thoroughfare, car or omnibus or at any public gathering or assembly, or lounging around any courtroom, private dwelling houses or out-houses or are found in a nay house of ill-fame, gambling house, tippling shop, shall be deemed to be and they are declared to be vagabonds, and upon conviction they are fined not to exceed one-hundred dollars.

Hutchinson, *Laws and Ordinances,* statute 1306.

7. Foote, "Vagrancy-Type Law," 615. William Chambliss argues that the first vagrancy statute appears in 1349. See Chambliss, "Sociological Analysis," 67–77, and Steinfeld, *Invention of Free Labor,* 36.

8. The Act for the Punishment of Vagabonds and for Relief of the Poore and Impotent punished "all Common Labourers being persons able in Bodye using loitering and refusinge to worke for such reasonable wages as is taxed and commonly given in suche parts where suche persons do or shall happen to dwell." See 5 Eliz. c. 4 (1562) and 14 Eliz. c. 5. (1572) in Ribton-Turner, *History of Vagrants and Vagrancy,* 101–107.

9. Quoted from 5 Eliz. c. 4 (1562) and 14 Eliz. c. 5. (1572) and printed in Ribton-Turner, 101–107. For discussion of the rise of the employment contract and early vagrancy law, see Steinfeld, *Invention of Free Labor,* 23, and Morris, *Government and Labor,* 3.

10. Statute 17 George II, c. 5 (1744). Quoted in Ribton-Turner, 101–107. Italics in original.

11. According to Blackstone, when Athens's Court of Areopagus "punished idleness, and exerted a right of examining every citizen in what manner he spent his time," it established a precedent for punishing vagrancy as a public offense. Blackstone, *Commentaries on Laws of England.*

12. Chambliss, "Sociological Analysis," 75; Morris, *Government and Labor,* 4–5.

13. Massachusetts, *General Laws and Liberties.*

14. Morris, *Government and Labor,* 24–25, 289.

15. Morris, 289.

16. Franklin is quoted in *New England Anti-Masonic Almanac for the Year of Our Lord 1832* (Boston: John Marsh, 1831), "Sayings for Farmers," n.p. Article IX of the Articles of Confederation reads, "The free inhabitants of each of these States, paupers, vagabonds, and fugitives from justice excepted, shall be entitled to all privileges and immunities of free citizens in the several States." Morris, 24.

17. Wood, *Creation of American Republic,* 53–65.

18. For workers' status in early national-era America, see Nash, *Urban Crucible,* 217, and Morgan, *American Slavery, American Freedom,* 339, 383. For creating a new status of workers as employees, see Johnson, *Shopkeeper's Millennium.*

19. For the decline of indentured labor in the 1830s, see Steinfeld, *Invention of Free Labor,* 147–172.

20. Legal commitments to white male autonomy also flourished outside Chicago. A couple of legal opinions point to how these statutes were created.

In 1824, New York State passed a law that blocked white men who were classified as paupers and vagabonds from entering the state through its ports. After
a ship's captain challenged the law — and his duty to uphold it — the United
States Supreme Court endorsed the right of states to exclude jobless and poor
men. See *City of New York v. Miln*. In 1837, a Pennsylvania court seized John
Morser's house and his land — the individual's principal unit of economic production and legal autonomy in an agrarian society. In the process, it brought
his economic status as a poor man into alignment with his legal status as a
prospectively criminal dependent, or public charge. See *Forks v. Easton*.

21. "Police Intelligence," *Chicago Tribune*, January 21, 1856.

22. "Vagrants — What Is Done with Them and What Might Be Done," *Chicago Tribune* May 26, 1855.

23. "A Vagrant," *Chicago Tribune*, July 11, 1864.

24. "A Notorious Vagrant Sent Up," *Chicago Tribune*, November 25, 1867.

25. "Another Vagrant," *Chicago Tribune*, October 23, 1866.

26. Children were also arrested and charged with violating vagrancy law. In
fact, poverty reformer W. H. Hadley, who called for the more severe punishment of juvenile vagrants, argued that city and state government might apply
vagrancy law against the young with "great advantage." See W. H. Hadley, "The
Poor of Chicago," *Chicago Tribune*, February 16, 1858. Meanwhile, Lewis Ren-
stall, accused of obtaining money under false pretenses in 1856, experienced
that "advantage" when he was convicted of vagrancy and sent to reform school
rather than jail when he could not pay his ten-dollar fine. "Police Intelligence,"
Chicago Tribune, January 24, 1856.

27. Their experiences are described in the *Chicago Tribune* on November 18,
1853, and March 24, 1854. Also, see Bloom, "The Floating Population," 131–134.

28. "Commercial and Collection Agencies — Explain Actions," *Chicago Tribune*, March 7, 1856.

29. *Chicago Tribune*, August 26, 1857. Described in Bloom, "Floating Population," 133.

30. Dubber, *Police Power*, 130–135.

31. "Police," *Chicago Tribune*, November 23, 1859.

32. "A Home for Vagrant Girls," *Chicago Tribune*, November 4, 1859.

33. For the Wentworth case, see "Recorder's Court," *Chicago Tribune*, June
14, 1859.

34. *Nelson v. People*. Nelson was likely enslaved. Martha Jones has argued
that courts typically referred to enslaved individuals by their first names and
often included a reference to their race, such as "a mulatto" or "a negro," alongside their name. See Jones, "Time, Space, and Jurisdiction," 1050.

35. Scholars' descriptions of convict-leasing schemes implicated local judges, sheriffs, and employers in efforts to convict African Americans on bogus charges and force them into treacherous, unpaid industrial, agricultural, and mining work. See "Sold Into Slavery," *Chicago Tribune*, December 19, 1880. Vagrancy law was, perhaps, most commonly used in southern legal schemes that saw African Americans convicted on minor infractions, such as vagrancy, and sold into convict leasing where they were forced to work in private industries ranging from coal and ore mining to cotton and turpentine farming. See Mancini, *One Dies, Get Another*; Oshinsky, *"Worse Than Slavery"*; Kusmer, *Down and Out*, 68; and Blackmon, *Slavery by Another Name*.

36. The state of California passed a vagrancy act that was popularly known as the "Greaser Act" because it attempted to exclude "greasers," or the "issues of Spanish and Indian blood," from the state. See Haney-López, *White by Law*, 102. In the decade after the 1849 gold rush, authorities described imported, contracted Chinese labor, or "coolie" labor, as a threat to "free White labor" and created a law to tax Chinese workers. See Burrill, *Servants of the Law*, 162.

37. Journalists praised local judges for their mass imprisonment of homeless and jobless men. See "Law for Banyon," *Chicago Tribune*, September 5, 1873. Bessie Louise Pierce also describe accounts of journalists praising judges. See Pierce, *History of Chicago*, 240, 242.

38. Chicago Relief, *Chicago Relief and Aid Society*, 4–6.

39. Chicago Relief and Aid Society, *Report of Chicago Relief*, 10.

40. For descriptions of the night, see Chicago Relief and Aid Society, 7–9.

41. Sawislak, *Smoldering City*, 89–90.

42. Brown, *History of Public Assistance in Chicago*, 54–70.

43. See Booth, "Inhabitants of Tower Hamlets," 326–391, and Brown, 36, 114–125.

44. The procedure, developed by employment bureau chairman and famed Chicago industrialist Nathaniel Fairbanks, was to give unskilled workers tickets that the society described as "certificates of character." After acquiring the ticket at a relief station, the prospective worker would present it at the employment bureau in exchange for a job. In late 1871, within weeks of the Fire, Chicago Relief and Aid Society authorities considered the failure to return a ticket "presumptive evidence that the bearer preferred to eat the bread of idleness rather than work for his own subsistence." For officials, the ticket became a voucher of "worth." For employment bureau, see Sawislak, *Smoldering City*, 97.

45. For the Stewart fund — fifty thousand dollars pledged within days of the Fire — see Chicago Relief and Aid Society, *Report Chicago Relief*, 279–281.

46. See *Chicago Tribune*, October 22, 1871.

47. See "Charity in Chicago," *New York Times,* December 26, 1875.

48. Brown, *History of Public Assistance,* 22–24. In fact, public trials in the mid-1870s and mid-1880s would expose systematic corruption and graft among — and undermining the authority of — private reformers. Stunningly, they would reveal that commitments to scientific charity masked attempts to pillage assets assembled to coordinate relief. See Brown, 91–94.

49. Sawislak, *Smoldering City,* 98.

50. Closson, "Unemployed in American Cities," 189–195; Phelps, "Idled Outside, Overworked Inside," 31–36.

51. Labor statistics summarized in Phelps, "Idled Outside, Overworked Inside," 42.

52. Pierce, *History of Chicago,* 269, 269n.

53. Phelps argues that in the late nineteenth century, prisons were the only place with continuous, full employment. Phelps, "Idled Outside, Overworked Inside." See also Robinson, *Should Prisoners Work?*

54. The explosion amplified this wrath — intended for labor organizers — as the hunt for perpetrators intensified and spilled over into popular media. "A Wild Mob's Work," *Chicago Tribune,* May 4, 1886. According to the *Tribune,* the women were "afflicted with a malignant form of the eight-hour malady." See "Shouting Amazons," *Chicago Tribune,* May 4, 1886.

55. The *New York Times* and the *New York Star* were quoted, along with other national presses, in the *Chicago Tribune,* May 5, 1886; "Two More Dead Heroes," *Chicago Tribune,* May 7, 1886; "Down with Anarchy," *Chicago Tribune,* November 20, 1891.

56. In Chicago newspapers, workers were depicted alternatively as "unruly hoards" who were "defying law and authority" or as "serfs" controlled by labor organizer Eugene Debs, whom the papers described as a "czar" or a "sovereign." The strike at Pullman began in May 1894 during the Panic of 1893 and was led by Debs's American Railway Union. Because most trains pulled a Pullman sleeper car, the strike quickly shut down activity on most of the nation's railroads, including the movement of mail cars, which transformed the local strike into a national strike. President Grover Cleveland crushed the strike with federal troops, despite Debs's repeated assurance that mail cars would not be obstructed. For newspaper coverage, see "Sovereign's Edicts," *Chicago Tribune,* July 13, 1894; "Debs' Czar's Crazy Letter to Cleveland," *Chicago Tribune,* July 9, 1894; and "Great Strike of '77," *Chicago Tribune,* July 8, 1894.

57. The town of Pullman may have been created to facilitated workers' uplift — through clean housing with running water, electricity, and indoor plumbing. But the town also prevented workers from ever owning their

homes; each belonged to namesake George Pullman. See Ely, "Pullman," 452, 455, 459. Upon Pullman's death in 1897, the Illinois Supreme Court ordered the company town dissolved because it was incompatible with good public policy. See *People ex rel. Molony v. Pullman's Palace-Car Co.*

58. "Pullman Strike Not Warranted," *Chicago Tribune,* December 11, 1894.

59. According to reports, Fire victims were fortunate to collect 20 percent from private insurance companies. Most insurers were bankrupted by the conflagration, and most dwellers got nothing. Sawislak, *Smoldering City,* 79.

60. Harvey also oversaw the building of "isolated homes" for Fire victims — modest barracks for survivors who owned or leased land. See Chicago Relief and Aid Society, *Report off Chicago Relief,* 188–193.

61. Chicago Relief and Aid Society, 184.

62. Brown, *History of Public Assistance,* 25–27; Bloom, "Floating Population," 240–260.

63. Bloom, *Floating Population,* 21.

64. Bloom, 15–52, 173, 193.

65. Hoyt, "One Hundred Years," 96–97.

66. Brown, *History of Public Assistance,* 30–35.

67. See Parton, "Chicago," 335–345. A similar view to Parton's can be found in "Workingmen's Homes," *Chicago Tribune,* April 18, 1875. Thomas Lee Philpott repudiates Parton's claims, arguing that Chicago had extensive tenement conditions after the Civil War. See Philpott, *Slum and Ghetto,* 8–9.

68. Abbott, *Tenements in Chicago,* 51; "Tenement Housing," *Chicago Tribune,* September 13, 1883; "Tenement House Reform," *Chicago Tribune,* September 14, 1884.

69. These statistics reflect national census material assembled by Joanne Meyerowitz. See Meyerowitz, *Women Adrift,* 47–48, 71.

70. Philpott notes that for two cents you could get accommodation on the floor of a flophouse, while some saloons allowed patrons to sleep on the floor. Men without money found shelter in stables and outhouses. See Philpott, *Slum and Ghetto,* 98; Slayton, "Flophouse," 379–381; and Embree, "Housing of the Poor," 375–376.

71. According to Embree, the Chicago Police Department used their facilities to shelter over thirty thousand men from November 1894 to February 1895. See Embree, "Housing of Poor," 373. For saloon lodging and public lodging, see Stead, *If Christ Came to Chicago,* 18–20, 127, 139, and Monkonnen, *Walking to Work,* 8, 10–12, 58, 174, 193–195. For "where wretched homeless wanderers may kennel themselves for the night," see "About Pauperism," *Chicago Tribune,* February 20, 1856.

72. Antilynching activist Ida B. Wells publicly criticized the exclusion of African Americans. See Ida B. Wells, "Letter to the Editor," *Record Herald,* January 26, 1912, quoted in Spear, *Black Chicago,* 46–47. According to the report *The Negro in Chicago,* migrants faced a "lack of lodging or hotels where lodging could be had at reasonable prices." This, the report explained, was partly responsible for this swarm of migrants seeking shelter in private homes." See Chicago Commission on Race Relations, *Negro in Chicago,* 166.

73. Bogue, *Chicago, Cheap Lodging Houses,* 3–4.

74. Abbott, *Tenements in Chicago,* 44. Codes were not entirely common in the late nineteenth century but were developed for housing built in the city's core after the 1871 Fire, when the City of Chicago required that rebuilding be done in brick. Because brick was more expensive, this policy limited workers' ability to rebuild within the city after the Fire. See Sawislak, *Smoldering City,* 139; Abbott, *Tenements of Chicago,* 16; and Philpott, *Slum and Ghetto,* 10, 13–14.

75. "The great drawback to self improvement," the Housing Association announced, "is the general condition of accommodation offered the lodger in Chicago." See Pierce, *History of Chicago,* 53.

76. Abbott, *Tenements of Chicago,* 44, 47, 51. Chicago Board of Health Report quoted in Abbott, 45. For continued use of sewers, see Pierce, *History of Chicago,* 55.

77. Pierce, *History of Chicago,* 311–321.

78. Riis, *How the Other Half Lives.*

79. Philpott, *Slum and Ghetto,* 26–27.

80. Hunter, *Tenement Conditions in Chicago,* 145–146.

81. Hunter, 71.

82. Embree, "Housing of Poor," 366, 374.

83. Feldman, *Citizens without Shelter,* 110–118.

84. For claims about being inadequate, see "Evils in the Police Court of Chicago," *Chicago Tribune,* May 23, 1897; Burke, "Official Complicity with Vice," 1240; and "Justice for the Poor," 4. For descriptions of the police court as inadequate, see McCormick, "Problems of Criminal Judicature," 287; Waterloo, "Revolution in Chicago's Judicial System," 452–453; and Olson, "Proper Organization and Procedure," 80.

85. For "go and sin no more," see "Our Old Police Court," *Chicago Tribune,* December 14, 1890. Michael Grossberg uses the term "judicial patriarchy" to describe the attitude of courts to women in the nineteenth century. Paul Boyer discusses reform as a shift away from "village" practices. See Grossberg, *Governing the Hearth,* and Boyer, *Urban Masses and Moral Order,* 122.

86. According to Almena Dawley, the police court was largely a "political

organizations" that "obeyed the orders of alderman" who instructed magistrates on how to manage the cases. The fee basis of the police courts, Dawley explains, operated as a "pecuniary motive for increasing the amount of litigation and the number of continuances." It also led to "judgments for the plaintiff," particularly if they were "in the habit of patronizing that particular court." Meanwhile, Dawley explains, bailiffs were vetted by aldermen and "owed their first duty to the alderman, their second duty to the court." As a result, those violating misdemeanors often "escaped prosecution." In other cases, "misdemeanor cases were not tried until the expiration of from three months to three years after the offense had been committed." Dawley describes how justice was thwarted — bought and sold — and judges instructed to either "liberate the prisoner or to assess a heavy fine, whatever the facts may be." See Dawley, "Study of Social Effects," 3–4. Elizabeth Dale also suggests in her review of Michael Willrich's *City of Courts* that law was being bought and sold. See Dale, "Michael Willrich," 548.

87. For blanket conviction, see "Courts Blamed for Outlawry," *Chicago Tribune,* November 29 1903. When the Illinois Bar Association backed a proposal for a new legal system to replace the police court in 1905, it cited, among other things, the court's failure to keep order, exemplified by its failure to punish the teamsters involved in a violent and disruptive stockyard strike in 1905. See Willrich, *City of Courts,* 26.

88. The charter convention was composed of men deeply invested in Chicago's business community, including Mayor Carter H. Harrison II, then completing his fourth term; circuit court judge Murray F. Tuley; attorney John S. Miller, who was employed by Standard Oil; attorney John P. Wilson; Civic Federation president Bernard E. Sunny, a western manager for the General Electric Company; and Robert A. Eckhart, a merchant. See Willrich, 34–36.

89. "Deadlock over City Court Bill," *Chicago Tribune,* February 28, 1905.

90. "Justice System Gets Its Finish," *Chicago Tribune,* April 22, 1905; Gilbert, "New Municipal Court System," 4.

91. Willrich, *City of Courts,* 47–49.

92. Bledstein, *Culture of Professionalism,* 53–65, 115–120.

93. City of Chicago, Municipal Court, *Fifth Annual Report of the Municipal Court of Chicago: For the Year December 5 1910 to December 3 1911, Inclusive* (Chicago: n.p., n.d.), 68; Waterloo, "Chicago's Judicial System," 453–455; McMurdy, "Law Providing," 252; Gilbert, "Legal Tract Series," 105.

94. Gilbert thought that the court should be like Marshall Fields, Chicago's famed department store: efficient and unencumbered by the lengthy delays characteristic of the police court. See Gilbert, "Legal Tract Series," 97.

95. "Defends Court of Chicago," *Chicago Tribune,* December 20, 1908.

96. Pound, "Administration of Justice," 312–313.

97. Olson boasted in lectures he gave outside Chicago that a "Court should be organized like a corporation." See Olson, *Municipal Court of Chicago,* 4, 9; Greene, "Municipal Court of Chicago," 344; McCormick, "Problems of Criminal Judicature," 279–280.

98. Blackstone, *Commentaries on Laws of England.*

99. Tiedeman, *Treatise on Limitations,* 118, 120; Freund, *Police Power,* 98–99.

100. Tiedeman, *Treatise on Limitations,* 118.

101. The compulsion to steady work was also arbitrary, Tiedeman added. "A man may spend his whole life in idleness and wandering from place to place" if "he has sufficient means of support," Tiedeman explained. For legal treatises, see Tiedeman, 118, 120, and Freund, *Police Power,* 100.

102. Although municipal court historian Michael Willrich has claimed that the new court aligned most closely with Pound's legal thinking, it nevertheless emerged in a context of diverse thinking about poverty and governance, where the legal meanings of autonomy, virtue, and isolation were not yet worked out. For Pound and the municipal court, see Willrich, *City of Courts,* 27. Pound embraced greater legal regulation and broader legal intervention into everyday life. He was interested in using law to reform social issues, such as poverty. See McLean, *Law and Civilization,* 191–205, and Pound, "Theories of Law," 114, 146. Pound also makes a similar argument about law's social role in "Administration of Justice," 310–321.

103. McMurdy, "Law Providing," 194, 199.

104. "The New Vagrancy Law," *Chicago Tribune,* July 1, 1877.

105. "The Vagrancy Law," *Chicago Tribune,* December 7, 1877.

106. For journalists criticizing McAllister, see "The Vagrancy Law," *Chicago Tribune,* February 1, 1877; "The Vagrancy Law," *Chicago Tribune,* March 8, 1877; "The Vagrancy Law," *Chicago Tribune,* December 7, 1877; and "Hickey's Message: The Police Superintendent's Report for Last Year," *Inter Ocean,* February 2, 1878.

107. Frank Hitchcock appealed his conviction and demanded a right to a trial by jury. McCulloch rejected the appeal and explained that jury deliberations would slow down the processing of jobless and homeless men, cause delays, and make the law less effective. "The People ex. rel., Cain v. Frank Hitchcock," *Chicago Legal News,* 329–330.

108. "City Brevities," *Inter Ocean,* August 15, 1879.

109. Henry Hyde, "New Methods in Public Life, Olson's Forte," *Chicago Tribune,* June 30, 1915.

110. "Olson Would Rid City of Crooks," *Chicago Tribune,* February 13, 1907.

111. Olson communicated with lawmakers about vagrancy, but it is not clear which incarnation of vagrancy law, if any, his advice helped shape. Judge Harry Olson, "Correspondences Addressing the 1907 Vagrancy Law," box 1, folder 3, Chicago Municipal Court Records, Research Center, Chicago History Museum.

112. "Vagrancy," *Chicago Tribune,* April 22, 1907.

113. This statement was made before the National Conference of Charities in Minneapolis. See "The Cost of Tramps," *Chicago Tribune,* June 16, 1907.

114. "Police and Judge in Steady Strife," *Chicago Tribune,* January 30, 1908.

115. City of Chicago, Municipal Court, *Second Annual Report,* 32–33.

116. Edward F. Roberts, "McKenzie Cleland of the Municipal Court," *Chicago Tribune,* April 23, 1908.

117. Willrich, *City of Courts,* 63–65.

118. Cleland rejected the idea that all jobless should be imprisoned. See Cleland, "New Gospel in Criminology," 362, 359, and "Husbands to Be Paroled," *Chicago Tribune,* January 31, 1907. Phelps suggests that full employment only existed in jails. See Phelps, "Idled Outside, Overworked Inside."

119. Cleland, "New Gospel in Criminology," 358.

120. "Husbands to Be Paroled," *Chicago Tribune,* January 31, 1907; "Judge Paroles 50; Wives Are Happy," *Chicago Tribune,* February 2, 1907.

121. Stella also brought charges against local saloonkeeper Joseph Szymanski, whom she accused of making her husband drunk. Cleland threw out this complaint. *People v. Leo Szulczaski.*

122. "Paroled Wife Beater No. 2 Again behind Bars," *Chicago Tribune,* February 5, 1907.

123. It was a "common thing for substantial business men to appear in Court and offer employment," Cleland boasted. See Cleland, "New Gospel in Criminology," 359.

124. Adult probation would become law in Illinois in 1911, signed in by Governor Charles Deneen. See Willrich, *City of Courts,* 93.

125. E. C. Cook pleaded with Olson to let Cleland's "experiential work continue in the interest of the community at large." Officials at Chicago's Henry Booth Settlement wrote Olson and formally requested that he reconsider Cleland's transfer. See controversy over the probation policies of Judge McKenzie Cleland, including letters from business and civic leaders, available in Chicago Municipal Court Records, box 2, folder 8.

126. In both letters, Olson used spousal abuse to illustrate a larger point

about legal restraint: "Some people believe that wife beaters should be pun-ished by public flogging, but it would not do for one of our courts to sentence a man to be thus publicly punished, without [laws] permitting it to be done." See Chicago Municipal Court Records, box 2, folder 8.

127. Materials on the controversy over the probation policies of Judge McKenzie Cleland, including letters from business and civic leaders, available in Chicago Municipal Court Records, box 2, folder 8.

128. City of Chicago, Municipal Court, Court of Domestic Relations, *Annual Report* (Chicago 1912), 4–5.

129. City of Chicago, Municipal Court, *Fourth Annual Report: The Municipal Court of Chicago; For the Year December 7, 1909 to December 4, 1910, Inclusive* (Chicago: W. J. Hartman, n.d.), 56, 60–61. The new court's expressed logic was straightforward. The Court of Domestic Relations had three aims: to "keep husband and wife together," to compel "delinquent deserters" to sup-port "those dependent on him," and to "provide watchful care over deserving and unfortunate women." See City of Chicago, Municipal Court, *Fifth Annual Report*, 68–72.

130. City of Chicago, Municipal Court, Court of Domestic Relations, *Annual Report*, 4–5. Judges also sought to compel labor through statute. For in-stance, in the court's first annual report (for the year 1912–1913), Judge Charles Goodnow recommended that the Abandonment Act of 1903, which autho-rized the court to punish men who abandoned their wives and children, be used to punish "delinquent" husbands "in perpetuity" by requiring that they pay child support past age nine. Goodnow also wanted to make the bastardy law — which targeted men who fathered children outside of wedlock — into an extraditable crime, so that men who left the state could be transported, tried, and compelled to provide. See City of Chicago, Municipal Court, Court of Domestic Relations, *Annual Report*, 6–9. Unemployment was criminal in a couple different ways. According to vagrancy law, irregularly and unemployed men were criminal. However, in the late nineteenth century, full and con-tinuous employment only existed in jails and prisons. Also see Phelps, "Idled Outside, Overworked Inside."

131. According to the court's first report, "sufficient time is given to make this payment, and unless the party is reported sick or out of work, an attach-ment is issued at once and payment compelled, or defendant sent to the House of Correction for failure to pay." See City of Chicago, Municipal Court, Court of Domestic Relations, *Annual Report*, 11, and City of Chicago, Municipal Court, *Sixth Annual Report of the Municipal Court of Chicago: For the Year December 4, 1911 to November 30, 1912, Inclusive* (Chicago: n.p., n.d.), 84.

132. For cases, see *People v. George Bowing*, *People v. Thomas Cayton*, and *People v. George Matter.*

133. According to Joanne Meyerowitz, eight dollars was a widely acknowledged subsistence wage for workingwomen in the early twentieth century. See Meyerowitz, *Women Adrift*, 34. The eight-dollar mark was also used in the *Senate Report on Vice* in 1916 to describe the impact of low wages on sex work. See Illinois General Assembly Senate Vice Committee, *Report of the Illinois Senate Vice Committee* (1916), 111.

134. City of Chicago, Municipal Court, *Sixth Annual Report*, 84–86.

135. Moral "crimes" ranged from selling salacious pictures and books to abduction, seduction, pandering, fornication, and concubinage to keeping, maintaining, patronizing, or leasing a house of ill fame. Each, according to the court, threaten women's status as mothers and nurturers. City of Chicago, Municipal Court, *Seventh Annual Report of the Municipal Court of Chicago: For the Year December 2, 1912 to December 30, 1913, Inclusive* (Chicago: n.p., n.d.); Willrich, *City of Courts*, 195; City of Chicago, Municipal Court, *Tenth and Eleventh Annual Report of the Municipal Court of Chicago: For the Year December 6, 1915 to December 2, 1917, Inclusive* (Chicago: n.p., n.d.), 85.

136. Chaired by University of Chicago social scientist Charles Merriam and assembled in response to a perceived crime wave in spring 1914, the committee endorsed the claim that joblessness was criminal. In its report, the committee proposed the active surveillance of "idle" and suspicious men and the institution of a card index system. "All you have to do is to find them [idling] a few times, [and] after you find they have no lawful means of support, you can arrest [them] all for vagrancy. It is not hard to secure a conviction under this statute," the committee explained, "if handled properly." Merriam, "Findings and Recommendations," 345. The committee was composed of the city's leading social scientists; Edith Abbott did the report's statistical work. Drawing on materials from 1913, she argued that those arrested and convicted were overwhelmingly men, typically single and native born, and disproportionately employed as unskilled laborers or skilled laborers. In addition, the greatest number of men and women arrested and charged with a crime were from twenty to thirty-nine years of age — prime working years. Chicago City Council, *Committee on Crime*, 52, 57, 46. The committee spent ten months gathering statistics and conducting investigations and produced its report in March 1915. The study examined the causes and prevalence of crime in the city and recommended a number of preventive schemes. Perhaps the most outstanding element of the study was that it collected, organized, and publicized all available information on crime in the city, from arrests and prosecutions

to the criminal complaints cataloged in the police department's "squeal book," previously regarded as a "private police document." Chicago City Council, *Committee on Crime,* 170–172.

137. At the Vagrancy Court, jobless men "were tried on the record at time of arrest, and not on promises" to get work. See Chicago City Council, *Vagrancy Court.* The Chicago City Council's compiled the following crime statistics for larceny, robbery, and burglary in the first five months of 1917: January, 1,540; February, 1,333; March, 1,666; April, 1,525; May, 1,508. Statistics for the same months in 1918 were January, 974; February, 750; March, 852; April, 776; May, 801. The report does not address the impact on crime statistics of the Selective Service and America's entry into World War I. Chicago City Council, *Vagrancy Court.*

138. "Olson Would Rid City of Crooks," *Chicago Tribune,* February 13, 1907.

139. Haller, "Historical Roots of Police Behavior," 312–313; Chicago City Council, *Vagrancy Court.*

140. Turner, "City of Chicago," 587, 591.

141. Turner, 587, 591.

142. For migration patterns, see Cronon, *Nature's Metropolis,* 155, 183–199.

CHAPTER 2. AUTONOMY

1. Wyckoff, *Workers: The West,* 46–47, 77–78.

2. Pinkerton, *Strikers, Communists, Tramps and Detectives,* 30–31.

3. Anderson, *On Hobos and Homelessness,* 66.

4. For accounts of "tramps," see Monkkonen, *Walking to Work;* Kusmer, *Down and Out;* and Anderson, *On Hobos and Homelessness,* 50–100.

5. Black, "Space and Status," 227–244.

6. For hobo political activism and community building, see Higbie, *Indispensable Outcasts.* For homelessness, see DePastino, *Citizen Hobo.* For tramps and expert knowledge, see Cresswell, *Tramp in America.* For mobility and crime, see Friedman, "Crimes of Mobility," 637–658. According to Michael Denning, the figure of the tramp transformed poverty in to a "contested terrain." See Denning, *Mechanic Accents,* 3–5.

7. This legal duty was spelled out in Chicago's vagrancy law. The law of 1890, for instance, targeted "all persons who . . . are habitually found prowling around any steamboat landing, railroad depot, banking institution, broker's office, place of public amusement, auction room, store, shop or crowded thoroughfare, car or omnibus or at any public gathering or assembly, or lounging

around any courtroom, private dwelling houses or out-houses." See Hutchinson, *Laws and Ordinances,* statute 2190.

8. For instance, see Foner, *Free Soil, Free Labor;* DePastino, *Citizen Hobo,* 33–34; and Rodgers, *Work Ethic in Industrial America,* 30–33.

9. "The Question of Tramps," *New York Times,* February 6, 1875.

10. "The Tramp."

11. Holland, "Once More the Tramp," 882.

12. "Hickey's Message: The Police Superintendent's Report for Last Year," *Inter Ocean,* February 2, 1878.

13. "The New Vagrancy Law," *Chicago Tribune,* July 1, 1877. The amendment to the law was ruled "hopelessly unconstitutional" in 1877 and thrown out. See "The Vagrancy Law," *Chicago Tribune,* December 7, 1877.

14. Middle-class depictions of poverty abound in the late nineteenth century and include "The Tramp"; "How to Give Alms," *Harper's Weekly,* October 6, 1877, 778–779; "Charity in Chicago," *New York Times,* December 26, 1875; Croffut, "What Rights Have Laborers?," 294; Holland, "Once More the Tramp," 882; and "Alms and Wages," *Harper's Weekly,* September 22 1877, 739.

15. "The Tramp."

16. "Prisoners and Vagrants."

17. "City Ordinances Are Defective," *Chicago Tribune,* December 10, 1892.

18. "Cause of Crime," *Chicago Tribune,"* December 20, 1892; "To Make Laws Effective," *Chicago Tribune,* January 12, 1893. According to Chicago's mayor and police chief, the jobless were "steeped in vice and utterly devoid of character." See "Live by Imposture: Chicago Beggers and Their Tricks and Manners," *Chicago Tribune,* February 10, 1893.

19. "Authorities hardly know how to handle it," they complained. See "Invaded for Bread: Chicago the Mecca for the Whole Country's Unemployed," *Chicago Tribune,* December 14, 1893.

20. According to a *Tribune* headline, "Maj. McClaughry Would Reform the Hobo by Working Him." See "Sure Cure for the Tramp Habit," *Chicago Tribune,* February 18, 1896. This view of the provisionally employed poor as criminal was reflected in claims that Chicago was a "Tramp Mecca." See, for instance, "City Ordinances Are Defective," *Chicago Tribune,* December 10, 1892, and "Calls Chicago Tramp Mecca," *Chicago Tribune,* November 17, 1900. For forced removal, see "Vagrancy and Colonization," *Chicago Tribune,* March 11, 1902. For the authority that private charity exercised defining dependency, see Brown, *History of Public Assistance in Chicago,* 110–120.

21. "The Tramp."

22. Holland, "Once More the Tramp," 882.

23. Leavitt would argue that communities had a responsibility to provide a place where the jobless could clean up, eat, and "pay for the hospitality by work," rather than face conviction and be forced to "work out a five hour sentence on a stone pile, with ball and chain." See Leavitt, "Tramps and the Law," 190.

24. For Charles Booth, see Booth, "Inhabitants of Tower Hamlets," 326–391, and Booth, "Conditions and Occupations," 276–339. For Chicago, see Residents of Hull House, *Hull House Maps and Papers*, 57, 148, 144, 139, and Stead, *If Christ Came to Chicago*, 24, 30–31. Stead visited Hull House regularly while writing his book. See Addams, *Twenty Years at Hull House*, 160.

25. "Alms and Wages," 739; "How to Give Alms," 778–779.

26. Leavitt, "Tramps and the Law."

27. Holland, "Once More the Tramp," 882.

28. Justice Taney's spiteful declaration, which was directed at free and enslaved African Americans on the eve of the Civil War, might also be understood to include the experiences of jobless and roaming men, who were often described as outliers and criminals in the years after the war. See *Dred Scott v. Sandford*.

29. For Fairbanks, see Chicago Relief, *Chicago Relief and Aid Society*, 6–7. For Walker, see Chicago Relief, *Chicago Relief and Aid Society*, 32; Nelson, "Chicago Relief and Aid Society, 1850–1874," 62.

30. Sumner, *What Social Classes*, 39; Sklansky, "Pauperism and Poverty," 118, 119.

31. From Sumner's 1883 speech at the Brooklyn Historical Society. Quoted in Sandage, *Born Losers*, 248.

32. "How to Give Alms," 779.

33. Wayland, *Paper on Tramps*, 10–15. Wayland is also cited in Katz, *Poverty and Policy*, 93.

34. Dorothy Ross discusses the rise of American social sciences. In her study, she makes at least two important points. First, she suggests that labor struggles and the disorder they caused drove the rise of American social sciences. Second, she suggests that labor struggles signaled a contested social order. The impetus to social scientific inquiry, Ross argues, "was oriented first toward the social transformation of industrialization and the fate of the working class." This would change. While the appearance of local and national unions, dissident political parties, strikes, and violence certainly allowed "the working class to make its existence known in palpable ways," it also came to overshadow concerns about workers "increasingly tied by machine process to wage labor and to the vicissitudes of the business cycle." Ross argues that

business benefited from the association of workers and urban disorder and invested heavily in universities and social scientific research. Consequently, deviation from a certain economic ideology came to matter more than the conditions it fostered. Ross, *Origins of American Social Sciences*, 139. Park explained reform as "some sort of restriction or governmental control over our activities." Park, Burgess, and McKenzie, *The City*, 28.

35. Park, Burgess, and McKenzie, *The City*, 28.

36. McCook, "Tramp Census." See also Ringenbach, *Tramps and Reformers*, 17–18.

37. McCook's findings were wide-ranging. The study found that among tramps, American nativity predominated, at just over 56 percent. Just over half, or 57 percent, of the sample identified as skilled workers, and 46 percent engaged in employments that required their mobility. Those included in the sample were also relatively young, with 75 percent under forty years of age and 60 percent under thirty-five. Meanwhile, just over 85 percent identified their health as "good." The study also found that nearly 83 percent of men took to the road in search of work and that fewer than 5 percent had been on the road for more than one year. McCook's statistical summary also found that literacy rates were over 90 percent, while roughly 63 percent of respondents claimed to be "intemperate." In the study, the tramps' attitude toward alcohol was communicated by two statistical summaries: fewer than 6 percent of tramps admitted to having committed a crime, but over 38 percent admitted to having been convicted of drunkenness. "Possibly they regarded drunkenness as no crime," McCook suggested. Before concluding with a list of suggestions for solving the tramp menace, McCook identified the "cost" of these "public burdens" as approximately "one half the cost of the navy." McCook, "Tramp Census." For more on McCook, see Harring, "Class Conflict." The vagrant demographic on the Lake Street rolls was also overwhelmingly male, of working age (from seventeen to forty-seven), and — with the exceptions of two peddlers, a cigar maker, clerk, and saloonkeeper — unemployed. See Chicago Police Department, *First Precinct Arrest Book.*

38. Although the study was published in 1911, it was based on material gathered in 1903–1904. See Solenberger, *One Thousand Homeless Men.*

39. Of the one thousand men surveyed, 74 percent were single, just under 8 percent married, and roughly 12 percent widowed. The bulk of men surveyed, fewer than 72 percent, were of prime working age (from fifteen to forty-nine). While a small percentage identified as professionals and businessmen, 21 percent identified as skilled workers, 9 percent as partly skilled, and just over one-third of the entire sample as unskilled workers. See Solenberger, *One Thousand Homeless Men.*

40. Wyckoff, *Workers*, 41.

41. Bogue, *Chicago Cheap Lodging Houses*, 3–4.

42. For the experiences of Mexicans and Asian immigrants, see Ngai, *Impossible Subjects*, 70, 131, 205. For McCook's proposal, see McCook, "Tramp Census," 766. Vagrancy laws, enticement laws, and emigrant agent laws were commonly used in the South to restrict the mobility of freedmen. For race, see Bernstein, *Only One Place of Redress*, 8–15, and Blackmon, *Slavery by Another Name*, 53, 124.

43. For Charles Booth, see Booth, "Inhabitants of Tower Hamlets," 50, 326–391, and Booth, "Conditions and Occupations," 51, 276–331. For Solenburger, see Solenberger, *One Thousand Homeless Men*, 10.

44. Reportedly, the anonymous tramp also explained, "I like to travel and I can get a living without working. I know you don't like the way I'll get it, but I've made up my mind; I'm done with work. There's no use in trying to argue with me, for I know what I'm going to do, but you treated me so White I thought I ought to let you know.'" See Solenberger, *One Thousand Homeless Men*, 81.

45. Solenberger, 81.

46. Cronon, *Nature's Metropolis*, 231–235, 328.

47. Solenberger, *One Thousand Homeless Men*, 143–144. Italics added for "ought"; italics for "right" are in original.

48. They noted that the "forlorn and bedraggled" women present were the "lowest grade of prostitute." See "Chicago: Hobo Capital of America," 287–290, 303–305.

49. Margot Canaday describes how the word was used by federal officials responsible for public charges and moral turpitude offenses in the context of immigration policy in the early twentieth century. See Canaday, *Straight State*, 24–28.

50. According to a 1911 vice commission report, male prostitution "begot children that were defective and deformed." See Chicago (Ill.), *Social Evil in Chicago*, 290.

51. In other instances, reformers were not sure how to interpret male sex workers and even doubted "whether any spread of actual knowledge of these practices is in any way desirable." See Chicago (Ill.), 295–298.

52. Chicago (Ill.), 296–298.

53. Anderson's case studies on homosexual practices among homeless and jobless men include "Document 122: Boy Tramp, Great Wanderer, Homosexual, Intelligent, Two Years on the Road," "Document 124: An Evening Spent on the Benches in Grant Park; Description of Men and Their Talk," "Document 125: Observations upon the Unnatural: Attachments of Some Homeless Men

and Boys," "Document 120: Young Man, Well Dressed, Homosexual Prostitute, Loafs in Grant Park," and "Document 82: Case of Boy in Teens, Tramp,
'Flirting' with Men in Grant Park," Ernest Watson Burgess Papers, box 210,
folder 9.

54. Adrian, "Organizing the Rootless," 1.

55. Anderson, *On Hobos and Homelessness*, 32–41.

56. For a description of Hobohemia, see Anderson, 32, 35.

57. Michael Denning refers to dime novels as "contested territories." See
Denning, *Mechanic Accents*, 3–5. Historians have generally scoffed at the
idea that work made workers self-sufficient in the late nineteenth century.
For instance, Amy Dru Stanley has argued that features of the bound-labor
economy were incorporated into the free-labor economy. The prosecution of
vagrants and their consignment to workhouses, Stanley writes, was perhaps
most emblematic of this incorporation. Part of this was due to the operation of
the market. "Wage labor contracts obeying the market," she writes, "revolved
around the same quid pro quo as slavery." Stanley adds, "The untrammeled
freedom of the marketplace was only ultimately assured by legal coercions."
Stanley, *From Bondage to Contract*, 137, 163.

58. Kusmer, *Down and Out*, 35–37.

59. Davis, "Forced to Tramp," 151.

60. Quoted in Davis, 147.

61. Quoted in Davis, 151.

62. Quoted in Davis, 151.

63. Wyckoff, *Workers: The West*, 215.

64. Anderson, *On Hobos and Homelessness*, 33; Harry M. Beardsley, "Along
the Main Stem with Red: Being an Account of Hobohemians," March 27, 1917,
box 127, folder 1, Ernest Watson Burgess Papers.

65. DePastino, *Citizen Hobo*, 105.

66. How was the grandson of James Buchanan, the renowned architect of
the Eads Bridge, connecting St. Louis and East St. Louis across the Mississippi River, and the son of the James F. How, general manager of the Wabash
Railroad. Born into privilege and educated at elite universities, How reportedly spurned his upbringing and even handed the twenty thousand dollars
he inherited upon his father's death to the mayor of St. Louis, "asking that it
be turned over to the people who had earned it — the poor." With subsequent
inheritances, he funded a "crusade for social justice." According to historian
Roger Burns, the "benefactor of his work was the American hobo." See Burns,
Damndest Radical, 21–22.

67. Ben Reitman, Chicago's famous physician to prostitutes, organized the
Hobo College. He recalled in his unpublished autobiography the college's gen-

esis in a chance 1907 stopover in St. Louis. Reitman said after the meeting that "for the first time in my life I really had something to say and an audience to say it to." See Reitman "Following the Monkey," 86–187, Ben Lewis Reitman Papers, box 2, folder 23.

68. According to Reitman, a medical doctor would explain "vagrant diseases, [and] industrial accidents"; railroad officials would "show how the railroads make vagrants, [and examine] the cost of confrontation"; judges would "lecture on the vagrant laws [and] how they work"; police would lecture on the likelihood of arrest and jail terms; and — testifying to the growing importance of social science to the study of urban life — a professor from the University of Chicago would lecture "on the vagrant's duty to society and society's duty to the vagrant." Reitman also proposed that a saloonkeeper "show why a vagrant drinks," a physiologist compare amounts of energy "a man expends when working and when not working," a representative from an employment agency instruct students "how to get a job," and "a reverend teach the influence of religion, home and women upon a man's life." See "The Reitman College for Vagrants," Ben Lewis Reitman Papers, box 30, folder 376. Emphasis in original.

69. DePastino, *Citizen Hobo*, 107.

70. Chas W. Allen, "Sociology Term Paper, March 16, 1923," box 150, folder 1, Ernest Watson Burgess Papers.

71. Beardsley, "Along the Main Stem."

72. Operating five evenings a week — possibly so its students could work during the day — the college also offered labor history and debates on Fridays and an open forum, with music, theater, and debates, on Sundays. See Beardsley.

73. "Hoboes: Judge Talks to Them about Their Rights under the Vagrancy Laws," *Chicago Tribune*, March 2, 1917.

74. The *"Hobo" News* claimed to "reflect the tramp's life and interests." It reportedly reached a maximum circulation of twenty thousand copies in winter, with lower numbers in the summer months, "when all the men [were] out of town, on the job." Anderson, *On Hobos and Homelessness*, 92–93.

75. "Document 104: Jewish Tramp, Sells Papers, Tin Worker, Served Time in Jail on Wife Desertion," box 127, folder 3, Ernest Watson Burgess Papers.

76. However, its content was not particularly radical — the paper's policy was "to keep the reds out." See Anderson, *Hobos and Homelessness*, 93, and DePastino, *Citizen Hobo*, 102.

77. E. J. Irvine, "The Hobo," *"Hobo" News*, December 1921.

78. Louis Angus Young, "Itinerant Philosopher: A Study in Wanderlust," *"Hobo" News*, July 1920.

79. Editorial, *"Hobo" News*, August 1922.

80. For W. B. Lamb, see editorial, *"Hobo" News*, August 1922. For Knibbs, see Knibbs, *Songs of the Outlands*, n.p.

81. J. J. O'Connell, "Editorial," *"Hobo" News*, June 1922.

82. Dan O'Brien, "Wage Slavery," *"Hobo" News*, June 1921 (page mutilated, n.p.).

83. "Document 77: Man Forced to Be Idle by Hard Times Learned to Get Along, Later Refused Work," box 127, folder 2, Ernest Watson Burgess Papers.

84. Anderson was accused of describing jobless men as criminally dependent. See "Book Review," *"Hobo" World*, November 1923.

85. D. H. Horn, "Trade Unions and Political Action," *"Hobo" News*, October 1922. Capitals in original.

86. Bill Quirks, "Work," *"Hobo" News*, February 1922.

87. The cover page of the November 1921 issue of the *"Hobo" News* pictured five unemployed men scanning job advertisements in a newspaper. The caption paraphrased President Harding's 1920 campaign motto "A Return to Normalcy." See "Back to Normalcy," *"Hobo" News*, November 1921.

88. Elmer T. Allison, "Phanton [*sic*] Democracy" *"Hobo" News*, July 1920.

89. In the early twentieth century, hobo union leader Robert Wilson solicited an endorsement from the Chicago Federation of Labor in his "scheme to declare all vagrancy laws unconstitutional." A public testimonial from the federation might have helped by declaring that irregularly employed men were entitled to the same rights, dignity, and protection as other workers. However, in this instance the federation declined the offer, instructing that "an itinerant toiler must go his own way." See "Union Men Turn Down Hoboes," *Chicago Tribune*, November 17, 1913. See also "Union Men Hear King of Hoboes," *Chicago Tribune*, November 13, 1913. Wilson had initially formed the hobo union in 1906 to "encourage habits of thrift and industry, [and] to provide [jobless men] with employment." Noting that "many hoboes are well informed," Wilson confirmed that "one of the first steps of the new organization will be to secure a modification of the vagrancy law as will insure the hobo against police as long as they are guilty of no actual crimes." See "Hoboes Form a Union for Their Protection," *Chicago Tribune*, April 22, 1906.

90. Roger Payne, who reportedly held degrees in the arts and law, dedicated his energies to traveling and selling his pamphlet *The Hobo Philosopher*, encouraging hobos to abandon the "hell" of wage work. See Payne, *Hobo Philosopher*, 2–3, 5–7.

91. "Vagrancy Writs to Sweep City," *Chicago Tribune*, September 8, 1905.

92. Olson proposed that "persons found guilty of vagrancy shall serve a

term on the 'rock pile.'" Endorsing expulsion — to "clear the scum of the earth from Chicago" — he recommended presenting "crooks and loafers" with two options: "work at honest labor" or "get out of Chicago." See "Olson Would Rid City of Crooks," *Chicago Tribune*, February 13, 1907.

93. "The new law went into effect last Monday, but they have not fled." See "The Vagrancy Act," *Chicago Tribune*, July 5, 1907.

94. "Police Must Check Crime," *Chicago Tribune*, November 28, 1909. The Chicago Council City Committee on Crime, which organized in 1915, also proposed to collect "records of every person found conducting himself in a manner making himself amenable to the vagrancy act." See Chicago City Council, *Committee on Crime*, 171.

95. "The Vagrancy Law," *Chicago Tribune*, January 31, 1908.

96. Vagabond Information by Individual, forms mixed in with vagrancy cases, Municipal Court of Chicago Criminal Records, Chicago Municipal Court Archives.

97. *People v. Theodore Ryanovski.*

98. *People v. Henry Geloss.*

99. *People v. Edward McNamara.*

100. *People v. John Williams*; *People v. G. Reed.*

101. *People v. Covey.*

102. *People v. O'Keefe.*

103. Callahan also acknowledged that he was a surety for others. *People v. David Miller*; *People v. Ed Brown.*

104. *People v. Harry Jacobs*, case number 99983, and *People v. Harry Morris*, case number 99982. Both also listed item number 12 on the vagrancy index: "Lodges in and was found in the nighttime in (a) an outhouse; (b) open air without giving a good assessment of himself."

105. "Document 80: Report of a Visit to Police Court, Hoboes Tried at Rate of One a Minute, August 28, 1922," box 127, folder 3, Ernest Watson Burgess Papers.

106. For Anton Cermak, see Green, "Anton J. Cermak," 100. Dependency charges included contributing to the delinquency of a minor or abandonment. *People v. George Bowing*; *People v. Charles Matter.*

107. The state of Illinois passed an adult probation law in 1911. See Illinois, "Notes on Current and Recent Events," *Journal of the American Institute of Criminal Law and Criminology* 5, no. 6 (March 1915): 928–929.

108. *People v. Fred Schultz*; *People v. Nicholas Wagner.*

109. In 1859, House of the Good Shepherd began reforming begging, unsupervised, abandoned, and homeless girls and women who might be "found

in a house of ill fame or in a house of prostitution." At the home, residents were instructed in cooking, embroidery, and knitting, as well as reading and writing, with the hopes that "when [women] are placed in a better moral atmosphere they [will] endeavor to lead good and virtuous lives." House of the Good Shepherd was located on the block edged by Elm, Market, and Hill Streets. See "A Noble Work," *Chicago Tribune*, February 8, 1886.

110. *People v. Nicholas Wagner*.

111. The committee was organized in response to a perceived increase in crime. Describing 1913, the most recent year for which it had statistic, its authors noted, "There was in the year 1913 an increase over the year 1912 of 9.0 per cent in arrests for felonies, an increase of 28.5 per cent in arrests for misdemeanors and an increase of 26.2 per cent in the total number of arrests." See Chicago City Council, *Committee on Crime*, 21–23, 10. The committee interpreted crime hierarchically: "The crime system is not a system in the sense that it is centrally organized, that it is completely organized, and under fairly close control. The degree of centralization differs in the various branches of crime. The pickpockets, for example, are probably the best organized, while the burglars and hold-up men are regarded as the lower grade of criminal. There are Dukes, counts, and lords in the criminal group, but there is no king who rules over the entire population." See Chicago City Council, 164.

112. According to the report, the category of "professional criminal" includes "pickpockets, burglars, holdup men, confidence men, gamblers, pimps, safe-blowers, shoplifters, and all-around crooks. Most of the burglary, robbery and larceny is committed by them." See Chicago City Council, 10.

113. Italics added. Chicago City Council, 10–13, 162, 170.

114. Chicago City Council, 170.

115. Chicago City Council, 171. For McCook, see McCook, "Tramp Census."

116. Chicago City Council, *Committee on Crime*, 55.

117. Chicago City Council, 12. For Samuel Leavitt, see Leavitt, "Tramps and the Law," 190, and Wyckoff, *Workers: The West*, 41.

118. Adrian, "Organizing the Rootless," 248, 259.

119. Livingston *Hobo Camp Fire Tales*, preface, 11, 26, 99.

120. The "A-No. 1" series was written by Leon Ray Livingston, who "grew up a pampered, well-educated child" in a wealthy California family. Livingston began publishing his stories through his vanity press in Cambridge Springs, Pennsylvania, but moved operations to Erie in the mid-1910s. Patterned "physically and in plot structure" on dime novel adventure tales, the "A-No. 1" series was designed for popular reading and marketed toward boys and young men. Adrian, "Organizing the Rootless," 236, 239–241.

121. Livingston, *Hobo Camp Fire Tales*, preface.
122. *People v. John Lewis.*

CHAPTER 3. VIRTUE

1. Dreiser, *Sister Carrie*, 64.
2. Kane may have borrowed these lyrics from an 1894 popular song, "What a Woman Will Do for a Man." See "What a Woman Will Do for a Man," Digital Collections, Music Division, New York Public Library.
3. Kane's argument also received coverage in the magazine the *American Lawyer*. See the first article (no title), *American Lawyer*, June 1900, 8. For more on Kane, see Dale, *Chicago Trunk Murder*, 38–39, and Black, "Citizen Kane."
4. For made to work, see "Free Woman from Work," Chicago Tribune, April 24, 1900.
5. Sex workers were sometime classified as "vagrants." In his treatise on police power, the University of Chicago's Ernst Freund wrote that the common prostitute "as a rule answers to the description of a vagrant, for she is without legitimate means of support and is apt to manifest her illegitimate livelihood in an offensive manner. She may therefore be dealt with under the laws of vagrancy, vagabondage and criminal idleness." Freund, *Police Power*, 98, 226, 228–230.
6. Catherine McCulloch, an attorney and president of the Illinois Equal Suffrage Association, criticized Kane for playing on the jury's sexism. See "Little Talk on Live Topics," *Chicago Tribune*, April 25, 1900.
7. Black, "Citizen Kane."
8. Turn-of-the century social scientists described workingwomen as inferior to male wageworkers. See Abbott, *Women in Industry*. Scholars point to the ways that judges and employers used women's domestic duty to justify subordination. See Winkler, "Revolution Too Soon," and Siegel, "She the People." Linda Gordon argues that workingwomen were not treated as breadwinners but as wage earners in a family economy. See Gordon, *Pitied but Not Entitled*, 36–38.
9. For economic arguments about sex work, see Peiss, *Cheap Amusements*, and Keire, *For Business and Pleasure*.
10. For "adrift," see Joanne Meyerowitz, *Women Adrift*. For "delinquent daughters," see Odem, *Delinquent Daughters*. For "sisterhood," see Rosen, *Lost Sisterhood*.
11. Michael Denning argues that working-class readers were attracted to

literary accounts that reflected their lives. See Denning, *Mechanic Accents*, 3–5.

12. Statement made by a tramp in J. J. McCook's "Tramp Census" in 1893. Quoted in DePastino, *Citizen Hobo*, 84. For prostitution and tramps, also see Higbie, *Indispensable Outcasts*, 15.

13. Anderson, *On Hoboes and Homelessness*, 11; Reitman, *Sisters of the Road*, 39, 199–200.

14. Camp, *Iron in Her Soul*, 12. Goldman ridiculed moral crusades against vice: "It is significant that whenever the public mind is to be diverted from a great social wrong, a crusade is inaugurated against indecency, gambling, saloons." See Goldman, "The Traffic in Women," in *Anarchism and Other Essays*, 179, 177, 194.

15. Donovan, *White Slave Crusades*, 57. In one of his many treatises on white slavery, Roe called for the creation of a Federal Bureau of Immigration in "great distributive centers," such as Chicago, to stop the "steady stream" of international pandering operations. Cautioning that immigrant panderers were innately devious, he instructed immigration officials to beware their "various simple subterfuges." See Roe, *Great War on White Slavery*, 391, 98, 211.

16. Hoy, "Caring for Chicago's Women and Girls," 49, 51; Hoy, *Good Hearts*, 53.

17. "Woes of Working Girls," *Inter Ocean*, August 28, 1887.

18. In the early 1890s, a small group of Chicago police escorted Women's Christian Temperance Union members, who — "convinced a trip to the Levee [Chicago's red-light district from the 1880s to 1912] would be a practical aid to their purpose and work" — encountered "'the other half of the world'" and then shuddered. Collecting stories "to enlighten future audiences," they discovered that "nearly all the inmates had come to Chicago seeking work." But because it was fixated on temperance, the organization reportedly shied away from a broader engagement with sex workers, explaining after the Levee tour "the union cannot cover too wide a field of action." "Go through Slums," *Chicago Tribune*, October 23, 1893; "Purity for Motto," *Chicago Tribune*, October 24 1897; "Place for Nice a Near-by Ward," *Chicago Tribune*, October 19, 1903; "Fight Levee Vice with Hymn Books," *Chicago Tribune*, June 14, 1907. Frances Willard typically viewed independence and domesticity as complementary, and her demands for women's independence led her to challenge gendered inequities in law and economics. "The femme covert" Willard asserted, "is not a character appropriate to our peaceful homelike communities." She proposed to make marriage "an affair of the heart and not of the purse." Willard, *White Life for Two*, 6, 11; Matthews, *Rise of the New Woman*, 20; Donovan, *White*

Slave Crusades, 41, 45. "For tempted and betrayed," see Women's Christian Association, *After Twenty-Five Years*. Quoted in Spain, *How Women Saved the City*, 156.

19. "Woes of Working Girls," *Inter Ocean*, August 21, 1887.

20. "Woes of Working Girls," August 12, 1887.

21. "Woes of Working Girls," September 11, 1887; "Woes of Working Girls," September 4, 1887.

22. "Woes of Working Girls," August 28, 1887.

23. "A Broken Hearted Father," *New York Times*, April 26, 1887; "Save the Girls: Who Will Watch the Trial of Mumford, the Betrayer of Little Julia Bernhardt?" *Inter Ocean*, April 30, 1887.

24. The trial was heated. Julia's father reportedly struck Frank Mumford with "a terrific backhand blow to the mouth, which stretched him almost senseless on the floor," and then returned to his seat, sobbing, "This miserable man has ruined my child." The conditions for statutory rape were narrow, including "every male person of the age 14 years and upward, who shall have carnal knowledge of any female child under the age of 10 years, either with or without her consent." "No Law to Punish Him: Frank Mumford, the Despoiler of Little Julia Bernhardt, a Free Man," *Inter Ocean*, November 26, 1887; "A Broken Hearted Father," *New York Times*, April 26 1887; "Save the Girls."

25. "Save the Girls."

26. Growth from 1870 to 1890 is reported in Pierce, *History of Chicago*, 237. In the half century after 1880, women's participation in wage labor increased from 2.6 million to 10.8 million, three times the rate of increase for workingwomen in the nation as a whole. See Meyerowitz, *Women Adrift*, 4–9. This growth also bears out in census data, which reveals that from 1880 to 1920, workingwomen were represented overwhelmingly among domestic service, laundry, needlework, and stenography — subsistence jobs that reinforced women's inability to become self-sufficient through work. Census material on women's occupations in Chicago from 1880, 1900, and 1920, as compared to men's, reveals striking consistency in the types of work that women performed. In 1880, 13,370 women were domestic servants (1,394 men), 1,450 in laundry (344 men), and 12,053 in needlework (4,848 men). In 1900 in Chicago, 35,340 women were servants (11,674 men), 2,963 were housekeepers (297 men), 13,205 were dressmakers (124 men), and 3,432 were milliners (118 men). Meanwhile, in the new category of stenographers/copiers that appeared in 1900, 8,113 were women (1,662 men). In 1920 in Chicago, the pattern in which women's paid work resembled domestic work continued to hold. A total of 8,513 women were dressmakers (16 men), 26,184 women were servants (8,640

men), and 6,638 women worked in laundries that were not industrial (644 men). Meanwhile, in the category of people paid to copy the words of others, 42,152 women were stenographers (3,023 men). See *Statistics of the Population, 1880*; Department of Commerce and Labor Bureau of the Census 1900, *Special Report*; and Department of Commerce, *Fourteenth Census*.

27. "Women out of Work; Hundreds of Destitute Females without Employment," *Inter Ocean*, December 17, 1893; "The Black Hole," *Inter Ocean*, January 14, 1882.

28. "Our Working Women," 5.

29. Addams, *New Conscience and Ancient Evil*, 63, 77.

30. Addams, 49, 59, 76.

31. On the contributions of working women, Edith Abbott writes that women have been "from the beginning of our history an important factor in American industry as secondary workers where they receive not "unequal pay for equal work, but unequal pay for different and probably inferior work." Abbott, *Women in Industry*, 6, 313–317. C. D. Wright backed Abbott's claim. He found that most women only worked for a short period before marriage. He also found that the wages of young workingwomen were barely adequate. See "Our Working Women," 5.

32. Della Carson, "Problems of the Working Girls," *Chicago Tribune*, April 7, 1907. In the "garment trades," women typically outnumbered men by two to one, and hours were long, conditions unsanitary, and workloads heavy. Production was characterized by a sweating system — a term denoting the pace of sewing-related work and the cheapness of the goods produced — both of which were "attained solely at the cost of the victim," or worker. *Hull-House Maps and Papers*, 86, 70; Stansell, *City of Women*, 19.

33. "Saved by the Needle," *Chicago Tribune*, January 4, 1894.

34. Miss Newton of Chicago's Siegel Cooper and Co. Employment Agency recalled that it was often a challenge to fill domestic jobs when the economy was strong. But during the Panic of 1893, she explained, "The trouble suburbanites used to have in obtaining help was all done away with now. Women were glad to go anywhere, no matter how lonesome, just so they got a job." "Women out of Work: Hundreds of Destitute Females without Employment," *Inter Ocean*, December 17, 1893. The conditions of domestic workers were also described before the Illinois General Assembly Senate Vice Committee. Illinois and O'Hara, *Report of Senate Vice Committee*, 40, 54.

35. Breckinridge, *Delinquent Child*, 78; Conyngton, *Report on Condition of Women and Child Workers*, 87–88; Deutsch, *Women and the City*, 57–60.

36. Sophonisba Breckinridge, *Delinquent Child*, 77; Stead, *If Christ Came to*

Chicago, 245. William Stead argued the "greatest evil" in Chicago was the "intermittent work, low wages, overwork and long hours of labor." After berating police for "raiding houses of ill-fame" and accusing city leaders of hypocrisy, he turned to his principal theme — Christian hypocrisy — and announced before an alarmed audience in Chicago that he would "rather take his chances on the day of judgment with" sex workers and vagrants "than with many of the men and women to be found in the churches and chapels of Chicago." See "Mr. Stead on Chicago: What the London Editor Thinks of the Garden City," *Inter Ocean*, November 13, 1893.

37. Addams, *New Conscience and Ancient Evil*, 64–65.

38. "Girl Who Comes to the City," 1005; Filene, "Betterments of Condition," 617.

39. Women's Auxiliary of Retail Clerks, *Are Your Women Clerks Earning*, 3–6.

40. Most of the material for the senate vice committee was collected in 1913. Illinois and O'Hara, *Report of Senate Vice Committee*, 932n8.

41. Chicago (Ill.), *Social Evil in Chicago*, 187, 189, 191.

42. Chicago (Ill.), 204.

43. "Justice Triumphs at Last," *Inter Ocean*, September 17, 1890. Hendrick Hartog examines this type of gap between law on the books and law on the streets in his study of pigs in antebellum New York. See Hartog, "Pigs and Positivism."

44. "State Street," *Chicago Tribune*, July 2, 1879.

45. "Mayor Harrison's Views: He Believes in Licensing Houses of Prostitution," *Inter Ocean*, July 7, 1879.

46. By the early 1880s, the criticism of Harrison's segregated vice policy was focused on the social implications of sex work. See "The Gate to Hades," *Inter Ocean*, February 4, 1882. For Ladies Social Evil Association, see Pierce, *History of Chicago*, 306.

47. In order to back up their strict construction of the statute, the court also turned to legislative intent, announcing that if lawmakers wanted to include the women with the keepers and patrons, "apt language to express such an intent would have been used." *Laura Raymond v. The People*.

48. "Justice Triumphs at Last," *Inter Ocean*, September 17, 1890.

49. Flinn and Wilkie, *History of Chicago Police*, 115, 461.

50. The first raid was at 42 S. Clark Street and produced eleven arrests, eleven charges of disorderly conduct, and eleven fines of two dollars. In the second raid, at 161 La Salle Street, Josie Howard, Jennie Spencer, Hattie Lawrence, and Alice Wright were arrested and charged with disorderly conduct.

Howard, Spencer, and Lawrence were fined two dollars, while Wright, who was likely the "keeper," or madam, was fined ten dollars. In the third raid, at 104 Randolph Street, Emma Adams and Annie Emerson were each fined fifty dollars for "Keep[ing] a House of Ill-fame," while Maggie Paterson, Nellie Smith, Tellie Walker, and Mary Gibbons, each listed as "day shift," were fined two dollars for disorderly conduct. The individual who recorded the arrests did not identify different functions. Charges and fines listed are identical. Chicago Police Department, *First Precinct Arrest Book*.

51. The practice of regulating vice was common in cities in the Midwest in the late nineteenth century. See, for instance, Best, *Controlling Vice*, and Adler, "Streetwalkers," 737–755.

52. "Local Law-Givers," *Inter Ocean*, January 6, 1881.

53. Binmore, *Laws and Ordinances*, ordinances 2194, 2196, 2197.

54. Printed in *Chicago Daily News*, June 1, 1887; cited in Pierce, *History of Chicago*, 306.

55. See ordinances 1456, 1457, 1458, 1459, and 1460 in Tolman, *Revised Municipal Code*, 405.

56. By the early twentieth century, the Women's Christian Temperance Union fought to criminalize wine rooms in Chicago, explicitly because they fostered prostitution. See "Place for Vice a Near-by Ward," *Chicago Tribune*, October 19, 1903, and "Fight Levee Vice with Hymn Books," *Chicago Tribune*, June 14, 1907.

57. Duis, *Saloon*, 254.

58. Ernst Freund, *Police Power*, 98, 226, 228–230.

59. Chicago (Ill.), *Social Evil in Chicago*, 25–50.

60. See ordinances 2729, 2730, and 2731 in Brundage, *Chicago Code of 1911*, 853.

61. Chicago (Ill.), *Social Evil in Chicago*, 281; Illinois and O'Hara, *Report of Senate Vice Committee*, 13, 23, 28, 35.

62. Chicago (Ill.), *Social Evil in Chicago*, 281; Illinois and O'Hara, *Report of Senate Vice Committee*, 13, 23, 28, 35.

63. Chicago (Ill.), *Social Evil in Chicago*, 280.

64. Chicago (Ill.), 263–264.

65. Fining for tardiness — common since the 1880s — deepened working-womens' precariousness by diminishing already paltry wages. "In order to ensure prompt attendance," Wright explained in the late 1880s, employers "adopted an oppressive system of fines." "Our Working Women: Annual Report of C. D. Wright, Commissioner of the Department of Labor," *Inter Ocean*, February 1, 1889. Fining could also target clerical errors, such as those com-

mitted by one clerk who in the early 1890s was fined thirty-five cents in one week — more than ten percent of her salary — fifteen cents of which was for a "mistake in a check." Jones, "Working Girls of Chicago," 168. Fining remained common in 1910–1911, as female clerks in department stores reported being charged ten cents "an error." Chicago (Ill.), *Social Evil in Chicago*, 206. According to the Chicago Vice Commission, a prostitute could earn twenty-five dollars a week, while "the average paid in a department store [was] $6.00 per week." Chicago (Ill.), 204, 271.

66. In the state senate vice commission report, O'Hara established that Sears employed "4,732 women and girls" and that those under sixteen began at five dollars a week and those over sixteen began at six dollars a week. In total, 1,465 women working at Sears earned less than eight dollars a week, a subsistence-level wage according to the commission. Illinois and O'Hara, *Report of Senate Vice Committee*, 178.

67. Illinois and O'Hara, 181, 186.

68. Illinois and O'Hara, 188. "Drivers" is a term often associated with antebellum plantation slavery, where drivers filled in for masters and got the most work out of enslaved men and women. See Howe, *What Hath God Wrought*, 403.

69. Illinois and O'Hara, *Report of Senate Vice Committee*, 189.

70. Illinois and O'Hara, 189–190.

71. Rosenwald collected newspaper articles describing the exchange, which included "Where Many Girls Work," *Chicago Daily News*, March 19, 1913; "What Should Be Man's Minimum Wage," *Dallas Morning News*, June 6, 1913; "Faith in Our Girls," *News* (Grand Rapids, MI), March 10, 1913; "Anti-Humanity Lobby Is Called Work of Glenn and Rosenwald," *San Francisco Examiner*, July 5, 1913; "Financier Sees End of Watered Stock," *Public Ledger* (Philadelphia), June 9, 1913. "Vice and Wages," scrapbook 12, Julius Rosenwald Papers. A *Washington Post* article, which was not included in Rosenwald's scrapbook, discussed the role of other senators and business leaders in the vice investigation. See "Vice Not Due to Wage," *Washington Post*, March 8, 1913.

72. "Miss Adams Hits Nail on the Head," *Inter Ocean*, 1914.

73. Addams, *New Conscience and Ancient Evil*, 91.

74. The new court would have jurisdiction over all criminal and quasi-criminal offenses associated with "keeping, maintaining, leasing and patronizing houses of prostitution and places for the practice of prostitution." The court especially targeted those who were "enticing females into or detaining females in houses of prostitution" but also policed "acts of indecency tending to debauch the public morals," such as fornication, adultery, abduction

and pandering. City of Chicago, Municipal Court, *Seventh Annual Report of the Municipal Court of Chicago: December 2, 1912 to November 30, 1913, Inclusive*, 81.

75. Interestingly, this distinction also reflected a nineteenth-century policy of nuisance abatement, in that it kept "the streets clean and the business [of sex work] hazardous." See "Our Old Police Court," *Chicago Tribune*, December 14, 1890.

76. Prosecution of houses of ill fame soared from 205 in 1911 to over three thousand in the first two years of the Morals Court and would remain over one thousand. In the 1910s, prosecutions for pandering, which first appeared in the municipal court records in 1910, would remain under a hundred a year. City of Chicago, Municipal Court, *Tenth and Eleventh Annual Reports of the Municipal Court of Chicago for the Years December 6, 1915 to December 2, 1917,* 87, 92; City of Chicago, Municipal Court, *Twelfth, Thirteenth and Fourteenth Annual Report of the Municipal Court of Chicago: For the Three Years December 2, 1917, to December 5, 1920, Inclusive*, 81.

77. Judge Hopkins complained that "the only thing the Court can do in the Morals branch is to fine the person" and that, if she is unable to pay, "she goes to the house of correction." See "Recommends Special Homes for Morals Laws Infringers Run by State," *Chicago Evening American*, April 14, 1914, in Olsen's Disassembled Scrapbooks, Research Center, Chicago History Museum. See also "All Get a Chance in the Morals Court," *Chicago Tribune*, April 8, 1913.

78. "Women Oppose Fine for Delinquent Girls," *Chicago Record Herald*, May 28, 1913. Olsen's Disassembled Scrapbooks, Research Center, Chicago History Museum; City of Chicago, Municipal Court, *Nineteenth, Twentieth, Twenty-first and Twenty-Second Annual Reports for the Municipal Court of Chicago for the Years December 1, 1924 to December 2, 1928, Inclusive*, 113; Willrich, *City of Courts*, 175.

79. City of Chicago, Municipal Court, *Tenth and Eleventh Annual Reports of the Municipal Court of Chicago for the Years December 6, 1915 to December 2, 1917, Inclusive*, 93.

80. The 25 percent statistic is based on the average of the highest and lowest numbers in the five years preceding and the three years after the opening of the court. City of Chicago, Municipal Court, *Twelfth, Thirteenth and Fourteenth Annual Report of the Municipal Court of Chicago: For the Three Years December 2, 1917, to December 5, 1920, Inclusive*, 81.

81. Arnold Prowess, a "barber" whose personal wealth exceeded $17,000 "above indebtedness," paid the bail of each woman. *People v. Mary Carter, People v. Rose Murphy, People v. Pearl Lucas, People v. Marcie Murphy, People v. Ethel Smith.*

82. *People v. Thomas Venos*, Chicago Committee of Fifteen Records, vol. 25, 298.

83. *People v. William Connors*, Chicago Committee of Fifteen Records, vol. 25, 85.

84. *People v. Claude Powers*, Chicago Committee of Fifteen Records, vol. 25, 86.

85. *People v. C. W. Scott*, Chicago Committee of Fifteen Records, vol. 26, 44.

86. Kate Adams ran the Coulter House and was the namesake of the Illinois State law, passed in June 1915, that made it a misdemeanor to be an "inmate" of a house of ill fame or to solicit on the streets. Willrich, *City of Courts*, 185; *People v. George Wine*, Chicago Committee of Fifteen Records, vol. 25, 294.

87. Lewicky's prosecution was interrupted several times by legal technicalities and retrials. One technicality was "on the ground[s] the information was not properly made out." Chicago Committee of Fifteen Records, vol. 25, 144, 152; "Jury Convicts Enticer of Girls," *Chicago Tribune*, July 23, 1911; "Bonds Are Forfeited," *Record Herald*, August 16, 1911.

88. The minority opinion in the *Slaughter-House Cases* was refined in subsequent opinions in *Powell v. Pennsylvania* (1888) and *Allgeyer v. Louisiana* (1897) and would convene in *Lochner v. New York* (1905), when the Supreme Court granted workingmen a full liberty to contract their employment without any interference from the government. The court acknowledged in *Lochner* that states could regulate high-risk employment, an issue that was discussed in *Holden v. Hardy* (1898), a case about mining work. The court would discuss whether women possessed the same liberty as men to contract their employment in *Muller v. Oregon* (1908). It ruled that they did not.

89. Justice Joseph Bradley expressed some of the opinion's most famous — and galling — language in a concurring opinion, "the paramount destiny and mission of women are to fulfill the noble and benign offices of wife and mother." *Bradwell v. Illinois*.

90. The decision rejected hour limits for workingwomen Kelly, "Sweating System," 7–72; *Ritchie v. People*.

91. *Muller v. Oregon*.

92. Brandeis, *Women in Industry*, 109–111.

93. *Muller v. Oregon*; Brandeis, *Women in Industry*, 42–46, 83–92. Thirty years after *Muller* was decided, when the Supreme Court upheld a minimum wage law as a legitimate exercise of state police power in *West Coast Hotel Co. v. Parrish* — overruling in spirit (if not law) *Adkins v. Children's Hospital*, a Fifth Amendment decision that established a robust liberty of contract for working women — the court made similar argument about the relationship between low wages and immorality. *West Coast Hotel Co. v. Parrish*.

94. United States Department of Labor, *Women in Industry Service.*

95. Sophonisba Breckinridge, "The Illinois Ten Hours Law," *Journal of Political Economy* 18 (June 1910): 467–469.

96. Violators of the ten-hour law, such as Napoleon Hill who ran the Betsy Ross Candy Company, faced fines up to one hundred dollars. See *People v. Betsy Ross Candy Company.* Deputy factory inspector Robert Mitchell investigated violations of child labor and hours law. On January 11, 1915, he brought a case against William Kennedy, who employed John Kelley, who was under sixteen, after 7:00 p.m. See *People v. William Kennedy.* Mitchell also brought suit against Louis Bruschko that same day for failing to keep a record of hours worked by his female employees. See *People v. Louis Bruschko.*

97. The group originated in the efforts of white-slave activist Clifford Roe, then an "energetic, young assistant in the States Attorney office." Initial members of the committee, including Clifford Barnes, Joseph Rosenwald, and packer Harold Swift, secretly furnished Roe with money for "special investigations and prosecutions." Although the committee was initially formed to fight pandering, it reorganized itself in 1911, the same year as the Chicago Vice Commission, and began to target prostitution exclusively. Barnes recalled that decision a few years later, noting that the committee had never "taken formal action against the practice of prostitution when thoroughly segregated, and certain of its members were still of the opinion that careful regulation was the best method of handling the social evil." Ultimately, the committee turned against regulated vice completely, "confident the city [would] be morally in a far more wholesome state than was possible with a protected red-light district." See Barnes, "Story of Committee of Fifteen," 145, 146, 148; Duis, "Evening with Committee of Fifteen"; and Donovan, *White Slave Crusades,* 163n27.

98. Duis, "Evening with Committee of Fifteen."

99. From April 1917 to April 1924, the cost of visiting a sex worker increased from about two dollars to roughly five dollars per "jazz," or "visit to the holy land." Chicago Committee of Fifteen Records, April 8, 12, 1918; November 1, 1920; April 24, 1922; and November 10, 11, 15, 1920.

100. Investigators' surveillance often extended beyond prostitutes to include police caught drinking in uniform. Such was the case with "Officer #1260," caught "drinking the full contents of a bottle of malt marrow" in April 1918 and, a week and a half later, "Officer #230," who enjoyed "two glasses of whisky over the bar." Standing at arm's length from local officials, vigilante committee investigators viewed their mandate broadly and in some cases extended their regulation to police. Such was the case when investigators noted

in their report that uniformed officers working for the barkeeper at the Fountain Inn in April 1918 "watched us and tried to get close to us." The secretive nature of the Committee of Fifteen was made apparent several years later when police arrested a couple investigators in a raid just before midnight on March 5, 1926. While their detachment from the police may have reflected concerns about police corruption, it also underscored the exclusivity of the committee's secretive, corrective crusade. See Committee of Fifteen Records, April 9, 18, 1918; April 13, 1918; and March 5, 1926. Also see City of Chicago, Municipal Court, *Seventh Annual Report of the Municipal Court of Chicago: December 2, 1912 to November 30, 1913, Inclusive*, 97 and City of Chicago, Municipal Court, *Twelfth, Thirteenth and Fourteenth Annual Reports of the Municipal Court of Chicago: December 2, 1917 to December 5, 1920, Inclusive*, 88.

101. Committee of Fifteen Records, April 8, 20, 1918

102. Flinn and Wilkie, *History of Chicago Police*, 454.

103. Flinn and Wilkie, 454.

104. Bowen, *Girl Employed in Hotels and Restaurants*; Bowen, *Department Store Girl*; Bowen, *Study of Bastardy Cases*; Bowen, *Public Dance Halls*.

105. Illinois and O'Hara, *Report of Senate Vice Committee*, 462; "Harrison Wants 10 Policewomen," *Chicago Tribune*, July 8, 1913.

106. "Harrison Wants 10 Policemen," *Chicago Tribune*, July 8, 1913; Daggett, "City as Mother," 111–117; "Fashions Not Degrading Women, Jane Addams Says," *Chicago Tribune*, September 26, 1913; "Ten Policewomen Chosen by Mayor: On Duty Monday," *Chicago Tribune*, August 2, 1913; "New Stars Ready for Policewomen," *Chicago Tribune*, August 3, 1913.

107. The Chicago Women's Aid Society hired travelers' aides during World War I to protect women who traveled to Chicago from "unfair inducement" and "wrong relationships" by stationing aides at major ports. Everett L. Meservey, "The Travelers' Aid Society: Report of the General Secretary for the Year Ending March 31, 1919," *Annual Report*, Chicago Women's Aid Society, folder 34, "The Travelers' Aid Society Department of 1919," University of Illinois at Chicago Special Collections.

108. The Chicago Bureau of Charities developed the Friendly Visitors program, which sent reformers to working-class homes where they advised mothers on efficient methods of cooking, cleaning, and childrearing. United Charities of Chicago, "Visiting Housekeeper," *Annual Report* (1911), 35–37; Getis, *Juvenile Court*, 14–21; United Charities of Chicago, "Visiting Housekeeper," *Annual Report* (1911), 35–37.

109. "They Talk for Charity" *Chicago Tribune*, October 31, 1896. The Bureau

of Charities boasted between four hundred and eight hundred "friendly visitors" at the end of the nineteenth century. Kusmer, "Functions of Organized Charity," 669.

110. Nesbitt, "Estimating a Family Budget," 11, 40, 51; United Charities of Chicago, "Visiting Housekeeper," *Annual Report* (1911), 35–37; Vera Kirkpatrick, "Wartime Work of the Visiting Housekeeper," United Charities of Chicago, *Annual Report* (1916–1917), 17; Hunter, *Tenement Conditions in Chicago*, 71.

111. Sears, *Charity Visitor*, 4–5.

112. "Science in Charity," *Chicago Tribune*, December 6, 1896. The idea of pensions for mothers spread quickly. San Francisco, Milwaukee, and St. Louis instituted pensions before Chicago, which pensioned mothers in 1913, the same year as fourteen other states. Programs existed under various names: Mother's Allowance, Parent's Allowance, Mother's Compensation, and Act to Protect Home Life for Dependent Children. Howe and Howe, "Pensioning the Widow and Fatherless," 286–287. Illinois's variant was the Funds to Parents Act, which was administered through the Juvenile Court in Chicago and designed to "ensure that families met their legal obligations to provide for their relations." Tanenhaus, "Growing Up Dependent."

113. In the summer of 1912, Mabel Daggett explained, roughly twelve hundred children were cared for on this plan, "costing the community an average of $5.75 per month per child, as against $10 per month per child under the old institutional plan." Daggett, "City as Mother," 113. According to Frederic C. Howe and Marie Jenney Howe, this social duty was a "more valuable service to the state than bearing arms." See Howe and Howe, "Pensioning the Widow and Fatherless," 284–86, 289, and Tanenhaus, "Growing Up Dependent." The pension, which reflected nineteenth-century reformers' insistence that workingwomen be virtuous, was influential into the 1930s. See Goodwin, *Gender and the Politics of Welfare Reform*, 13.

114. Goodwin, "American Experiment," 329.

115. "Hungry Woman Offers Self to Highest Bidder," *"Hobo" News*, November 1921.

116. Kellor, "Southern Colored Girls," 584–585; Blair, "We Must Live Anyhow," 123, 140.

CHAPTER 4. ISOLATION

1. Baldwin, "James Baldwin Tells Us," 49.

2. According to *The Negro in Chicago*, "restricted opportunity is evident

from the fact that, in 1910, almost two thirds of the gainfully occupied Negro women in Chicago were engaged in two occupational groups, 'servants' and 'laundresses not in laundries.'" See Chicago Commission on Race Relations, *Negro in Chicago*, 378.

3. See "No Place for Sick Woman but the Bridewell," *Chicago Defender*, February 7, 1914. The exclusion of African Americans from private spaces was a feature of Progressive Era law. This exclusion was endorsed by the Supreme Court in the *Civil Rights Cases* in 1883 as the private right to exclude. This right was not formally overturned until the 1964 Civil Rights Act. In the Progressive Era, antilynching activist Ida B. Wells criticized this right to exclude when she singled out the Women's Model Lodging House, which gave all women a place to sleep, except drunks, "immoral women," and Black women. See Ida B. Wells, "Letter to the Editor" *Record Herald*, January 26, 1912, quoted in Spear, *Making of Negro Ghetto*, 46–47.

4. In the *Slaughter-House* opinions, the Supreme Court restricted the application of the Fourteenth Amendments to African Americans. See *Slaughter-House Cases*.

5. According to Miller, this "scheme" left African American workers "to loiter around the outer edges of industry," to pick up "menial work [such] as odds and ends." See Miller, "Economic Handicap," 84, 87.

6. See Justice Harlan's dissenting opinion in the *Civil Rights Cases*. In 1883, the Supreme Court weakened the 1875 Civil Rights Act by throwing out the social equality provisions outlined in its first two sections, ruling that government could not regulate private acts. As a result, private business could exclude private consumers, unless state law determined otherwise.

7. Because they were treated as fundamentally different and unequal, African Americans did not possess the same liberty of contract that white Americans possessed. This conclusion required reading a couple of different Supreme Court cases together: *Plessy v. Ferguson* and *Lochner v. New York*. According to Elizabeth Dale, *Plessy v. Ferguson* "decided that the Fourteenth Amendment gave political power but not social right to African Americans." See Dale, "Social Equality Does Not Exist," 311, 314. Two years after *Plessy*, in *Williams v. Mississippi*, the court upheld African American disenfranchisement — stripping them of these political rights. A few years later, in *Lochner v. New York*, the court identified a liberty of contract — theorized as a fundamental right to negotiate contracts free from government interference — as the basis of labor relations. Arguably, the inequality sanctioned in *Plessy* and *Williams* would make it impossible for Black Americans to contract their labor equitably, according to the theory set out in *Lochner*.

8. Du Bois was puzzled by what he observed as a movement that inspired tens of thousands of African American men and women in the South to risk much for distant and uncertain rewards in the urban North. See Du Bois, "Migration of Negroes," 65.

9. See Drake and Cayton, *Black Metropolis*, 267–268.

10. Arguably, Christopher Robert Reed and James Grossman offer optimistic assessments of the Great Migration. See Reed, *Rise of Chicago's Black Metropolis*, and Grossman, *Land of Hope*.

11. Khalil Gibran Muhammad, who examines the criminalization of race in the Progressive Era urban North, also stresses the impact of social practices on formal policies. See Muhammad, *Condemnation of Blackness*.

12. A spate of new scholarship stresses isolation. For housing and real estate, see Satter, *Family Properties*, and Rothstein, *Color of Law*. Rashad Shabazz describes the "carceral" space of the South Side kitchenette in "'Our Prisons': Carceral Power in and Black Masculinity during the Interwar Years," in Shabazz, *Spatializing Blackness*.

13. For instance, historian Arthur Waskow describes efforts to reinstitute the quarantine over the course of the riot. On Sunday, whites beat twenty-seven African Americans, stabbed seven, and shot four. Monday, Tuesday, and Wednesday were characterized by more stabbings, murders, assaults, dragging, and shootings — some targeted, some random — all before the city's mayor finally called in the National Guard late on Wednesday evening, when isolation was restored. See Waskow, *From Race Riot to Sit-In*, 40–44.

14. Baldwin, "James Baldwin Tells Us," 49.

15. For causal and domestic workers, R. R. Wright Jr. has used census material to demonstrate that in Chicago in 1900, "8,381 of the 13,005 Negro males in gainful occupation were in domestic service, and 3,998 of the 4,921 females were similarly employed . . . [as was] typical of the Negro at work in the large cities in the north." See Wright, "Negro in Unskilled Labor," 25. Also see Pierce, *History of Chicago*, 517–519. In the era of the Civil War, Illinois's Black Codes, which had barred African Americans from entering and settling in the state, were relaxed under pressure from advocates such as John Jones, a successful Black tailor who challenged the their constitutionality and pushed for the ratification of the Thirteenth Amendment. Jones's pamphlet was titled *The Black Laws of Illinois, and a Few Reasons Why They Should Be Repealed.* The state's Black Codes, which originated in its first general assembly, March 30, 1819, provided that "no black or mulatto could reside in the state without a certificate of freedom" and prohibited manumission. In 1829, bond for entrance from African Americans, free and slave, was set at a thousand

dollars, and a revision in 1845 prohibited miscegenation. As late as 1862, a constitutional convention received significant popular support to sustain the racial exclusion. Angle, "Illinois Black Laws."

16. In the late nineteenth century, Black organizations included the Colored Masons. The Colored Men's Library Association offered lectures and reading material, and there were two Black newspapers, the *Chicago Conservator* and *Chicago Observer*, and a number of educational and benevolent associations. The *Conservator* reportedly had a circulation of a thousand to twelve hundred. Only snippets of the *Conservator* survive and are printed in Davis, "Negro Newspapers in Chicago," 10, 17, 20, 26. The Black professional and business directory, published after 1885, also supported claims of a Black middle class. See Pierce, *History of Chicago*, 48–49, and Dale, "Social Equality Does Not Exist," 314.

17. For growth from the upper North, see Wright, "Migration of Negroes to the North," 99. For growth over time, Thomas Lee Philpott has used census data to chart the growth of Chicago's Black population from 1840. In 1840, African Americans were 53/4,470 (1.2 percent). In 1850, 323/29,963 (1.1 percent). In 1860, 955/109,260 (0.9 percent). In 1870, 3,691/298,977 (1.2 percent). In 1880, 6,480/503,185 (1.3 percent). In 1890, 14,271/1,099,850 (1.3 percent). In 1900, 30,150/1,698,575 (1.8 percent). In 1910, 44,103/2,185,283 (2.0 percent). In 1920, 109,458/2,701,705 (4.1 percent). In 1930, 233,803/3,376,438 (6.9 percent). See Philpott, *Slum and Ghetto*, 117. For early migrations, see Wright, "Negro in Unskilled Labor," 24; Wright, "Migration of Negroes," 107; and Dale, "Social Equality Does Not Exist," 314.

18. Blair, *I've Got to Make My Livin'*, 112–113. The judge ruled that the theater violated the Civil Rights Act and fined it one hundred dollars. See Dale, "Social Equality Does Not Exist," 318–319.

19. He was charged "$3.55 for a thirty-five-cent order of roast beef and a five-cent cup of coffee." See "Mr. Seales Roast Beef," *Chicago Tribune*, April 24, 1888.

20. In 1896, the Illinois State Supreme Court found the 1885 Civil Rights Act too vague to be enforced. The Illinois legislature promptly amended it in 1897. See Spear, *Black Chicago*, 41.

21. She would also accuse the "the so-called superior race" of a "contemptuous attitude." See Addams, "Social Control," 22–23.

22. Wright, "Negro in Unskilled Labor," 22, 24.

23. Washington announced before an audience at Chicago's venerable Quinn Chapel in 1905 that "the Negro will find his chief protection and development" in work and cites his failure to "bear up under the pressures of

new industrial conditions." See "Work the Hope of the Negro Race," *Chicago Tribune*, April 4, 1905. According to University of Pennsylvania sociologist Kelsey, "the absolutely crucial thing is that [Black migrants] learn to work regularly and intelligently. He asserted that they were "not ready to work alone and get the best results" and get "economic freedom." See Kelsey, "Evolution of Negro Labor," 74–76.

24. "Negro Rights in Chicago," *Chicago Tribune*, June 14, 1916.

25. The right was outlined in the *Civil Rights Cases*, which overruled section 2 of the Civil Rights Act of 1875. See *Civil Rights Cases,* 109 U.S. 3 (1883). The private right to discriminate remained intact legally until 1964, when Congress passed the Civil Rights Act.

26. See "Negro Rights in Chicago," *Chicago Tribune*, June 14, 1916. The proposed amendment gave rise to a debate in the editorial pages about the meaning of social equality. See, for instance, Edward H. Wright, "Voice of the People: Civil Rights and Social Equality," *Chicago Tribune*, June 22, 1916, and John H. Owens, "Do Negroes Want Social Equality?," *Chicago Tribune*, June 28, 1916.

27. "Negro Rights in Chicago," *Chicago Defender*, June 17, 1916.

28. The same report described the ordeal of sixteen-year-old Josephine Rominsky, on her way home with Annie Schmack and Georgie Doestal "after completing her day's work in the dried beef department in the Armour Plant." They were the target "of stone and mud from every direction." Their stories, along with Raglan's, was described in "Girl Mobbed by 1,000," *Chicago Tribune*, July 23, 1904.

29. Herbst, *Negro in Slaughtering Industry*, xxi, 15–19.

30. The slaughterhouse workers struck in sympathy with Eugene Debs's America Railroad Union. See Tuttle, *Race Riot*, 112.

31. Tuttle, 113.

32. Hoyle's attack followed a miniriot that developed after Thomas Johnson shot John Stokes in self-defense. See "Fight and Riot near the Yards," *Chicago Tribune*, July 27, 1904. For mob and stabbed both eyes out, see Tuttle, 119.

33. "Negroes on a Street Car Attack Members of Union," *Chicago Tribune*, September 4, 1904.

34. For padrones, see Peck, "Reinventing Free Labor," 848–871. According to Tuttle, Black strikebreakers were a principal scapegoat in the failed 1904 stockyard strike. See Tuttle, *Race Riot*, 114–117, and Tuttle, "Some Strikebreakers' Observations," 193–196.

35. Editorial, *Broad Ax*, May 6, 1905, and quoted in Spear, *Black Chicago*, 40. The *Tribune* considered the use of Black strikebreakers "a terrible injustice

and wrong to the negroes already employed as teamsters in the city." See "The Race Issue in the Strike," *Chicago Tribune*, May 13, 1905.

36. Quoted in Spear, *Black Chicago*, 37.

37. "Workers," *Chicago Tribune*, August 1, 1904; *Chicago Tribune*, August 29, 1904; Herbst, *Negro in Slaughtering Industry*, 25–26; Tuttle, "Some Strikebreakers' Observations," 193–196; Tuttle, *Race Riot*, 119.

38. For unions and racial exclusion, see Spear, *Black Chicago*, 159–160, and Grossman, *Land of Hope*, 211.

39. Grossman, *Land of Hope*, 215, 219; Spear, *Black Chicago*, 160. Some scholars have attributed this mistrust to southern agricultural practices and a "rural psychology." See Tuttle, *Race Riot*, 147–150.

40. For Anna Julia Cooper, see Gaines, *Uplifting the Race*, 128–152. For Washington describing his opposition to unions in a Chicago speech, see "Work the Hope of the Negro Race," *Chicago Tribune*, April 4, 1905. Also see Kelsey, "Evolution of Negro Labor," 74–76.

41. Grossman, *Land of Hope*, 215–217.

42. Before a New York meeting of the National Negro Business League, Williams asserted that strikebreaking has "demonstrated that the Negro who is called to do difficult work under difficult conditions is very much a man." See "Jolt for the Negro Race," *Chicago Tribune*, August 18, 1905.

43. While white settlement house worker Graham Taylor was initially appointed by the mayor to lead the commission on the race riot, African American sociologist Charles Johnson would take over and become de facto leader. See Muhammad, *Condemnation of Blackness*, 236, and Chicago Commission on Race Relations, *Negro in Chicago*, 429.

44. Park may not have been optimistic about the future of American race relations, Arvarh Strickland points out, but he was a recognized "authority on the negro problem" and committed to an ethic of equality and opportunity. See Strickland, *History of Chicago Urban League*, 40, and Reed, *Chicago NAACP*, 28. For an example of Park's approach to racial issues, see Park, "Racial Assimilation." Chicago Urban League, *First Annual Report of the Chicago League on Urban Conditions among Negroes* (1917), 3; Chicago Urban League, *Second Annual Report of the Chicago League on Urban Conditions among Negroes* (1918), 4, 11.

45. Bowen, *Colored People of Chicago*, n.p.; Grossman, *Land of Hope*, 123.

46. White, "Chicago and Its Eight Reasons," 296.

47. Wood, *Negro in Chicago*, 23–24.

48. Wells, "Letter to the Editor," *Record Herald*, January 26, 1912.

49. Quoted in Wood, *Negro in Chicago*, 23–24.

50. For Park, see Park, *The City*, 8. Cities were also interpreting racial problem in patterns of city settlement. The Supreme Court struck down Louisville, Kentucky's 1914 racial zoning ordinance in a 1917 legal opinion, citing the due process, or property, clause of the Fourteenth Amendment, rather than the equal protection clause. See *Buchanan v. Warley*. Christopher Silver discusses the case in Silver, "Racial Origins of Zoning," 23–42.

51. Ms. Josephine Mulcahy made the purchase at 4506 Forestville Avenue and transferred it to Davis for costs and a fifty-dollar commission. "Whites Buy Davis House," *Chicago Daily News*, May 3, 1915.

52. "Race War Fades—Flares Up Again," *Chicago Tribune*, May 4, 1915. Richard Rothstein has argued that the claim that African Americans—who typically paid higher rents in cities—drove real estate prices down is inaccurate and continues to distort our understanding of the impact of race on housing prices. See Rothstein, *Color of Law*, 93–95.

53. "Negro to Gain White Apology," *Chicago Tribune*, May 5, 1915.

54. White, "Chicago and Its Eight Reasons," 296.

55. Chicago (Ill.), *Social Evil in Chicago*, 38; Blair, *I've Got to Make My Livin'*, 16, 146.

56. Black women encountered widespread exclusion from the labor market. According to sociologists St. Clair Drake and Horace Cayton, vice simply testified to the absence of jobs available to African American women: "The colored girl does not have the chance to work." See Drake and Cayton, *Black Metropolis*, 597–599. This problem stemmed from the migrations' earliest days. Labor shortages during the World War I created opportunities for Black women in hundreds of previously closed firms. For example, in 1910, women were more than 40 percent of breadwinners in African American households, statistically "more than double the proportion of White women employed." See Bowen, *Colored People of Chicago*, n.p. Also see Herbst, *Negro in Slaughtering Industry*, 220–225; Chicago Commission on Race Relations, *Negro in Chicago*, 155–170. However, according to a Department of Labor official in 1919, Black women's hold on jobs was always tenuous: "As soon as the situation clears itself no more colored help will be employed," one official explained. See Grossman, *Land of Hope*, 184–185. According to vice historian Cynthia Blair, the era of vice prohibition, when sex work was scattered to the corners of the informal economy, was also the era when vice was made racial—producing the figure of the "Black jezebel." Cynthia Blair argues that the regulation of sex work helped to produce the figure of the Black jezebel. See Blair, *I've Got to Make My Livin'*, 3–20.

57. Frazier, *Negro Family in Chicago*, 100–101. Louise deKoven Bowen de-

scribed a similar restriction in the years before the bulk of the Great Migration, when Black households were required to board strangers. See Bowen, *Colored People of Chicago*.

58. Hill, "Housing for Negro Wage Earner," vi, 309–313; Breckinridge, "Color Line," 575–576; Drake and Cayton, *Black Metropolis*, 55.

59. Song lyric quoted in editorial, *Chicago Defender*, October 7, 1916.

60. "Judge Uhlir Saves Man from Southern Sheriff," *Chicago Defender*, September 22, 1917.

61. James Grossman argues that the *Chicago Defender* communicated "easily with so many Black southerners," combining editorial "militancy" and "sensationalism" with a "vast promotion and distribution network" that saw circulation rocket along with the Great Migration from 33,000 in 1916 to 90,000 in 1917, 125,000 in 1918, and 130,000 in 1919, "pumping a constant flow of trusted information" into "some of the most remote corners of the south." See Grossman, *Land of Hope*, 79–80. The *Defender* self-consciously placed itself at the center of narratives of northern success. It solicited letters, asking "What did the *Defender* do for you? Write and send your picture." See "What the *Defender* Has Done," *Chicago Defender,* February 2, 1918. Alternatively, the paper reminded readers that "the *Chicago Defender* is taking information and inspiration into all sections of the south, in such a way as no paper published there can do and live." See Ben Baker, "Our Political and Economic Statues," *Chicago Defender*, March 13, 1918.

62. *Chicago Defender*, January 9, 1915; editorial, *Chicago Defender*, October 7, 1916, quoted in Drake and Cayton, *Black Metropolis*, 59.

63. See "Black Man, Stay South," *Chicago Tribune*, May 30, 1917. In a similar vein, columnist Henry Hyde argued that because Black migrants might never assimilate, they were likely to become criminals and burdens on their communities. "They are compelled to live crowded together in dark unsanitary rooms," he argued. "They are surrounded by constant temptations in the way of wide open saloons and other worse resorts; they find a complete absence of all restrictions as to their use of the street." "The Negro problem" — which Hyde appeared to view in terms of criminal poverty — "has moved north with a vengeance." See Henry M. Hyde, "Half a Million Darkies from Dixie Swarm the North to Better Themselves," *Chicago Tribune*, July 8, 1917.

64. In 1910, white New York socialite Ruth Standish Baldwin convened representatives of "many social welfare organizations" to found the National League on Urban Conditions among Negroes. Six years later, the league opened a branch in Chicago, which quickly became the foremost advocacy group for migrants assimilating into life in the urban North. The branch focused on im-

proving the joblessness, low wages, poor housing, and degraded social status of Chicago's new urban citizens "without a hyphen." See Strickland, *History of Chicago Urban League*, 11–12. The allocation and organization of the league before 1914 is also described in "National League on Urban Conditions among Negroes," 43–46. Despite its national presence, the NAACP would not become a significant presence in Chicago until the 1930s. See Reed, *Chicago NAACP*.

65. The Chicago Urban League also advised new migrants on the "necessity of being orderly citizens, efficient workers and good housekeepers." See Chicago Urban League, *First Annual Report*, 11. Also, many southern migrants arrived from primarily agricultural communities with "employment structures radically different" from what they would find in industrial Chicago. In addition, concerns that Blacks lacked skills immediately "transferable to Chicago's urban industrial economy" further defined the efforts and initiatives of the Chicago Urban League. Chicago Urban League, *First Annual Report*, 11; Grossman, *Land of Hope*, 182–183.

66. Chicago Commission on Race Relations, *Negro in Chicago*, 350.

67. Chicago Urban League, *First Annual Report*, 3. James Grossman notes that in its early years, "the League had only as much influence over working condition as employers would grant. . . . More importantly, its contributions relied heavily on stockyards firms, Julius Rosenwald of Sears, Roebuck, a few steel companies, and International Harvester." Basically, corporate contributions increased as it demonstrated its "usefulness." See Grossman, *Land of Hope*, 203. Also, although Black Americans composed almost 75 percent of the Chicago Urban League's members and contributors, their donations amounted to only 10 percent of monies raised in its first year. Strickland, *History of Chicago Urban League*, 33–34, 47–8.

68. Reed, *Chicago NAACP*, 28. Park may not have been optimistic about the future of American race relations, Arvarh Strickland points out, but he was a recognized "authority on the negro problem" and committed to an ethic of equality and opportunity. See Strickland, *History of Chicago Urban League*, 40. For an example of Park's racial ethic, see Park, "Racial Assimilation," 606–623. Chicago Urban League, *First Annual Report*, 3. For Du Bois, see Du Bois, "Social Equality," 16–18.

69. The question was posed two years after heavyweight boxing champion Jack Johnson was accused of transporting his white girlfriend, Lucille Cameron, across state line in 1912 for "immoral purposes." For Mann Act, see "Legal Help," *Chicago Defender*, October 3, 1914.

70. For intentionally inserting false client information, see "Legal Helps," *Chicago Defender*, May 2, 1914. For delayed payment, see "Legal Helps," *Chi-*

cago Defender, March 13, 1915. For disputed benefactor, see "Legal Helps," *Chicago Defender*, September 26, 1914. For keeping and withholding receipts, see "Legal Helps," *Chicago Defender*, August 22, 1914. For hiring an attorney, see "Legal Helps," *Chicago Defender*, April 17, 1915.

71. For tenement lights, see "Legal Helps," *Chicago Defender*, March 6, 1915.

72. In his column, Westbrooks explained basic legal concepts to his readers. For testifying in court, see "Legal Helps," *Chicago Defender*, December 26, 1914. For duty to appear, see "Legal Helps," *Chicago Defender*, May 15, 1915. For costs of using courts, see "Legal Helps," *Chicago Defender* July 4, 1914. For attorney's fees, see "Legal Helps," *Chicago Defender*, July 25, 1914. For deadline for payment, see "Legal Helps," *Chicago Defender*, September 5, 1914. For setting aside ruling, see "Legal Helps," *Chicago Defender*, July 10, 1915. For pace at which cases are tried, see "Legal Helps," *Chicago Defender*, February 20, 1915.

73. Westbrooks encouraged readers to use law to their benefit, writing that "the time in Chicago has arrived for the citizens to rise up and put [the officer] in his proper place." "Legal Helps," *Chicago Defender*, October 24, 1914. Regarding the stationmaster, he advised that "remedies offered to the race by statute should be promptly and vigorously invoked against any such discrimination." See "Legal Helps," *Chicago Defender*, June 6, 1914.

74. For right to an attorney, see "Legal Helps," *Chicago Defender*, August 15, 1914. For treatment by police, see "Legal Helps," *Chicago Defender*, October 24, 1914. For beating in jail and fraudulent white attorneys, see "Legal Helps," *Chicago Defender*, November 14, 1914.

75. According to the paper, "If we do not fight at home, with the great weapon of the secret ballot, for what they are fighting for abroad with guns and gas and liquid fire," then "those of us left behind will be a disgrace to our name," the *Defender* announced patriotically. See "Our Political and Economic Statutes," *Chicago Defender*, March 23, 1918.

76. Du Bois, "Close Ranks," 111.

77. "The Negro and the War," *Chicago Defender*, March 23, 1918. Abbott claimed that the war universalized the struggle for jobs in "mills and factories that have been closed to us" and advocated taking the struggle abroad, to a new frontier. See Drake and Cayton, *Black Metropolis*, 60.

78. African Americans not only served in Europe but also "helped to prepare the meat that kept the life and fight in the boys at the front in Europe." See "Chicago," *Crisis*, 214.

79. He also said, "Patriotism is as deeply rooted under Black skin as under any other." See "Judge Carter Bids Good-By to 8th Infantry," *Chicago Tribune*, September 1, 1917. Historian Adrian Lenz-Smith describes how the Illinois

Eighth tore a raucous strip across the American South, flirting with white women, taunting white men, and pillaging stores that refused them service. See Lentz-Smith, *Freedom Struggles*, 89–96.

80. Medals were presented by the American and French governments. See "Throngs Greet Eighth," *Chicago Defender*, February 22, 1919, and Grossman, *Land of Hope*, 179.

81. Tuttle, *Race Riot*, 218.

82. In *The Colored People of Chicago*, Bowen tells the story of nineteen-year-old Chicagoan George W., who was "not allowed to sleep, beaten, cuffed and kicked" after he was arrested and then convicted of rape despite the presiding judge's comments on the weakness of the prosecution's case. She also described a case involving a young African American facing murder charges. He was tried and convicted in sixteen minutes, "from the time the negro [*sic*] was brought into the court to the time he left it." George W. was found guilty and sentenced to fourteen years' incarceration. See Bowen, *Colored People of Chicago*, n.p.

83. For investigating the court, see "Legal Helps," *Chicago Defender*, August 5, 1916.

84. According to Reckless, the increase was due to "restricted occupational outlets," the "disorganized neighborhood conditions in which most Negroes must live," and "greater liability of police arrest." See Reckless, *Vice in Chicago*, 26, 31.

85. *People v. George Mason*.

86. *People v. Ike Holiday*.

87. Armstrong had moved from Louisiana with his wife, Daisy, in the late 1910s to Chicago, where he earned a good income playing at clubs, including the Sunset Cabaret on the West Side. However, despite his stable income, Daisy claimed that Louis failed to support her, and she argued that he had also disregarded an earlier order issued by the Domestic Relations Court in New Orleans, where they had lived previously. Louis Armstrong filed for divorce in Chicago on August 30, 1923. The case was heard on November 15, and the divorce was granted on December 18, 1923. In the 1923 case, she asked for alimony, explaining that she lived in a manner "becoming a good, true, and virtuous wife." Louis Armstrong responded that the couple had lived separately for several years. See *Armstrong v. Armstrong*. The complete Armstrong file is available at the Cook County Archives. See also Teachout, *Pops*, 76. Albert Bailey George hailed from Washington, DC, and moved to Chicago to study law at Northwestern University; he practiced privately and even served a stint as secretary of the Chicago Urban League. See "First Colored Judge Looks to Race Advantage," *Chicago Tribune*, November 6, 1924.

88. For journalists' accounts of Judge George's election, see "George Elected Judge," *Chicago Defender*, November 8, 1924; Philip Kinsley, "Negro Judge's Election Seen as Racial Hope," *Chicago Tribune*, November 10, 1924; Philip Kinsley, "Colored Judge Wins Respect in Court Work," *Chicago Tribune*, July 3, 1925; and "Chicago's First Colored Judge Takes Office," *Chicago Tribune*, December 2, 1924.

89. Chicago Commission on Race Relations, *Negro in Chicago*, 400.

90. The story of the race riot began on July 27 with conflicting claims to access to the beach at Twenty-Ninth Street. A couple of blocks north, and oblivious to the violence erupting at the Twenty-Seventh Street beach, four African American boys kicked their homemade raft through the waters of Lake Michigan. John Harris, one of the boys on the raft, later recalled ducking the rocks a white person threw from seventy-five feet as the raft drifted toward the Twenty-Ninth Street beach. "As long as we could see him," Harris explained later, "he never could hit us, because after all a guy throwing a rock that far is not a likely shot. And, you could see the brick coming." Eugene Williams must have not seen the rock that struck his forehead and caused him to drown in fifteen feet of water. Reportedly, Williams's friends identified the rock thrower to the police officer stationed at the "white" beach, but he refused to make an arrest. The white officer even stopped a Black officer, brought from the "Black" beach on Twenty-Fifth Street, from making an arrest. Williams's death sparked the riot that would spread across the city and into the South Side. William Tuttle uses oral interviews and local media to reconstruct the hours and minutes preceding the race riot. See Tuttle, *Race Riot*, 3–10.

91. Chicago Commission on Race Relations, *Negro in Chicago*, xv, 1.

92. For racial violence at schools, see "Judge Dismisses Case after Street Fight," *Chicago Defender* July 7, 1917, and "Race Trouble Again at Wentworth and 57th," *Chicago Defender*, October 6, 1917. For racial violence at a ballpark when rioting began after a baseball game, see "Game Ends in Near Race Riot," *Chicago Defender*, June 15, 1918. For housing and, in particular, Black families moving into new neighborhoods, see "Race Riot Scare Keeps Cops on Jump," *Chicago Defender*, August 31, 1918.

93. "Memorandum on Work of Investigations on Public Opinion," March 12, 1920, box 6, folder 4, Julius Rosenwald Papers; "Chicago," *Crisis*, 213.

94. According to the *Defender*, Thomas and his friends "repelled the attack," but as they ran through the intersection at 67th and Vernon Streets, they were pelted with rocks and bricks from a crowd attending a nearby baseball game. While the paper notes that the "miniature riot" occurred after school, implying the boys are school age, it does not give their age. "Boys Fight on South Side," *Chicago Defender*, June 7, 1919.

95. For Robinson and Mitchell, see "Ragan's Colt's Start Riot," *Chicago Defender*, June 28, 1919. The headline "No 'Race Riots' on the Fourth of July: What Do You Know about That?" in Tuttle, *Race Riot*, 237–239.

96. Chicago Commission on Race Relations, *Negro in Chicago*, xvi; "Minutes of the Chicago Race Commission: Summary of Industrial Questionnaire to Date," 11, Julius Rosenwald Papers, box 6, folder 4.

97. See Chicago Commission on Race Relations, *Negro in Chicago*, 436.

98. See Chicago Commission on Race Relations, 2. For references to strikebreaking, see Chicago Commission on Race Relations, 75, 182, 364, 367, 383, 404.

99. See Chicago Commission on Race Relations, 167.

100. See Chicago Commission on Race Relations, 365–367, 370, 390.

101. According to the report, "they felt that the Negroes were receiving all the benefits secured for the workers by the unions without paying their portion of the expense of organization." See Chicago Commission on Race Relations, 314.

102. For instance, see Herbst, *Negro in Slaughterhouse Industry*, 65–72, and Addams, "Social Control," 22–23.

103. According to University of Pennsylvania sociologist Kelsey, "the absolutely crucial thing is that [Black migrants] learn to work regularly and intelligently." He asserted that they were "not ready to work alone and get the best results" and get "economic freedom." See Kelsey, "Evolution of Negro Labor," 74–76.

104. See Chicago Commission on Race Relations, *Negro in Chicago*, 439.

105. Major employers of migrants also tended to diminish their status with unsteady work and poor conditions. "Minutes of Chicago Race Commission."

106. "Suggested Question to Solicit Opinions from Persons Called into Industrial Conference," box 6, folder 5, Julius Rosenwald Papers.

107. Chicago Commission on Race Relations, "Montgomery Ward," box 6, folder 4, Joseph Rosenwald Papers.

108. According to Alma Herbst, packers relied on excess Black labor to break strikes. See Herbst, *Negro in Slaughterhouse Industry*, 65–72.

109. "Industrial Survey," box 6, folder 5, Julius Rosenwald Papers.

110. See Chicago Commission on Race Relations, *Negro in Chicago*, 118.

111. Language is reproduced in the report from a "dodger" announcing the meeting. See Chicago Commission on Race Relations, *Negro in Chicago*, 118.

112. See Chicago Commission on Race Relations, 195.

113. Waskow, *From Race Riot to Sit In*, 55.

114. See Booth, "Inhabitants of Tower Hamlets," 326–391; Du Bois, *Philadelphia Negro*, 170–175; and Solenberger, *One Thousand Homeless Men*.

115. See Chicago Commission on Race Relations, *Negro in Chicago*, 192.

116. Rothstein, *Color of Law*, vii–viii.

117. Chicago (Ill.), *Social Evil in Chicago*, 38

118. See Chicago Commission on Race Relations, *Negro in Chicago*, 52.

119. For lodging houses, see Chicago Commission on Race Relations, 201. For high rents and lodgers, see Chicago Commission on Race Relations, 93.

120. According to the report, a "lack of lodging or hotels where lodging could be had at reasonable prices was partly responsible for this swarm of migrants seeking shelter in private homes." See Chicago Commission on Race Relations, 165.

121. See Chicago Commission on Race Relations, 171.

122. For Judge Scalan, see Chicago Commission on Race Relations, 352. For Judge Kersten, see Chicago Commission on Race Relations, 353. For Judge Pam, see Chicago Commission on Race Relations, 354.

123. Chicago Commission on Race Relations, 355. Mary Bartelme — assistant to municipal court judge Victor Arnold — claimed that migrants' "mental development has not been the same" as whites'. See Chicago Commission on Race Relations, 333.

124. See Chicago Commission on Race Relations, 335.

125. J. J. McCook also proposed a passbook scheme. See McCook, "Tramp Census."

126. Hill, "Negro in Chicago," 112.

127. Waskow, *From Race Riot to Sit-In*, 104.

128. Chicago Commission on Race Relations, *Negro in Chicago*, 385.

129. Quoted in Strickland, *History of Chicago Urban League*, 72.

130. Editorial in *Chicago Defender* quoted in Hill, "Why Southern Negroes," 185.

131. See Chicago Commission on Race Relations, *Negro in Chicago*, 602.

CHAPTER 5. FALL

1. Sumner, *Forgotten Man*, 468.

2. Franklin D. Roosevelt, "Radio Address from Albany, New York: 'The "Forgotten Man" Speech,'" April 7, 1932; cited in DePastino, *Citizen Hobo*, 302. Ubiquitous in the early 1930s, the phrase "forgotten man" made a dramatic appearance in song and cinema, as a tribute to Bonus Marchers — World War I veterans who were violently rebuffed after they demanded early payment of promised bonuses in 1932. The ordeals of the "forgotten man" was put to lyrics by Al Dubin and Harry Warren in the song "Remember My Forgotten Man,"

sung by Joan Blondell in the climax of the motion picture *Gold Diggers of 1933*. See Rubin, *Showstoppers*, 105.

3. "Carl Kolins Case Study," box 135, folder 2, Ernest Watson Burgess Papers.

4. "Chicago Jobless Colonize," *New York Times*, November 12, 1930; "Chicago Gets Shanty Town," *Los Angeles Times*, November 16, 1930.

5. For description of jobless men in the *New Republic*, see Josephson, "Other Nation"; Vorse, "School for Bums"; and Israel, "Shanty Town."

6. "U.S. Reveals 'Hunger March' as Red Joy Ride," *Chicago Tribune*, November 29, 1931.

7. Hunger march organizer Karl Lochner demanded protection from eviction "for non-payment," free gas and electricity for heating, and relief from cuts in grocery orders. "Jobless to Ask for Permit to Parade Downtown Monday," *Chicago Tribune*, October 26, 1932.

8. Percy Wood, "Hunger Amy Asks State for a $15 a Week Dole," *Chicago Tribune*, June 16, 1931.

9. Historians have partitioned the era. See, for instance, Leuchtenburg, *Supreme Court Reborn*. For economic inequality, encroaching poverty, and weakening state authority, see Turkel, *Hard Times*, 3–8, and McElvaine, *Down and Out*, 3–32. For poverty and the federal government, see Cohen, *Making a New Deal*; Sanchez, *Becoming Mexican American*; Simon, *Fabric of Defeat*; and Ferguson, *Black Politics*.

10. For Sonsteby's initiation, see "Sonsteby to Sit in Many Courts to Learn His Job," *Chicago Tribune*, December 4, 1930; and Sonsteby, *Address by Honorable John J. Sonsteby*, 2–4. For Olson and older values of the lower court, see Olson, *Municipal Court of Chicago*, 4.

11. Arthur Evans, "Hobo Farmhand Nearly Extinct: Machinery Foe," *Chicago Tribune*, August 22, 1926; DePastino, *Citizen Hobo*, 77–87; Higbie, *Indispensable Outcasts*, 207–209. Mechanization and increased competition strengthened the hand of employers. See *"Hobo" News*, February 1923, and Cohen, *Making a New Deal*, 102. In 1930, there were just over two thousand Filipino workers in Illinois. See Espiritu, *Filipino American Lives*, 9. Gabriela F. Arredondo estimates that twenty to twenty-five thousand Mexicans lived in Chicago in 1930. See Arredondo, *Mexican Chicago*, 16.

12. For tramp families, see "Foes of Hobo Kingdom Mass for Big Drive," *Chicago Tribune*, December 18, 1924, and "Calls 'Tramp' Family Life Growing Factor in Chicago Conditions," *Chicago Tribune*, March 30, 1929.

13. Park, Burgess and McKenzie, *The City*, 160.

14. Anderson, *On Hobos and Homelessness*, 29.

15. Zorbaugh, *Gold Coast and Slum*, 105–109. The Eureka Hotel provision-

ally sheltered over four hundred men a night at 737-7 South State Street, including men like "Hutchison," a typical hobo-workman, "Henry Jeckle," who did "not mean any harm to anyone" but also "did not work," and "Chicago Jack," a jobless man who always "had money" and felt "there was not any use of working." See George F. David, "A Dozen Hobo Hotels in the Loop, Documents 151," box 127, folder 5, Ernest Watson Burgess Papers.

16. W. A. Evans, "How to Keep Well," *Chicago Tribune*, August 4, 1923. Predictably, editorials published in the *"Hobo" News* rejected the claims of men like Dr. Evans and criticized residential housing as a health menace and a threat to "the workers who are forced to abide there." See Editorials, *"Hobo" News*, November 1923.

17. "Spring Brings Highway Hobos into Open Again," *Chicago Tribune*, March 30, 1930.

18. For entrepreneurs of leisure, see Denning, *Mechanical Accents*, 16.

19. "A $100 Hobo," *Chicago Tribune*, July 22, 1921.

20. Samuel G. Blythe, "Tapering Off on Work," *Saturday Evening Post* 198 (August 8, 1925), 3–4.

21. F. C. Kelly, "Our Need for Wasting More Time," *Harper's Monthly* 150 (1925), 659–662. For an example of an earlier advice manual, see Payne, *Hobo Philosopher*.

22. See "An Amateur Hobo Finds the Road Not So Bad," *Literary Digest*, June 8, 1928, 63–67.

23. The term "civilized leisure" was coined by H. A. Overstreet in *A Guide to Civilized Leisure*.

24. Kusmer, *Down and Out*, 183, 190–191; Todd DePastino, *Citizen Hobo*, 165.

25. In early 1922, journalist Gustav Schaefer puzzled over the "sincerity of those folks who imagine there is a job at all times for all the jobless." See Gustav Schaefer, "Do the Hoboes Like to Work," *"Hobo" News*, 1922. The *"Hobo" News* also complained about wages that were "barely sufficient to pay one's way while the job lasts" and criticized employment bureaus for making workers "pay for the right to work." See Holiday Special, *"Hobo" News*, December 1923 / January 1924, and Editorials, *"Hobo" News*, November 1923. For the mayor's plan, see "All Law Forces Join to Drive Beer and Booze from City," *Chicago Tribune*, September 19, 1923.

26. According to the *Tribune*, the purpose of the Sadler Act was "to penalize gun-toting." According to police chief Morgan Collins, it targeted "gangsters" arrested *with* guns and provided for up to ten years in prison. See "All Law Forces Join," 2. For the Sadler Act, see "The Sadler Act Repeal," *Chicago Tribune*, April 25, 1925.

27. For hoodlums, see "New Warrant Names 25 Gunmen and Gangster," *Chicago Tribune*, April 17, 1928.

28. *Nineteenth, Twentieth, Twenty-First and Twenty-Second Annual Reports off the Municipal Court of Chicago: For the Years December 1, 1924 to December 2, 1928, Inclusive* (Chicago: Fred J. Ringley). Vagrancy prosecution rates appear to have fallen off in the 1920s. This may have been because vagrancy law was doing a number of different things, such as punishing bootleggers, and not just targeting hobos and itinerants. Variation might also be attributable to difference among judges. See "Judges, Divided, Ask One Policy Concerning 'Vags,'" *Chicago Tribune*, May 27, 1919.

29. "Gangsters and the Vagrancy Law," *Chicago Tribune*, September 10, 1930.

30. "Gunman Slays Alfred Lingle in I. C. Subway," *Chicago Tribune*, June 10, 1930.

31. "Gangsters Put on Rock Pile as Vagrants," *Chicago Tribune*, September 4, 1930.

32. Despite the fact that Alderman and Condi were not charged with, or guilty of, the Lingle murder, the lawmakers involved in their trials were divided over the meaning of vagrancy law. After their convictions, Alderman and Condi's attorney, Benjamin Feldman, filed a writ of habeas corpus in the Criminal Court of Cook County, a separate court where cases were typically bound over after receiving a first hearing in the Chicago municipal court. See "Use of Vagrancy Act Marks New Attack on Gangs," *Chicago Tribune*, September 7, 1930. Feldman told a criminal court judge that his clients were denied access to council. Presiding judge John McGoorty, acknowledging "that the Criminal Court of Cook County has no general authority to review the judgment of the Municipal Court of Chicago," ordered Alderman and Condi released. "When basic legal principles are violated," McGoorty explained, "such as access to an attorney, all courts have a duty to review." See "Freed Hoodlums Rearrested as They Quit Court," *Chicago Tribune*, September 9, 1930. Within eighteen hours, Judge Lyle had both men rearrested. But by this point the legal issue had shifted. It was not whether they had information about the murder of Alfred Lingle — it was "whether notorious Chicago hoodlums may be imprisoned under the state vagrancy act." See "Lyle Jails Two Hoodlums Again: Cites Bondsman," *Chicago Tribune*, September 10, 1930. Lyle increased the men's bond from twenty thousand to thirty thousand dollars and up to forty thousand dollars in real estate. See "Invoke Vagrant Act to Lock Up 2 More Gangmen," *Chicago Tribune*, September 11, 1930. Alderman and Condi were released again after their bondsman had municipal court judge Alfred

Erickson approve a midnight appeal. Lyle again moved to immediately cancel the bond approval, hoping to institute a new precedent that "lawless hoodlums" could be imprisoned "for six-month hard labor under the vagrancy act."

The two judges would publicly disagree over the lower court's application of vagrancy law. Erickson argued that the bond for vagrancy should be no more than a hundred dollars because "the offence is so trivial." See "Judge Explains Freeing of Two on False Bonds," *Chicago Tribune*, September 12, 1930. Meanwhile, veteran municipal court judge Harry Fisher, explaining that while he "applaud[ed] what the serious minded men in this community are doing," said, "I am true to my oath of office. . . . I must lay aside all considerations save that which the law requires of me in the trial of a human whose liberty is at stake." See "Bail Cut Again by Judge Fisher in Condi Case," *Chicago Tribune*, October 23, 1930. Condi and Alderman were ultimately acquitted of vagrancy after about a year. The postscript to Condi's story confirms Lyle's hostility. In June, one year after the Alfred Lingle slaying that triggered a wholesale reexamination of vagrancy law in Chicago, Condi was rearrested, this time in connection with the robbery of *Tribune* employee and creator of *The Gumps* comic strip Sydney Smith. See "Condi Named in Sidney Smith Gem Robbery," *Chicago Tribune*, June 25, 1931. For more on Alderman and Condi, see "Two Gangsters Indicted under Vagrancy Act," *Chicago Tribune*, September 13, 1930; "Jury Ponders Fate of Condi as a Vagrant," *Chicago Tribune*, October 24, 1930; and "Condi, Alderman Get Extradition Hearing Delay," *Chicago Tribune*, October 29, 1930.

33. "Stege Launches Drive to Clear City of Hoboes," *Chicago Tribune*, January 11, 1930.

34. "37th Conviction Is Obtained in Vagrancy Drive," *Chicago Tribune*, April 23, 1931.

35. James O'Donnell Bennett, "Forty Hoodlums before Judge: 2 Win Freedom," *Chicago Tribune*, January 16, 1931.

36. "Bail Cut Again."

37. "Vagrancy Laws," *Chicago Tribune*, August 23, 1930.

38. "Supreme Court Kills Chicago Vagrancy Law," *Chicago Tribune*, April 22, 1934.

39. Virginia Gardner, "A Hobo Retires to His Estate in City 'Jungle,'" *Chicago Tribune*, August 7, 1930.

40. Virginia Gardner, "Hobo Village Turns Men to Domestic Arts," *Chicago Tribune*, August 20, 1931.

41. "Czarnecki Seeks to Clear Hobo Shacks from U.S. Property," *Chicago Tribune*, October 21, 1930.

42. *Adkins v. Children's Hospital* was a Fifth Amendment case involving a District of Columbia minimum wage law requiring that workingwomen be paid at a rate that ensured "good health and protect[ed] their morals." The decision upheld the complaints of the Washington, DC, children's hospital that the minimum wage law violated the liberty of contract that was endorsed in *Lochner v. New York.*

43. Because *Adkins* was decided on Fifth Amendment grounds, it did not overturn *Muller v. Oregon*, which was decided on Fourteenth Amendment grounds. Arguably, however, it disrupted the spirit of the *Muller* opinion.

44. *Adkins v. Children's Hospital.*

45. For workingwomen's declining wages, see Kessler-Harris, *Out to Work*, 228.

46. Eunice Fuller Barnard, "Home — Job — or Both? The Woman's Problem," *Nation*, June 2, 1926, 601–602.

47. Doris Blake, "Ambition Often Ruins Happiness," *Chicago Tribune*, January 5, 1930; Doris Blake, "How to Be Happy though Married," *Chicago Tribune*, July 16, 1923, 19; Doris Blake, "How to Be Happy though Married," *Chicago Tribune*, August 31, 1923.

48. "Well Groomed Look Is Great Big Asset in Landing That Job," *Chicago Tribune*, August 27, 1928.

49. "Finds Women Prefer Work in Loop District," *Chicago Tribune*, March 2, 1929.

50. "Rich Wife Should Pay Alimony," *Chicago Tribune*, July 20, 1924.

51. "The dress of women and their economic possibilities do not make ordinary hobo behavior practicable," Dr. W. A. Evans wrote in the *Tribune*. "Basically, the prostitute who moves around from city to city is a female hobo," he explained. For "female hobo," see W. A. Evans, "How to Keep Well," *Chicago Tribune*, August 4, 1923. "Female hoboes" were often equated with sex workers. Walter Reckless would describe a criminally dependent class of "female hoboes." Drawing on Transient Bureau records, Reckless described how "Mrs. Metzger," a Seventh-day Adventist, roamed in search of religious tolerance, lived modestly, and regularly encountered sexual violence. See Walter C. Reckless, "Why Women Become Hoboes," *American Mercury*, 175–180; Cliff Maxwell, "Lady Vagabonds," *Scribner's Magazine*, March 1929, 292; and "*Lady Hoboes*," *New Republic*, January 1930, 164–169.

52. Butler, *Two Paths to Equality*, 102–106.

53. Arthur Evans, "Bob 'Makes War' in Chicago," *Chicago Tribune*, October 12, 1924.

54. For criticism of Kate Kane, see "Little Talk on Live Topics," *Chicago Tribune*, April 25, 1900.

55. Catharine Waugh McCulloch, "Voice of the People," *Chicago Tribune*, March 8, 1923.

56. Valeska Bari, "Shall Women Be Protected?," *Nation*, February 9, 1927, 143–144.

57. *Adkins v. Children's Hospital.*

58. John Kelley, "Vice Barometer Shows Big Drop in Last Decade," *Chicago Tribune*, December 11, 1921.

59. Water Reckless argued the "delinquent" and "disordered" are better met with the full enforcement arm of the state. See Reckless, *Vice In Chicago*, 58–59, 68, 270. In 1929, of the 7,695 "women cases" in the Morals Court, Reckless noted that the vast majority (76.2 percent) were discharged, while smaller numbers were fined (10.9 percent), given probation (8.1 percent), or sentenced to the house of correction (4.1 percent). See Reckless, 64, 245, 270.

60. *Nineteenth, Twentieth, Twenty-First and Twenty-Second Annual Reports of the Municipal Court of Chicago*, 112–114; Willrich, *City of Courts*, 185.

61. Hassil was one of eighty-four people charged in Chicago's Municipal Court in 1928 with pandering. *Nineteenth, Twentieth, Twenty-First and Twenty-Second Annual Reports of the Municipal Court of Chicago.*

62. *People v. Hassil.*

63. Committee of Fifteen Records, April 23, 1924.

64. Investigators recalled taking a meal downtown at 416 South Wabash and, while dining, noticing "six unescorted women." After they joined two women, Edith and May, they duly noted they were being solicited. See Committee of Fifteen Records, April 22, 1922, April 21, 1924, and April 22, 1924.

65. Committee of Fifteen Records, April 5, 1922.

66. Committee of Fifteen Records, March 1 and March 2, 1926.

67. Committee of Fifteen Records, March 1, 1926.

68. Committee of Fifteen Records, March 2, 1926. According to these reports, the racial hierarchy of wage work was replicated in sex work. Black sex workers were typically paid half of what whites were paid and were generally shut out of high-end houses that served bootlegged alcohol. In these houses, rates increased dramatically and ranged from ten to fifteen dollars — nearly triple the standard rate — plus one dollar per drink. Based on the records, white women charged five dollars and Black women charged two dollars. There were exceptions. For instance, white women Mildred and Katherine working in a house on Indiana Avenue charged three dollars in April 1922. As

a rule, though, African American sex workers charged lower rates for their services. See Committee of Fifteen Records, April 15–21, 1922, April 29, 1924, and March 2, 1926.

69. Committee of Fifteen Records, March 2, 1926.

70. Committee of Fifteen Records, March 3, 1926.

71. Committee of Fifteen Records, April 14, 1924.

72. Newspaper and census data support claims about women's increasing participation in economic activity by the early 1930s. See Doris Blake, "Women Work from Necessity, Says Labor Bureau Head," *Chicago Tribune*, June 18, 1930. Newspaper reports of 1930 census results revealed that women represented one quarter of the steady industrial and clerical work force and that, with housekeepers factored in, women worked steadily in numbers comparable to those of men. See "One of Every 4 U.S. Women between 16 and 64 Work," *Chicago Tribune*, September 1, 1930. For "necessary" to the "modern industrial system," see "Open Inquiry into Slashes in Women's Pay," *Chicago Tribune*, April 4, 1933. For minimum wage, see Genevieve Forbes Herrick, "It's Ladies' Day for Hearing on Fixed Wage Bill," *Chicago Tribune*, April 26, 1933, and "Roosevelt Minimum Wage Plan Fought by Woman's Party," *Chicago Tribune*, April 16, 1933.

73. For minimum wage, see "Open Inquiry into Slashes in Women's Pay," *Chicago Tribune*, April 4, 1933, and Parke Brown, "Horner Urges Minimum Wage Law for Women," *Chicago Tribune*, May 26, 1933. For divided activists, see Percy Wood, "House Committee Indorses Women's Eight Hour Bill," *Chicago Tribune*, May 27, 1931.

74. While the concept of the New Negro emerged in Harlem, its significance reverberated well beyond New York City. The essay was originally published in *Survey Graphic* as "Enter the New Negro" in March 1925. It was republished in an anthology later that year as "The New Negro." See Locke, *New Negro*.

75. While the steel, meat-packing, and iron industries provided steady employment for Black men, there was a long list of jobs, including plumbing, electrical, printing, and woodwork, that were "practically closed." See Chicago Urban League Annual Reports, *Tenth Annual Report of the Chicago Urban League, for the Fiscal Year Ending October 31, 1926*, 5, 12–13, 16.

76. Chicago Urban League Annual Reports, *Fourth Annual Report for the Fiscal Year Ending October 31, 1920*, 6.

77. Sayre, "Negro Women in Industry," *Opportunity* (August 1924): 244.

78. Drake and Cayton argue in *Black Metropolis* that for a generation of Black migrants, racial inequality was self-replicating and flowed into all areas of Black life. See Drake and Cayton, *Black Metropolis*, 268.

79. Evans, "Negro in Chicago Industries," 15–16.

80. "'Walk Out' Makes Jobs for Those Who Are Barred," *Chicago Defender*, July 15, 1922; "The Right to Strike," *Chicago Defender*, August 12, 1922.

81. "Survey of Labor," *Chicago Defender*, February 28, 1925.

82. According to historian Rick Halpern, the time cards of African American workers were marked with Black stars "so the foremen could easily see and quickly identify them when the call came to reduce the size of the gang." Halpern, *Down on the Killing Floor*, 71–79. For physically separated, see "Feed Strikebreakers at the 'Hog Trough' in RR Shop," *Chicago Defender*, August 5, 1922.

83. "Colored Strikebreaker Hanged in Oklahoma," *Chicago Tribune*, January 18, 1922.

84. "Greater than the Law," *Chicago Defender*, September 2, 1922.

85. Bates, "Mobilizing Black Chicago, 196.

86. Halpern, *Down on the Killing Floor*, 87, 94; Cohen, *Making a New Deal*, 314–319.

87. Eric Arnesen, *Brotherhoods of Color* (Cambridge, MA: Harvard University Press, 2001), 90–93.

88. Bates, "Mobilizing Black Chicago," 197–199.

89. "Urban League Finds It Hard to Get Jobs," *Chicago Defender*, December 31, 1927.

90. "Constitutional Rights Fail to Aid Workers," *Chicago Defender*, October 20, 1928.

91. Frazier, "Chicago," 72.

92. Harris, "Negro Workers," 83.

93. White, "Negro and Communists," 62. The National Urban League met in late 1933 to establish boards and bureaucracies to "acquaint the Negro with the laws respecting the [National Recovery Administration's] codes, relief, re-employment" and to help Blacks "obtain the benefits of the various acts." See "Negroes to Be Taught Rights under New Deal" *Chicago Tribune*, October 7, 1933.

94. Drake and Cayton, *Black Metropolis*, 293.

95. Hill, "Picketing for Jobs," 216.

96. "US Acts to Curb 'Reds,'" *Chicago Defender*, August 8, 1931.

97. "Calls Chicago Battlefront of Red Agitators," *Chicago Tribune*, August 8, 1931.

98. For 1935 arrest, see "Co-Eds Freed after Promise to Quit Reds," *Chicago Tribune*, August 28, 1935. A similar configuration of African Americans and young white women was arrested on similar grounds in 1933. See "5 Men,

2 Women Reds Convicted by Jury; Fined," *Chicago Tribune*, February 11, 1933. Of course, the Scottsboro Trial exemplified the mistreatment of African Americans for interacting with white woman, in this case for supposedly sexually assaulting white women on a train in 1931. See Goodman, *Stories of Scottsboro*.

99. "Council of Social Agencies of Chicago Memorandum," box 204, folder 1, Social Welfare Collection Papers, Chicago History Society.

100. "12 of 36 Judges in City Court Accept Pay Cut," *Chicago Tribune*, May 4, 1933. Some judges challenged the cuts. See "Municipal Court Judges to Fight Pay Cut in Court," *Chicago Tribune*, July 1, 1933.

101. "Charge Chicago Court Fees Are Far Above Other Cities," *Chicago Tribune*, May 30, 1933. Despite the municipal court's dramatic growth under the Republican administration of Harry Olson, Republican judges complained vociferously under the administration of Democrat Chief Justice Sonsteby about fees, spending, and institutional organization. See "12 of 36 Judges in City Court," and Willrich, *City of Courts*, 310–311.

102. The branch was located at State Street and Eleventh Avenue. See "Special Court Set Up to Try Relief Cases," *Chicago Tribune*, November 3, 1933.

103. For Jakubik, see "Relief Cheater Is Sent to Cell for 9 Months," *Chicago Tribune*, January 16, 1936. For criticism of the court's prosecution of "relief cheaters," see Edward Larson, "Causes of Relief Violence," *Chicago Tribune*, February 3, 1935. It seems likely that Jakubik's wife worked and did not need his support. See "Relief Cheater Is Sent."

104. For the Leach trial, see "Relief Cheater Is Sent."

105. For John Sandilands, see "Relief Cheater Sentenced," *Chicago Tribune*, October 1, 1936.

106. "Municipal Court Becomes Proud Poppa of a New Book," *Chicago Tribune*, November 15, 1935.

EPILOGUE: THE NEW DEAL'S SOCIAL ORIGINS

1. Quoted in Charles, *Minister of Relief*, 86.

2. "Ruth Johnson," Ernest Watson Burgess Papers, addenda, box 135, folder 2. Johnson's race is not disclosed in the case study.

3. For economic inequality drove New Deal reforms, see Goluboff, *Lost Promise of Civil Rights*, which argues that economic rights ultimately became a "lost promise." George Lovell also describes the preponderance of right talk

focused on work in 1930s America. See Lovell, *This Is Not Civil Rights*. For New Deal reforms limited wholesale revolution, see Tomlins, *State and Unions*.

4. President Roosevelt's quote is from a statement he prepared for the exposition, "President's Message to the Fair," *New York Times*, May 28, 1933.

5. "Fireside Chat September 30, 1934," 413–422.

6. Quoted in Charles, *Minister of Relief*, 86.

7. For New Deal privileges white men, see DePastino, *Citizen Hobo*, 209. Unlike President Herbert Hoover, who responded to the Great Depression with a couple of banking and finance reforms in 1932, President Roosevelt responded extravagantly, expanding securities, lending, and banking reform while championing the poor through programs in infrastructure, agriculture, direct hiring, and relief. For examples of President Hoover's efforts, see the Reconstruction Finance Corporation Act, passed in January 1932; the Glass-Steagall Act, passed in February 1932; and the Federal Home Loan Bank Act, passed in July 1932. Roosevelt expanded the Glass-Steagall Act into the Banking Act in June 1933 and created the Securities Exchange Act in June 1934. His administration built infrastructure through the Tennessee Valley Authority Act, offered direct relief through the Federal Emergency Relief Act, hired through the Civilian Conservation Corps, the Reforestation Relief Act, and the Work Progress Administration, and tried to help farmers through the Agricultural Adjustment Act.

8. As Linda Gordon points out, relief to women was still "morals tested" in the 1930s, and workingwomen were largely excluded from New Deal employment programs. See Gordon, *Pitied but Not Entitled*, 192–196. Only 7 percent of the CWA's four million workers were women. See Gordon, 193. For humiliation, see Cohen, *Making a New Deal*, 247.

9. Wage floors and hours ceilings proposed by First Lady Eleanor Roosevelt and labor secretary Frances Perkins were aimed at basic protections. See Genevieve Forbes Herrick, "It's Ladies' Day for Hearing on Fixed Wage Bill," *Chicago Tribune*, April 26, 1933; "Roosevelt Minimum Wage Plan Fought by Woman's Party," *Chicago Tribune*, April 16, 1933; Cohen, *Making a New Deal*, 247.

10. According to Karen Ferguson, the New Deal benefited elite Black Atlanta. See Ferguson, *Black Politics*. And these programs included housing, where "redlining" policies prevented African Americans from receiving loans. See Rothstein, *Color of Law*.

11. For the de-employment of Black Americans, see Cohen, *Making a New Deal*, 242, and Drake and Cayton, *Black Metropolis*, 354. According to a "Black

Belt Police Station" captain, most sex workers were "poor women who are out of a job and can't make it any other way. If they could just get a job scrubbing floors, you wouldn't see them trying to be whores very long." According to an anonymous Morals Court official, "some of the people arrested for prostitution are not prostitutes. The race question enters in here. There are more accidental arrests for persons who are not prostitutes among the colored than would be true in cases of Whites." See Drake and Cayton, *Black Metropolis*, 595–597.

12. Initially Supreme Court justices resisted the New Deal and even overturned some of its programs. For instance, the court overruled New Deal programs when it decided against the National Industrial Recovery Act in 1935 in *Schechter Poultry v. United States.* In response — and after winning a second term in office — President Roosevelt threatened to "pack" the court with sympathetic junior justices. In response, justices began upholding New Deal legislations by the same slim majority they had been rejected them. This threat to New Deal programs ended when Justice Owen Roberts changed his vote in *West Coast Hotel Co. v. Parrish* and began supporting New Deal legislations. See Hall, *Magic Mirror*, 281–284.

13. *West Coast Hotel Co. v. Parrish.*

14. *National Labor Relations Board v. Jones & Laughlin Steel Corp.*

Bibliography

NEWSPAPERS

Chicago Daily News
Chicago Defender
Chicago Inter Ocean
Chicago Record Herald
Chicago Tribune
"Hobo" News
"Hobo" World
Los Angeles Times
New York Times

PERIODICALS

Crisis
Forum
Harper's Magazine
Literary Digest
McClure's Magazine
Nation
New Republic
Opportunity
Saturday Evening Post
Scribner's

SPECIAL COLLECTIONS

Archives Department of the Clerk of the Circuit Court of Cook County, Chi-
    cago, Illinois.
Ben Lewis Reitman Papers. University of Illinois at Chicago Special Collec-
    tions and University Archives.

Chicago Committee of Fifteen Records. Special Collections, Regenstein Library, University of Chicago.

Chicago Municipal Court Records. Research Center. Chicago History Museum.

Chicago Police Department. *First Precinct Arrest Book*, January 2, 1875–June 30, 1885. Chicago History Museum.

Ernest Watson Burgess Papers. Regenstein Library. University of Chicago Special Collections.

Harry Olson Disassembled Scrapbooks. Chicago History Museum.

"Hobo" News. Rare Books and Manuscript Library, University of Illinois at Urbana-Champaign.

Julius Rosenwald Papers. University of Chicago Special Collections.

Social Welfare Collection Papers, Chicago History Society.

CENSUS REPORTS

Department of Commerce and Labor Bureau of the Census 1900. *Special Report: Occupations at the Twentieth Census*. Washington: Government Printing Office, 1904.

Department of Commerce. Bureau of the Census 1920. *Fourteenth Census of the United States Taken in the Year 1920: Occupations*. Washington: Government Printing Office, 1923.

Statistics of the Population of the United States at the Tenth Census, 1880. Washington: Government Printing Office, 1993.

ANNUAL REPORTS

Chicago Municipal Court Annual Reports, 1906–1928. D'Angelo Law Library, University of Chicago.

Chicago Urban League Annual Reports, 1917–1926. Chicago History Museum.

Chicago Women's Aid Society Annual Reports. Chicago History Museum.

United Charities of Chicago Annual Reports. University of Illinois at Chicago Special Collections.

LEGAL DECISIONS

Federal

Adair v. United States, 208 U.S. 161 (1908).

Adkins v. Children's Hospital, 261 U.S. 525 (1923).

Allgeyer v. Louisiana, 165 U.S. 578 (1897).

Bradwell v. Illinois, 83 U.S. 130 (1872).

Buchanan v. Warley, 245 U.S. 60 (1917).

City of New York v. Miln, 36 U.S. 102 (1837).

Civil Rights Cases, 109 U.S. 3 (1883).

Coppage v. Kansas, 236 U.S. 1 (1915).

Dred Scott v. Sandford, 60 U.S. 393 (1856).

Edwards v. California, 314 U.S. 160 (1941).

Holden v. Hardy, 169 U.S. 366 (1898).

Lochner v. New York, 198 U.S. 45 (1905).

Minor v. Happersett, 88 U.S. 162 (1874).

Muller v. Oregon, 208 U.S. 412 (1908).

National Labor Relations Board v. Jones & Laughlin Steel Corp., 301 U.S. 1 (1937).

Palko v. Connecticut, 302 U.S. 319 (1937).

Papachristou v. City of Jacksonville, 405 U.S. 156 (1972).

Slaughter-House Cases, 83 U.S. 36 (1873).

United States v. Carolene Products Co., 304 U.S. 144 (1938).

West Coast Hotel Co. v. Parrish, 300 U.S. 379 (1937).

Williams v. Mississippi, 170 U.S. 213 (1898).

State

Forks v. Easton, 2 Whart. 405, 1837 WL 3175 (Pa.).

Laura Raymond v. The People, 9 Ill. App. 344, 1881.

Nelson v. People 33 Ill. 390 (1864).

People ex rel. Molony v. Pullman's Palace-Car Co., Supreme Court of Illinois, 1898, 175 Ill. 125.

People v. Covey, 179 Ill. App. 354 (1913).

People v. Hassil, 341 Ill. 286, 173 N.E. 355 (1930).

People v. O'Keefe, 178 Ill. App 86 (1913).

Powell v. Pennsylvania, 127 U.S. 678 (1888).

Ritchie v. People, 155 Ill. 98 (1895).

Stanley v. Wells, 71 Ill. 78 (1873).

Municipal Court of Chicago Criminal Records, Chicago Municipal Court Archives

Armstrong v. Armstrong. Case 101250. August 30, 1923.

People v. Betsy Ross Candy Company. Case 111413–111420. January 11, 1915.

People v. Charles Matter. Case 108690. May 12, 1914.

People v. Claude Powers. Chicago Committee of Fifteen Records. Vol. 25, 86.

People v. C. W. Scott. Chicago Committee of Fifteen Records. Vol. 26, 44.

People v. David Miller. Case 136202. September 16, 1915.

People v. Ed Brown. Case 136246. September 24, 1915.

People v. Edward McNamara. Case 103352. July 20, 1914.

People v. Ethel Smith. Case 187532–187537. April 21, 1917.

People v. Fred Schultz. Case 105851. June 5, 1914.

People v. George Bowing. Case 105859. April 28, 1914.

People v. George Mason. Case 413037. 1926.

People v. George Wine. Chicago Committee of Fifteen Records. Vol. 25.

People v. G. Reed. Case 101670. April 22, 1914.

People v. Harry Jacobs. Case 99983. November 9, 1914.

People v. Harry Morris. Case 99982. November 9, 1914.

People v. Henry Geloss. Case 124671. February 15, 1915.

People v. Ike Holiday. Case 413039. 1926.

People v. John Lewis. Case 105857. April 14, 1914.

People v. John Williams. Case 101669. April 22, 1914.

People v. Joseph Gworek. Case 108700. July 1914.

People v Joseph Szymanski. Case 109279. August 12, 1914.

People v. Leo Szulczaski. Case 109278. August 17, 1914.

People v. Louis Bruschko. Case 111411. January 11, 1915.

People v. Marcie Murphy. Case 187536. April 23, 1917.

People v. Mary Carter. Case 187537. April 20, 1917.

People v. Nicholas Wagner. Case 105852. June 16, 1914.

People v. Pearl Lucas. Case 187535. April 20, 1917.

People v. Rose Murphy. Case 187536. April 21, 1917.

People v. Theodore Ryanovski. Case 124656. February 2, 1915.

People v. Thomas Cayton. Case 105856. June 17, 1914.

People v. Thomas Venos. Chicago Committee of Fifteen Records. Vol. 25.

People v. William Connors. Chicago Committee of Fifteen Records. Vol. 25.

People v. William Kennedy. Case 111412. January 11, 1915.

PRIMARY SOURCES

A Century of Progress, Inc. *Chicago International Exposition of 1933: A State-ment of Its Plan and Purposes and of the Relation of States and Foreign Governments to Them.* Chicago: Century of Progress, 1930.

Addams, Jane. *A New Conscience and an Ancient Evil*. New York: Macmillan, 1911.

———. "Social Control." *Crisis* 1, no. 3 (January 1911): 22–23.

———. *Twenty Years at Hull House*. New York: MacMillan, 1910.

"Alms and Wages." *Harper's Weekly*, September 22, 1877, 739.

Anderson, Nels. *On Hobos and Homelessness*. Edited and introduction by Raffaele Rauty. Chicago: University of Chicago Press, 1999.

Baldwin, James. "James Baldwin Tells Us All How to Cool It This Summer." *Esquire*, April 29, 2015, 49–53, 116. First published July 1968.

Baldwin, William H. "The Court of Domestic Relations of Chicago." *Journal of the American Institute of Criminal Law and Criminology* 3 (September 3, 1912): 400–406.

Bari, Valeska. "Shall Women Be Protected?" *Nation* 124 (February 9, 1927): 143–144.

Barnard, Eunice Fuller. "Home — Job — or Both? The Woman's Problem." *Nation* 122 (June 2, 1926): 601.

Barnes, Clifford W. "The Story of the Committee of Fifteen of Chicago." *Journal of Social Hygiene* 4 (1918): 145–156.

Binmore, Harry. *Laws and Ordinances Governing the City of Chicago*. Chicago: E. B. Meyers, 1890.

Blackstone, William. *Commentaries on the Laws of England*. Chicago: University of Chicago Press, 1979. First published 1765–1769.

———. *Commentaries on the Laws of England*. Book 4: "Public Wrongs Section." Stat. 198: "Vagrants, Rogues and Vagabonds."

Blythe, Samuel G. "Tapering Off on Work." *Saturday Evening Post* (August 8, 1925): 198.

Bogue, John H. *Chicago Cheap Lodging Houses and Their Lodgers: A Report*. Chicago: Improved Housing Association, 1899.

Booth, Charles. "Conditions and Occupations of the People of East London and Hackney." *Journal of the Royal Statistical Society* 51, no. 2 (June 1888): 276–339.

———. "The Inhabitants of Tower Hamlets (School Board Division), Their Condition and Occupations." *Journal of the Royal Statistical Society* 50, no. 2 (1887): 326–401.

Bowen, Louise deKoven. *The Colored People of Chicago: An Investigation Made for the Juvenile Protective Association*. Chicago: Juvenile Protective Association, 1913.

Brandeis, Louis D. *Women in Industry: Decision of the United States Supreme Court in Court Muller vs. State of Oregon*. New York, 1908.

Breckinridge, Sophonisba. "The Color Line in the Housing Problem." *Survey* 40 (February 1, 1913): 575–576.

————. *The Delinquent Child and the Home.* New York: Charities Publication Committee, 1912.

Brundage, Edward J. *The Chicago Code of 1911.* Chicago: Callaghan, 1911.

Burke, W. H. "Official Complicity with Vice." *Christian Union* 45, no. 26 (June 25, 1892): 1240–1241.

Carnegie, Andrew, and David Nasaw. *The Gospel of Wealth Essays and Other Writing.* New York: Penguin, 2006.

"Chicago." *Crisis* 21, no. 5 (March 1921): 213–215.

"Chicago: Hobo Capital of America." *Survey* 50 (June 1, 1923): 287–290, 303–305.

Chicago City Council. *Report of the Activities from January 29, 1918, to June 24, 1918, or Vagrancy Court in Chicago.* Municipal Court Papers. Folder 35. Research Center, Chicago History Museum.

————. *Report of the City Council Committee on Crime.* Chicago: H. G. Adair, 1915.

Chicago Commission on Race Relations. *The Negro in Chicago: A Study of Race Relations and a Riot.* Chicago: University of Chicago Press, 1922.

Chicago (Ill.). *The Social Evil in Chicago: A Study of Existing Conditions with Recommendations by the Vice Commission of Chicago.* Chicago: Gunthorp-Warren Printing Co., 1911.

Chicago, Illinois. *Laws and Ordinances Governing the City of Chicago.* Chicago: E. B. Myers & Chandler, 1873.

————. *The Revised Municipal Code of Chicago, 1905.* Chicago: Lawyers' Co-operative, 1905.

Chicago Relief. *Chicago Relief and Aid Society.* Chicago: Culver, Page, Hoyne, 1871.

Chicago Relief and Aid Society. *Report of the Chicago Relief and Aid Society of Disbursement of Contributions for the Sufferers by the Chicago Fire.* Printed for the Chicago Relief and Aid Society, at the Riverside Press, 1874.

City of Chicago, Municipal Court. *Second Annual Report of the Municipal Court of Chicago: For the Year December 1, 1907 to December 6, 1908, Inclusive.* Chicago: Henry O. Shepard, n.d.

————. *Seventh Annual Report for the Municipal Court of Chicago for the Year December 2, 1912, to November 30, 1913.* Chicago: Henry O. Shepard, n.d.

Cleland, McKenzie. "The New Gospel in Criminology." *McClure's Magazine* 31 (July 1908): 358–363.

Closson, Carlos, Jr. "The Unemployed in American Cities." *Quarterly Journal of Economics* 8 (January 1894): 168–217.

Conyngton, Mary. *United States Bureau of Labor: Report on the Condition of Women and Child Workers in the United States.* Washington: Government Printing Office, 1910–1913.

Croffut, W. A. "What Rights Have Laborers?" *Forum* 1 (May 1886): 294–296.

Daggett, Mabel Potter. "The City as Mother." *World's Work* 25 (November 1912): 111–117.

Dawley, Almena. "A Study of the Social Effects of the Municipal Court of Chicago." MA thesis, University of Chicago, 1915.

Dreiser, Theodore. *Sister Carrie.* Mineola, NY: Dover, 2004. First published 1900.

Du Bois, W. E. B. "Close Ranks." *Crisis* 16 (July 1918): 111.

——. "The Migration of Negroes." *Crisis* 14 (June 1917): 63–66.

——. *The Philadelphia Negro: A Social Study.* Philadelphia: Published for the University, 1899.

——. "The Social Equality of Whites and Blacks." *Crisis* 21 (November 1920): 16–18.

Ely, Richard. "Pullman: A Social Study." *Harper's Magazine* 70 (February 1885): 452–466.

Embree, Frances Buckley. "The Housing of the Poor in Chicago." *Journal of Political Economy* 8 (June 1900): 354–377.

Evans, William L. "The Negro in Chicago Industries." *Opportunity* 1 (February 1923): 15–16.

"Fireside Chat September 30, 1934." In *The Public Papers and Addresses of Franklin D. Roosevelt, Vol. 3,* compiled by Samuel I. Rosenman, 413–422. New York: Macmillan, 1941).

Filene, Edward A. "The Betterment of the Condition of Working Women." *Annals of the America Academy of Political and Social Science* 27 (May 1906): 613–626.

Flinn, Joseph, and John Elbert Wilkie. *History of the Chicago Police from the Settlement of Community to the Present Time.* Chicago: Police Book Fund, 1887.

Flynt, Josiah. "In the World of Graft." *McClure's Magazine* 16 (February 1901): 327–334.

Frazier, E. Franklin. "Chicago: A Cross Section of Negro Life." *Opportunity* 7 (March 1929): 71–73.

——. *The Negro Family in Chicago.* Chicago: University of Chicago Press, 1932.

Freund, Ernst. *The Police Power: Public Policy and Constitutional Rights.* Chicago: Callaghan, 1904.

George, Henry. *Progress and Poverty: An Inquiry into the Cause of Industrial Depressions and of Increase of Want with Increase of Wealth; The Remedy.* New York: Modern Library, 1938.

Gilbert, Hiram. "Legal Tract Series: Practice of the Municipal Court of Chicago." *Illinois Law Review* 1 (1906), 94–105.

———. "New Municipal Court System: Address Delivered before the Union League Club of Chicago, April 10, 1906." Chicago, 1906.

Goldman, Emma. *Anarchism and Other Essays.* New York: Dover Publications, 1969.

Greene, J. Kent. "The Municipal Court of Chicago." *University of Pennsylvania Law Review and American Law Register* 58 (March 1910): 335–346.

Harris, Abram L. "The Negro Workers: A Problem of Progressive Labor." *Crisis* 37 (March 1930): 83–85.

Herberg, Will. "Shall the Negro Worker Turn to Labor of Capital?" *Crisis* 38 (July 1931): 227–228.

Hill, Augustus. "The Negro in Chicago." *Crisis* 25 (January 1923): 112.

Hill, T. Arnold. "Housing for the Negro Wage Earner." In *Housing Problems in America: Proceedings of the Sixth National Conference.* New York: National Housing Association, 1917, 309–313.

———. "Picketing for Jobs." *Opportunity* 8 (July 1930): 216.

———. "Why Southern Negroes Don't Go South." *Survey* 43 (November 29, 1919): 183–195.

Holland, J. G. "Once More the Tramp." *Scribner's Magazine* 15 (April 1878): 882–883.

Holmes, O. W. "The Path of Law." *Harvard Law Review* 110 (March 1897).

Howe, Frederic C., and Marie Jenney Howe. "Pensioning the Widow and Fatherless." *Good Housekeeping* 57 (September 1913): 282–291.

"How to Give Alms." *Harper's Weekly,* October 6, 1877, 778–779.

Hull-House Maps and Papers: A Presentation of Nationalities and Wages in a Congested District of Chicago, Together with Comments and Essays on Problems Growing Out of the Social Conditions. Urbana: University of Illinois Press, 2007. First published 1895.

Hunter, Robert. *Tenement Conditions in Chicago.* Chicago: City Homes Association, 1901.

Hutchinson, Jonas. *Laws and Ordinances Governing the City of Chicago.* Chicago: E. B. Meyers, 1890.

Illinois. *Report of the Senate Vice Committee Created under the Authority of the Senate of the Forty-Ninth General Assembly as a Continuation of the Com-*

mittee Created under the Authority of the Senate of the Forty-Eighth General Assembly, State of Illinois. Chicago, 1916.

Israel, Boris. "Shanty Town: USA." *New Republic* 75 (May 24, 1933): 39–41.

Jones, Katherine. "The Working Girls of Chicago." *Review of Reviews* 4 (September 1891): 168.

Josephson, Matthew. "The Other Nation." *New Republic* 17 (March 17, 1933): 14–16.

"Justice for the Poor." *Liberty: Not the Daughter but the Mother of Order* 297 (April 7, 1894).

Kelley, Florence. *The Autobiography of Florence Kelley*. Chicago: Charles H. Kerr, 1986.

———. "Our Need for Wasting More Time." *Harper's Monthly* 150 (1925), 659–662.

———. "The Sweating System." In *Hull House Maps and Papers*, edited by Residents of Hull House, 27–48. Urbana: University of Illinois Press, 2007. First published 1895.

Kellor, Frances A. "Southern Colored Girls in the North: The Problem of Their Protection." *Charities* 8 (March 18, 1905): 584–585.

Kelsey, Carl. "The Evolution of Negro Labor." *Annals of the American Academy of Political and Social Science* 21 (January 1903): 55–76.

Knibbs, Henry Herbert. *Songs of the Outlands: Songs of the Hoboes and Other Verse*. New York: Houghton Mifflin, 1914.

Leavitt, Samuel. "The Tramps and the Law." *Forum* 2 (October 1886): 190–200.

Lincoln, Abraham. "Address before the Wisconsin State Agricultural Society, Milwaukee, Wisconsin" (September 30, 1859). In *The Collected Works of Abraham Lincoln*, vol. 3, edited by Roy P. Basler. New Brunswick, NJ: Rutgers University Press, 1953, 478–479.

Livingston, Leon Ray. *Hobo Camp Fire Tales*. Cambridge Springs, PA: A-No. 1 Publishing, 1911.

Lloyd, Henry Demarest. *Wealth against Commonwealth*. Englewood Cliffs, NJ: Prentice Hall, 1963. First published 1894.

Locke, Alain, ed. *The New Negro*. New York: Atheneum, 1969. First published 1925.

Massachusetts. *The General Laws and Liberties of the Massachusetts Colony*. Cambridge, MA: 1675.

McCook, J. J. "A Tramp Census and Its Revelation." *Forum* 15 (August 1893): 753–766.

McCormick, Robert H. "Problems of Criminal Judicature in Chicago and

How They Have Been Solved by the Municipal Court." *Proceedings of the American Political Science Association* 4 (1907): 277–284.

McMurdy, Robert. "The Law Providing for a Municipal Court in Chicago." *Albany Law Journal* (August 1906): 246–252.

Merriam, Charles E. "Findings and Recommendations on the Chicago Council Committee on Crime." *Journal of the American Institute of Criminal Law and Criminology* 6 (September 1915): 345–362.

Miller, Kelly. "The Economic Handicap of the Negro in the North." *Annals of the American Academy of Political and Social Science* 27 (May 1906): 81–88.

"National League on Urban Conditions among Negroes." *Crisis* 8 (September 1914): 243.

Nesbitt, Florence. "Estimating a Family Budget." In *The Charity Visitor: A Handbook for Beginners*," edited by Amelia Sears, 50–59. Chicago: Chicago School of Civics and Philanthropy, 1918. First published 1913.

Olson, Harry. *The Municipal Court of Chicago: An Extemporaneous Address.* San Francisco: Rincon, 1916.

———. "The Proper Organization and Procedure of a Municipal Court." *Proceedings of the American Political Science Association* 7 (1910): 78–96.

Overstreet, H. A. *A Guide to Civilized Leisure.* New York: Norton, 1934.

Palmer, Alice Freeman. "Some Lasting Effects of the World's Fair." *Forum* 16 (December 1893): 517–523.

Palmer, Bertha. "Women's Part in the Columbian Exhibition." *Journal of American Politics* 1 (August 1892): 124–129.

Park, Robert E. "Racial Assimilation in Secondary Groups with Particular Reference to the Negro." *American Journal of Sociology* 19 (March 1914): 618–619.

Park, Robert, Ernest Burgess, and Roderick McKenzie. *The City.* Chicago: University of Chicago Press, 1967. First published 1925.

Parton, James. "Chicago." *Atlantic Monthly* 19 (March 30, 1867): 338–339.

Payne, Roger. *The Hobo Philosopher, the Philosopher of the Hobo Life, or, The Message of Economic Freedom.* Puente, CA: Payne, 1919.

"People ex rel. Scully and O'Leary v. The Superintendent of the Bridewell" (1878). In *Illinois Circuit Court Reports*, edited by Francis E. Matthews and Hal Crampton Bangs. Chicago: T. H. Flood, 1908.

Pinkerton, Alan. *Strikers, Communists, Tramps and Detectives.* New York: Carleton, 1882.

Pound, Roscoe. "The Administration of Justice in the Modern City." *Harvard Law Review* 26 (February 1913): 302–328.

————. "The Causes of Popular Dissatisfaction with the Administration of Justice." *American Bar Association Reporter* 29 (1906): 395–417.

————. "Common Law and Legislation." *Harvard Law Review* 21 (1908): 342–497.

————. "Liberty of Contract." *Yale Law Review* 18 (1909): 454–487.

————. "Mechanical Jurisprudence." *Columbia Law Review* 8 (1908): 605–623.

————. "The Need of a Sociological Jurisprudence." *Green Bag* 19 (1907): 607–615.

————. "The Scope and Purpose of Sociological Jurisprudence." *Harvard Law Review* 24 (1911–1912): 591–619.

————. "Theories of Law." *Yale Law Journal* 22 (December 1912): 114–150.

"Prisoners and Vagrants." *Harper's Weekly*, March 3, 1877, 162.

Reckless, Walter. *Vice in Chicago*. Montclair, NJ: Patterson Smith, 1969. First published 1933.

Ribton-Turner, C. J. *A History of Vagrants and Vagrancy, and Beggars and Begging*. London: Chapman & Hall, 1887.

Riis, Jacob A. *How the Other Half Lives: Studies among the Tenements of New York*. New York: C. Scribner's Sons, 1890.

Roe, Clifford Griffith. *The Great War on White Slavery, or, Fighting for the Protection of Our Girls*. Chicago: 1911.

Sayre, Helen B. "Negro Women in Industry." *Opportunity* 2 (August 1924): 242–244.

Solenberger, Alice. *One Thousand Homeless Men*. New York: Charities Publication Committee, 1911.

Sonsteby, John. *Address by Honorable John J. Sonsteby, Chief Justice, the Municipal Court of Chicago, at Annual Meeting, the Illinois State Bar Association*. Chicago: Champlin-Shealy, 1932.

Stead, William. *If Christ Came to Chicago*. Chicago: Chicago Historical Book Works, 1990. First published 1894.

Stoker, Bram. "The American 'Tramp' Question and the Old English Vagrancy Laws." *North American Review* 190 (November 1909): 605–614.

Sumner, William Graham. *The Forgotten Man and Other Essay*. New York: Cosimo, 2007. First published 1919.

————. *What Social Classes Owe Each Other*. New York: 1972. First published 1883.

"The Girl Who Comes to the City." *Harper's Bazaar* 42 (October 1908): 1005.

"The People ex. rel., Cain v. Frank Hitchcock." *Chicago Legal News* 10 (June 29, 1878): 329–330.

"The Tramp." *Harper's Weekly*, September 2, 1876, 718–719.

Tiedeman, Christopher Gustavus. *A Treatise on the Limitations of Police Power in the United States: Considered from Both a Civil and Criminal Standpoint.* St. Louis: F. H. Thomas Law Book Co., 1886.

Tolman, Edgar Bronson. *The Revised Municipal Code of Chicago of 1905.* Rochester, NY: Lawyer's Cooperative, 1905.

Turners, George Kibbe. "The City of Chicago: A Study of the Great Immoralities." *McClure's Magazine*, April 1907, 575–592.

United States Department of Labor. *Physical Standards for Working Children.* Washington: Government Printing Office, 1921.

———. *Women in Industry Service: Standards Governing the Employment of Women in Industry.* Washington: December 12, 1918.

Vinogradoff, Paul. "The Meaning of Legal History." *Columbia Law Review* 22 (December 1922): 673–705.

Vorse, Mary Heaton. "How Scottsboro Happened." *New Republic* 74 (May 10, 1933): 356–358.

———. "School for Bums." *New Republic* 66 (April 29, 1931): 292–294.

Ward, Lester. *Dynamic Sociology.* New York: D. Appleton, 1897.

———. *Glimpses of the Cosmos.* New York: Putnam, 1913–1918.

———. "The Utilitarian Character of Dynamic Sociology." *American Anthropologist* 5 (April 1892): 97–104.

Waterloo, Stanley. "The Revolution in Chicago's Judicial System." *American Monthly Review of Reviews* 35 (April 1907): 452–455.

Wayland, Francis. *A Paper on Tramps Read at the Saratoga Meeting of the American Social Science Association before the Conference of State Charities, September 6, 1877.* New Haven, CT, 1877.

Wells, Ida B., and Robert W. Rydell, eds. *The Reason Why the Colored American Is Not in the World's Columbian Exposition: The Afro-American's Contribution to Columbian Literature.* Urbana: University of Illinois Press, 1999. First published 1893.

White, Walter. "Chicago and Its Eight Reasons." *Crisis* 18 (October 1919): 293–297.

———. "The Negro and the Communists." *Harper's Monthly Magazine*, December 1931, 62–72.

Whitmore, William Henry. *The Colonial Laws of Massachusetts: Reprinted from the Edition of 1672, with the Supplements through 1686.* Boston: Rockwell & Churchill, 1887.

Willard, Frances Elizabeth. *A White Life for Two.* Chicago: Woman's Temperance Publishing Association, 1890.

Women's Auxiliary of the Retail Clerks International Protective Association, *Are Your Women Clerks Earning a Living Wage?* The Auxiliary, 1908.

Women's Christian Association. *After Twenty-Five Years: 1868–1893.* Cleveland: Western Reserve Historical Society, 1893.

Wood, Junius B. *The Negro in Chicago: How He and His Race Kindred Came to Dwell in Great Numbers in a Northern City, How He Lives and Works, His Successes and Failures, His Political Outlook; A First-Hand Study.* Chicago: Chicago Daily News, 1916.

Wright, R. R., Jr. "The Migration of Negroes to the North." *Annals of the American Academy of Political and Social Science* 27 (May 1906): 97–116.

———. "The Negro in Unskilled Labor." *Annals of the American Academy of Political and Social Science* 49 (September 1913): 19–27.

Wyckoff, Walter. *The Workers: An Experiment in Reality; The East.* New York: Scribner's, 1897.

———. *The Workers: An Experiment in Reality; The West.* New York: Scribner's, 1899.

Zorbaugh, Harvey W. *The Gold Coast and the Slum: A Sociological Study of Chicago's Near North Side.* Chicago: University of Chicago Press, 1929.

SECONDARY SOURCES

Abbott, Edith. *The Tenements of Chicago, 1908–1935.* Chicago: University of Chicago Press, 1936.

———. *Women in Industry: A Study of Economic History.* New York: D. Appleton, 1909.

Adler, Jeffrey. "A Historical Analysis of the Law of Vagrancy." *Criminology* 27 no. 2 (1989): 209–229.

———. "Streetwalkers, Degraded Outcasts and Good-for-Nothing Hussies: Women and the Dangerous Class in Antebellum St. Louis." *Journal of Social History* 25, no. 4 (1992): 737–755.

Adrian, Lynne Marie. "Organizing the Rootless: American Hobo Subculture, 1893–1932." PhD diss., University of Iowa, 1985.

Adrian, Lynne M., and Joan E. Crowley. "Hoboes and Homeboys: The Demography of Misdemeanor Convictions in the Allegheny County Jail, 1892–1923." *Journal of Social History* 25, no. 2 (1991): 345–371.

Alilunus, Leo. "Statutory Means of Impending Emigration of the Negro." *Journal of Negro History* 22, no. 2 (April 1937): 148–162.

Angle, Paul M. "The Illinois Black Laws." *Chicago History* 8, no. 3 (Spring 1967): 65–75.

Arnesen, Eric, ed. *The Black Worker: Race, Labor, and Civil Rights since Emancipation.* Urbana: University of Illinois Press, 2007.

Arredondo, Gabriela F. *Mexican Chicago: Race, Identity, and Nation, 1916–1939*. Urbana: University of Illinois Press, 2008.

Balkin, Jack. "Plessy, Brown and Grutter: A Play in Three Acts." *Cardozo Law Review* 26 (2005): 1689–1730.

Ballam, D. A. "Exploding the Original Myth Regarding Employment-at-Will: The True Origins of the Doctrine." *Berkeley Journal of Employment and Labor Law* 17 (1996): 91–130.

Balogh, Brian. "State of the State among Historians." *Social Science History* 27, no. 3 (Fall 2003): 455–463.

Barnett, Randy. "The Three Narratives of the Slaughter-House Cases." *Journal of Supreme Court History* 41, no. 3 (November 2016): 295–309.

Bates, Beth Thompkins. "Mobilizing Black Chicago: The Brotherhood of Sleeping Car Porters and Community Organizing, 1925–1935." In Arnesen, *Black Worker*, 195–221.

Beck, Frank. *Hobohemia*. Chicago: Charles H. Kerr, 2000.

Beckett, Katherine, and Steven Kelly Herbert. *Banished: The New Social Control in Urban America*. Oxford: Oxford University Press, 2010.

Berlin, Ira. *Many Thousands Gone: The First Two Centuries of Slavery in North America*. Cambridge, MA: Belknap Press of Harvard University, 1998.

Bernstein, Dave E. *Only One Place of Redress: African Americans, Labor Regulations, and the Courts from Reconstruction to the New Deal*. Durham, NC: Duke University Press, 2001.

Best, Joel. *Controlling Vice: Regulating Brothel Prostitution in St. Paul, 1865–1883*. Columbus: Ohio State University Press, 1998.

Black, Joel E. "Citizen Kane: The Everyday Ordeals and Self-Fashioned Citizenship of Wisconsin's 'Lady Lawyer,'" *Law and History Review* 33, no. 1 (2015): 201–230.

———. "Space and Status in Chicago's Legal Landscapes," *Journal of Planning History* 12, no. 3 (August 2013): 227–244.

———. "A Theory of African-American Citizenship: Richard Westbrooks, the Great Migration, and the Chicago Defender's 'Legal Helps' Column." *Journal of Social History* 46, no. 4 (Summer 2013): 896–915.

Blackmon, Douglas. *Slavery by Another Name: The Re-Enslavement of Black Americans from the Civil War to World War II*. New York: Anchor Books, 2008.

Blair, Cynthia. *I've Got to Make My Livin': Black Women's Sex Work in Turn-of-the-Century Chicago*. Chicago: University of Chicago Press, 2010.

———. "We Must Live Anyhow: Africa American Women and Sex Work in Chicago." In Arnesen, *Black Worker*, 122–146.

Bledstein, Burton J. *The Culture of Professionalism: The Middle Class and the Development of Higher Education in America.* New York: Norton, 1976.

Bloom, Alan. "The Floating Population: Homelessness in Early Chicago, 1833–1871." PhD diss., Duke University, 2001.

Boyer, Paul. *Urban Masses and Moral Order in America.* Cambridge, MA: Harvard University Press, 1978.

Brown, James. *The History of Public Assistance in Chicago, 1833–1893.* Chicago: University of Chicago Press, 1941.

Bruns, Roger. *The Damndest Radical: The Life and World of Ben Reitman, Chicago Celebrated Social Reformer, Hobo King and Whorehouse Physician.* Urbana: University of Illinois Press, 1987.

Burrill, Donald R. *Servants of the Law: Judicial Politics on the California Frontier, 1849–89; An Interpretative Exploration of the Field-Terry Controversy.* Lanham, MD: University Press of America, 2010.

Butler, Amy. *Two Paths to Equality: Alice Paul and Ethel M. Smith in the ERA Debate, 1921–1929.* Albany: State University of New York Press, 2002.

Camp, Helen C. *Iron in Her Soul: Elizabeth Gurley Flynn and the American Left.* Pullman: Washington State University Press, 1995.

Canaan, Gareth. "'Part of the Loaf': Economic Conditions of Chicago's African-American Working Class during the 1920's." *Journal of Social History* 35, no. 1 (2001): 147–174.

Canaday, Margot. *The Straight State: Sexuality and Citizenship in Twentieth-Century America.* Princeton, NJ: Princeton University Press, 2011.

Caputo, Richard K. *U.S. Social Welfare Reform: Policy Transitions from 1981 to the Present.* New York: Springer Verlag, 2011.

Certeau, Michel de. *The Practice of Everyday Life.* Berkeley: University of California Press, 1984.

Chambliss, William. "A Sociological Analysis of the Law of Vagrancy." *Social Problems* 2, no. 1 (1964): 67–77.

Charles, Searle F. *Minister of Relief: Harry Hopkins and the Depression.* Syracuse, NY: Syracuse University Press, 1963.

Chazkel, Amy. *Laws of Chance: Brazil's Clandestine Lottery and the Making of Urban Public Life.* Durham, NC: Duke University Press, 2011.

Cohen, Lizabeth. *Making a New Deal: Industrial Workers in Chicago, 1919–1939.* New York: Cambridge University Press, 1989.

Cowie, Jefferson. *Staying Alive: The 1970s and the Last Days of the Working Class.* New York: New Press, 2010.

Cresswell, Tim. *The Tramp in America.* London: Reaction Books, 2001.

Cronon, William. *Nature's Metropolis: Chicago and the Great West*. New York: W. W. Norton, 1992.

Curtis, Michael Kent. *Free Speech, the People's Darling Privilege: Struggles for Freedom of Expression in American History*. Durham, NC: Duke University Press, 2000.

Dale, Elizabeth. *The Chicago Trunk Murder: Law and Justice at the Turn of the Century*. DeKalb: Northern Illinois University Press, 2011.

———. "Michael Willrich. *City of Courts: Socializing Justice in Progressive Era Chicago*." *American Historical Review* 109, no. 2 (2004): 548–549.

———. *The Rule of Justice: The People versus Zephyr Davis*. Columbus: Ohio State University Press, 2001.

———. "'Social Equality Does Not Exist among Themselves, nor Among Us': *Baylies v. Curry* and Civil Rights in Chicago, 1888." *American Historical Review* 102, no. 2 (April 1997): 311–339.

Davis, Michael. "Forced to Tramp: The Perspective of the Labor Press, 1870–1900." In Monkkonen, *Walking to Work*, 141–170.

Davis, Ralph Nelson. "Negro Newspapers in Chicago." MA thesis, University of Chicago, 1939.

D'Emilio, John, and Estelle B. Freedman. *Intimate Matters: A History of Sexuality in America*. Chicago: University of Chicago Press, 1998.

Denning, Michael. *Mechanic Accents: Dime Novels and Working-Class Culture in America*. London: Verso, 1998.

DePastino, Todd. *Citizen Hobo: How a Century of Homelessness Shaped America*. Chicago: University of Chicago Press, 2003.

Deutsch, Sarah. *Women and the City: Gender, Space, and Power in Boston, 1870–1940*. New York: Oxford University Press, 2002.

Donovan, Brian. *White Slave Crusades: Race, Gender and Anti-Vice Activism, 1887–1917*. Urbana: University of Illinois Press, 2006.

Douglas, William O. "Vagrancy and Arrest on Suspicion." *Yale Law Journal* 70 (November 1960): 1–14.

Downey, Dennis. "The Congress on Labor at the World's Columbian Exhibition." *Journal of the Illinois State Historical Society Journal* 76 (Summer 1983): 131–138.

Drake, St. Clair, and Horace R. Cayton. *Black Metropolis: A Study of Negro Life in a Northern City*. Chicago: University of Chicago Press, 1993. First published 1945.

Dubber, Markus D. *The Police Power: Patriarchy and the Foundations of American Government*. New York: Columbia University Press, 2005.

Duis, Perry R. "An Evening with the Committee of Fifteen." University of Chicago Special Collections, n.d.

———. *The Saloon: Public Drinking in Chicago and Boston 1880–1920*. Urbana: University of Illinois Press, 1983.

Edwards, Laura. "The Civil War and Reconstruction." In Grossberg and Tomlins, *Cambridge History of Law in America*, 313–344.

———. *The People and Their Peace: Legal Culture and the Transformation of Inequality in the Post-Revolutionary South*. Chapel Hill: University of North Carolina Press, 2009.

Espiritu, Yen Le. *Filipino American Lives*. Philadelphia: Temple University Press, 1995.

Evans, Peter B., Dietrich Rueschemeyer, and Theda Skocpol, eds. *Bringing the State Back In*. New York: Cambridge University Press, 1985.

Feinman, Jay M. "The Development of the Employment at Will Rule." *American Journal of Legal History* 20 (April 1976): 118–135.

Feldman, Leonard. *Citizens without Shelter: Homelessness, Democracy and Political Exclusion*. Ithaca, NY: Cornell University Press, 2004.

Ferguson, Karen. *Black Politics in New Deal Atlanta*. Chapel Hill: University of North Carolina Press, 2002.

Fine, Lisa M. *The Soul of the Skyscraper: Female Clerical Workers in Chicago*. Philadelphia: Temple University Press, 1990.

Finkelman, Paul. "The Taney Court: The Jurisprudence of Slavery and the Crisis of the Union." In *The United States Supreme Court: The Pursuit of Justice*, edited by Christopher Tomlins. Boston: Houghton Mifflin, 2005, 75–99.

Fleming, Anne. "The Borrower's Tale: A History of Poor Debtors in *Lochner* Era New York City." *Law and History Review* 30, no. 4 (2012): 1053–1098.

Foner, Eric. *Free Soil, Free Labor, Free Men: The Ideology of the Republican Party before the Civil War*. New York: Oxford University Press, 1995.

———. *Nothing but Freedom: Emancipation and Its Legacy*. Baton Rouge: Louisiana State University Press, 1982.

Foote, Calib. "Vagrancy-Type Law and Its Administration." *University of Pennsylvania Law Review* 104 (1956), 603–650.

Forbath, William. "The Ambiguities of Free Labor: Labor and the Law in the Gilded Age." *Wisconsin Law Review* 767, no. 4 (1985): 767–817.

———. "Social and Economic Rights in the American Grain." In *The Constitution in 2020*, edited by Jack Balkin and Reva Siegel. New York: Oxford University Press, 2009, 55–68.

Friedman, Lawrence M. "Crimes of Mobility." *Stanford Law Review* 43 (February 1991): 637–658.

Gaines, Kevin. *Uplifting the Race: Black Leadership, Politics and Culture in the Twentieth Century*. Chapel Hill: University of North Carolina Press, 1996.

Getis, Victoria. *The Juvenile Court and the Progressives*. Urbana: University of Illinois Press, 2000.

Gilfoyle, Timothy. *City of Eros: New York City, Prostitution and the Commercialization of Sex*. New York: W. W. Norton, 1993.

———. "Prostitutes in History: From Parables of Pornography to Metaphors of Modernity." *American Historical Review* 104, no. 1 (February 1999): 117–141.

Goluboff, Risa. *The Lost Promise of Civil Rights*. Cambridge, MA: Harvard University Press, 2007.

Goodman, James. *Stories of Scottsboro*. New York: Vintage, 1995.

Goodwin, Joanne L. "An American Experiment in Paid Motherhood: The Implementation of Mother's Pensions in Early Twentieth Century Chicago." *Gender and History* 4, no. 3 (Autumn 1992): 364–386.

———. *Gender and the Politics of Welfare Reform: Mothers' Pensions in Chicago, 1911–1929*. Chicago: University of Chicago Press, 1997.

Gordon, Linda. *Pitied but Not Entitled: Single Mothers and the History of Welfare, 1890–1935*. New York: Free Press, 1994.

Green, Paul. "Anton J. Cermak: The Man and His Machine." In *The Mayors: The Chicago Political Tradition*, edited by Paul Green and Melvin Holli, 99–110. Carbondale: Southern Illinois University Press, 2005.

Grossberg, Michael. *Governing the Hearth: Law and the Family in Nineteenth Century America*. Chapel Hill: University of North Carolina Press, 1988.

Grossberg, Michael, and Christopher L. Tomlins, ed. *The Cambridge History of Law in America: Volume 2*. Cambridge: Cambridge University Press, 2011.

Grossman, James. *Land of Hope: Chicago, Black Southerners and the Great Migration*. Chicago: University of Chicago Press, 1989.

Gullett, Gayle. "'Our Great Opportunity': Organized Women Advance Women's Work at the World's Columbian Exposition of 1893." *Illinois Historical Journal* 87, no. 4 (Winter 1994): 259–276.

Hall, Kermit. *The Magic Mirror: Law in American History*. New York: Oxford University Press, 2009.

Haller, Mark H. "Historical Roots of Police Behavior: Chicago, 1890–1925." *Law and Society Review* 10, no. 2 (Winter 1976): 303–323.

Halpern, Rick. *Down on the Killing Floor: Black and White Workers in Chicago's Packinghouses*. Urbana: University of Illinois Press, 1997.

Hamm, Richard. *Shaping the Eighteenth Amendment: Temperance Reform, Legal Culture and the Polity, 1880–1920.* Chapel Hill: University of North Carolina Press, 1995.

Haney-López, Ian. *White by Law: The Legal Construction of Race.* New York: New York University Press, 1996.

Harring, Sidney. "Class Conflict and the Suppression of Tramps in Buffalo, 1892–189." *Law and Society Review* 11, no. 5 (Summer 1977): 873–911.

Hartog, Hendrik. "Pigs and Positivism." *Wisconsin Law Review* no. 4 (1985): 899–935.

Harvey, David. *A Brief History of Neoliberalism.* Oxford: Oxford University Press, 2005.

Herbst, Alma. *The Negro in the Slaughtering and Meat-Packing Industry in Chicago.* New York: Arno, 1971. First published 1932.

Higbie, Frank Tobias. "Between Romance and Degradation: Navigating the Meanings of Vagrancy in North America, 1870–1940." In *Cast Out: A Global History of Vagrancy,* edited by Augustus Lee Beier and Paul Ocobock, 250–269. Athens: Ohio University Press, 2008.

———. *Indispensable Outcasts: Hobo Workers and Community in the American Midwest.* Urbana: University of Illinois Press, 2003.

Holton, Woody. *Unruly Americans and the Origins of the Constitution.* New York: Hill & Wang, 2008.

Horwitz, Morton. *The Transformation of American Law, 1870–1960: The Crisis in Legal Orthodoxy.* New York: Oxford University Press, 1994.

Howe, Daniel Walker. *What Hath God Wrought: The Transformation of America, 1815–1848.* New York: Oxford University Press, 2009.

Hoy, Suellen. "Caring for Chicago's Women and Girls." *Journal of Urban History* 23, no. 3 (March 1997): 260–294.

———. *Good Hearts: Catholic Sisters in Chicago's Past.* Urbana: University of Illinois, 2006.

Hoyt, Homer. "One Hundred Years of Land Values in Chicago." PhD diss., Department of Economics, University of Chicago, 1933.

Hunt, Alan. *Governing Morals: A Social History of Moral Regulation.* New York: Cambridge University Press, 1999.

———. *The Sociological Movement in Law.* Philadelphia: Temple University Press, 1978.

Jacobs, Jane. *The Death and Life of Great American Cities.* New York: Vintage, 1992.

Johnson, Paul. *A Shopkeeper's Millennium: Society and Revivals in Rochester, New York, 1815–1837.* New York: Hill & Wang, 1978.

Jones, Martha. "Time, Space, and Jurisdiction in Atlantic World Slavery: The Volunbrun Household in Gradual Emancipation New York." *Law and History Review* 29, no. 4 (2011): 1031–1060.

Kalman, Laura. *The Strange Career of Legal Liberalism*. New Haven, CT: Yale University Press, 1996.

Katz, Michael B. *Poverty and Policy in America History*. New York: Academic Press, 1983.

Keire, Mara. *For Business and Pleasure: Red Light Districts and the Regulation of Vice in the United States, 1890–1933*. Baltimore: Johns Hopkins University Press, 2010.

———. "The Vice Trust: A Reinterpretation of the White Slavery Scare in the United States, 1907–1917." *Journal of Social History* 35 (2001): 5–41.

Kelley, Robin D. G. "'We Are Not What We Seem': Re-Thinking Black Working Class Opposition in the Jim Crow South." *Journal of American History* 80, no. 1 (June 1993): 75–112.

Kessler-Harris, Alice. *Gendering Labor History*. Urbana: University of Illinois Press, 2007.

———. *In Pursuit of Equity: Women and the Quest for Economic Citizenship in 20th Century America*. New York: Oxford University Press, 2001.

———. *Out to Work: A History of Wage-Earning Women in the United States*. New York: Oxford University Press, 1982.

Kramer, Larry. *The People Themselves: Popular Constitutionalism and Judicial Review*. Oxford: Oxford University Press, 2005.

Kusmer, Kenneth. *Down and Out, and on the Road: The Homeless in American History*. New York: Oxford University Press, 2002.

Kusmer, Kenneth L. "The Functions of Organized Charity in the Progressive Era: Chicago as a Case Study." *Journal of American History* 60, no. 3 (1973): 657–678.

Kyvig, David E. "The Character of the Cork Determines the Flow from the Flask." *Reviews in American History* 24, no. 1 (1996): 114–119.

Labbe, Ronald M., and Jonathan Lurie. *The Slaughterhouse Cases: Regulation, Reconstruction, and the Fourteenth Amendment*. Lawrence: University Press of Kansas, 2005.

Lambert, Josiah. *If the Workers Took a Notion: The Right to Strike and American Political Development*. Ithaca, NY: Cornell University Press, 2005.

Lefebvre, Henri. "The Everyday and Everydayness." Translated by Christine Levich. *Yale French Studies* 73 (1987): 7–11.

Lentz-Smith, Adriane. *Freedom Struggles: African American and World War I*. Cambridge, MA: Harvard University Press, 2009.

Leuchtenberg, William E. *Franklin D. Roosevelt and the New Deal: 1932-1940.* New York: Harper & Row, 1963.

———. "The Pertinence of Political History: Reflections on the Significance of the State in America." *Journal of American History* 73, no. 3 (December 1986): 585–600.

———. *Supreme Court Reborn: The Constitutional Revolution in the Age of Roosevelt.* New York: Oxford University Press, 1996.

Levy, Jonathan. *Freaks of Fortune: The Emerging World of Capitalism and Risk in America.* Cambridge, MA: Harvard University Press, 2012.

Lichtenstein, Alexander. *Twice the Work of Free Labor: The Political Economy of Convict Labor in the New South.* London: Verso, 1996.

Lovell, George. *This Is Not Civil Rights: Discovering Rights Talk in 1939 America.* Chicago: University of Chicago Press, 2012.

Mack, Kenneth W. "Rethinking Civil Rights Lawyering and Politics in the Era before Brown." *Yale Law Journal* 115 (2005): 256–355.

Mackey, Robert A. "Criminal Law: Vagrancy: Single Offense Theory: Evidence for Previous Acts: Number of Acts Necessary to Establish Vagrancy Status." *California Law Review.* 39 (December 1951): 579–584.

Mackey, Thomas. *Red Lights Out: A Legal History of Prostitution, Disorderly Houses and Vice Districts, 1870–1917.* New York: Garland, 1987.

Mancini, Matthew. *One Dies, Get Another: Convict Leasing in the American South, 1866–1928.* Columbia: University of South Carolina Press, 1996.

Marshall, T. H. *Class Citizenship and Social Development.* Garden City, NY: Doubleday, 1964.

Matthews, Jean. *The Rise of the New Woman: The Women's Movement in America, 1875–1920.* Chicago: Ivan R. Dee, 2003.

McElvaine, Robert. *Down and Out in the Great Depression: Letters from the Forgotten Man.* Chapel Hill: University of North Carolina Press, 1983.

McGerr, Michael. *A Fierce Discontent: The Rise and Fall of the Progressive Movement in America.* New York: Oxford University Press, 2003.

McLean, Edward B. *Law and Civilization: The Legal Thought of Roscoe Pound.* Lanham, MD: University Press of America, 1992.

Meier, August, and Elliott M. Rudwick. "Black Man in the 'White City': Negroes and the Columbian Exposition, 1893." *Phylon* 26, no. 4 (1965): 354–361.

———. "Negro Protest at the Chicago World's Fair, 1933–1934." *Journal of the Illinois State Historical Society* 59, no. 2 (1966): 161–171.

Meyerowitz, Joanne. *Women Adrift: Independent Wage Earner in Chicago.* Chicago: University of Chicago Press, 1988.

Monkkonen, Eric, ed. *Walking to Work: Tramps in America, 1790–1935.* Lincoln: University of Nebraska Press, 1984.

Moreton, Bethany. *To Serve God and Wal-Mart: The Making of Christian Free Enterprise.* Cambridge, MA: Harvard University Press, 2009.

Morgan, Edmund. *American Slavery, American Freedom: The Ordeal of Colonial Virginia.* New York: W. W. Norton, 1975.

Morris, Richard. *Government and Labor in Early America.* Boston: Northeastern University Press, 1946.

Muhammad, Khalil Gibran. *The Condemnation of Blackness: Race, Crime and the Making of Modern Urban America.* Cambridge, MA: Harvard University Press, 2010.

Nash, Gary. *Urban Crucible: Social Change, Political Consciousness and the Origins of the American Revolution.* Cambridge, MA: Harvard University Press, 1979.

Nelson, Otto M. "The Chicago Relief and Aid Society, 1850–1874." *Journal of the Illinois State Historical Society* 59, no. 1 (Spring 1966): 48–66.

Ngai, Mae. *Impossible Subjects: Illegal Aliens and the Making of Modern America.* Princeton, NJ: Princeton University Press, 2004.

Nieman, Donald. *Promises to Keep: African Americans and the Constitutional Order, 1776 to the Present.* New York: Oxford University Press, 1991.

Nimmer, Raymond. "Court Directed Reform of Vagrancy-Type Law." *Judicature* 54, no. 2 (August/September 1970): 50–54.

Novak, William. "The Myth of the 'Weak' American State." *American Historical Review* 113, no. 3 (2008): 752–772.

———. *The People's Welfare: Law and Regulation in Nineteenth Century America.* Chapel Hill: University of North Carolina Press, 1996.

O'Connor, Alice. *Poverty Knowledge: Social Science, Social Policy, and the Poor in Twentieth-Century U.S. History.* Princeton, NJ: Princeton University Press, 2001.

Odem, Mary. *Delinquent Daughters: Protecting and Policing Adolescent Female Sexuality in the United States, 1885–1920.* Chapel Hill: University of North Carolina Press, 1995.

Oshinsky, David. *"Worse Than Slavery": Parchman Farm and the Ordeal of Jim Crow.* New York: Simon & Schuster, 1996.

Ott, Julia C. *When Wall Street Met Main Street: The Quest for an Investors' Democracy.* Cambridge, MA: Harvard University Press, 2011.

Parmet, Wendy. "From Slaughter-House to Lochner: The Rise and Fall of the Constitutionalization of Public Health." *American Journal Legal History* 40, no. 4 (October 1996): 476–505.

Peck, Gunther. "Reinventing Free Labor: Immigrant Padrones and Contract Laborers in North America, 1885–1925." *Journal of American History* 83, no. 3 (1996): 848–871.

————. *Reinventing Free Labor: Padrones and Immigrant Workers in the North American West, 1880–1930*. Cambridge: Cambridge University Press, 2000.

Peiss, Kathy. *Cheap Amusements: Working Women and Leisure in Turn-of-the-Century New York*. Philadelphia: Temple University Press, 1986.

Phan, Hoang Gia. "'A Race So Different': Chinese Exclusion, the Slaughterhouse Cases and Plessy v. Ferguson." *Labor History* 45, no. 2 (May 2004): 133–163.

Phelps, Margaret Dorsey. "Idled Outside, Overworked Inside: The Political Economy of Prison Labor during Depressions in Chicago, 1871–1897." PhD diss., University of Iowa, 1992.

Philpott, Thomas Lee. *The Slum and the Ghetto: Immigrants, Blacks and Reformers in Chicago, 1880–1930*. New York: Oxford University Press, 1978.

Piccato, Pablo. *City of Suspects: Crime in Mexico City, 1900–1931*. Durham, NC: Duke University Press, 2011.

Pierce, Bessie Louise. *A History of Chicago, Vol. 3: The Rise of a Modern City, 1871–1893*. Chicago: University of Chicago Press, 1957.

Reed, Christopher Robert. *The Chicago NAACP and the Rise of Black Professional Leadership, 1910–1966*. Bloomington: Indiana University Press, 1987.

————. *The Rise of Chicago's Black Metropolis, 1920–1929*. Urbana: University of Illinois Press, 2011.

Reitman, Ben. *Sisters of the Road: The Autobiography of Boxcar Bertha*. Edinburgh, UK: AK Press/Nabat, 2002. First published 1937.

Residents of Hull House, eds. *Hull House Maps and Papers*. Urbana: University of Illinois, 2007. First published 1895.

Ringenbach, Paul. *Tramps and Reformers*. Westport, CT: Greenwood, 1973.

Robinson, Louis N. *Should Prisoners Work? A Study of the Prison Labor Problem in the United States*. Philadelphia: John C. Winston, 1931. First published 1923.

Rockman, Seth. *Scraping By: Wage Labor, Slavery, and Survival in Early Baltimore*. Baltimore: Johns Hopkins University Press, 2009.

Rodgers, Daniel T. *The Work Ethic in Industrial America, 1850–1920*. Chicago: University of Chicago Press, 1974.

Rosen, Ruth. *The Lost Sisterhood: Prostitution in America*. Baltimore: Johns Hopkins University Press, 1982.

Ross, Dorothy. *The Origins of American Social Sciences*. New York: Cambridge University Press, 1992.

Ross, Michael A. "Justice Miller's Reconstruction: The Slaughter-House Cases, Health Codes, and Civil Rights in New Orleans, 1861–1873." *Journal of Southern History* 64, no. 4 (November 1998): 649–676.

———. *Justice of Shattered Dreams: Samuel Freeman Miller and the Supreme Court during the Civil War Era*. Baton Rouge: Louisiana State University Press, 2003.

Rothman, David. *The Discovery of the Asylum: Social Order in the New Republic*. Boston: Little, Brown, 1971.

Rothstein, Richard. *The Color of Law: A Forgotten History of How Our Government Segregated America*. New York: Liveright, 2017.

Rubin, Martin. *Showstoppers: Busby Berkeley and the Tradition of Spectacle*. New York: Columbia University Press, 1993.

Ryan, Mary. *Civic Wars: Democracy and Public Life in the America City during the Nineteenth Century*. Berkeley: University of California Press, 1977.

Rydell, Robert W. *All the World's a Fair: Visions of Empire at American International Expositions, 1876–1916*. Chicago: University of Chicago Press, 1987.

———. "Editors' Introduction." In Wells and Rydell, *Reason Why the Colored American*, xxxiii–xxxvii.

Sanchez, George. *Becoming Mexican American: Ethnicity, Culture, and Identity in Chicano Los Angeles, 1900–1945*. New York: Oxford University Press, 1995.

Sandage, Scott. *Born Losers: A History of Failure in America*. Cambridge, MA: Harvard University Press, 2005.

Sandburg, Carl. *The Complete Poems of Carl Sandburg*. New York: Harcourt, 2003.

Satter, Beryl. *Family Properties: How the Struggle over Race and Real Estate Transformed Chicago and Urban America*. New York: Picador, 2010.

Sawislak, Karen. *Smoldering City: Chicagoans and the Great Fire, 1871–1874*. Chicago: University of Chicago Press, 1995.

Scott, James. *Seeing like a State: How Certain Schemes to Improve the Human Condition Have Failed*. New Haven, CT: Yale University Press, 1998.

Semonche, John. *Censoring Sex: A Historical Journey through American Media*. New York: Rowman & Littlefield, 2007.

Shabazz, Rashad. *Spatializing Blackness: Architectures of Confinement and Black Masculinity in Chicago*. Urbana: University of Illinois Press, 2010.

Sherry, Arthur H. "Vagrants, Rogues and Vagabonds: Old Concepts in Need of Revision." *California Law Review* 48, no. 4 (October 1960): 557–573.

Siegel, Reva. "She the People: The Nineteenth Amendment, Sex Equality, Federalism, and the Family." *Harvard Law Review* 115, no. 4 (2002): 947–1046.

Silver, Christopher. "The Racial Origins of Zoning in American Cities." In *Urban Planning and the African American Community: In the Shadows*, edited by Marsha Ritzdorf and June Manning Thomas, 23–42. Thousand Oaks, CA: SAGE, 1997.

Simon, Bryant. *A Fabric of Defeat: The Politics of South Carolina Millhands, 1910–1948*. Chapel Hill: University of North Carolina Press, 1998.

Sklansky, Jeff. "Pauperism and Poverty: Henry George, William Graham Sumner and the Ideological Origins of Modern American Social Science." *Journal of the History of the Behavioral Sciences* 35, no. 2 (Spring 1999): 111–138.

Skowronek, Stephen. *Building a New American State: The Expansion of National Administrative Capacities*. New York: Cambridge University Press, 1982.

Slayton, Robert A. "The Flophouse: Housing and Public Policy for the Single Poor." *Journal of Public History* 1, no. 4 (1989): 373–390.

Smith, Carl. *Urban Disorder and the Shape of Belief: The Great Chicago Fire, the Haymarket Bomb, and the Model Town of Pullman*. Chicago: University of Chicago Press, 1994.

Smith, Stacey. *Freedom's Frontier: California and the Struggle over Unfree Labor, Emancipation and Reconstruction*. Chapel Hill: University of North Carolina Press, 2013.

Spain, Daphne. *How Women Saved the City*. Minneapolis: University of Minnesota Press, 2002.

Spear, Alan. *Black Chicago: The Making of a Negro Ghetto*. Chicago: University of Chicago Press, 1966.

Spicker, Paul, Sonia Álvarez Leguizamón, and David Gordon, eds. *Poverty: An International Glossary*. London: Zed Books, 2007.

Standing, Guy. *The Precariat: The New Dangerous Class*. London: Bloomsbury Academic, 2011.

Stanfield, Robert. *The Invention of Free Labor: The Employment Relationship in English and American Law*. Chapel Hill: University of North Carolina Press, 1991.

Stanley, Amy Dru. "Beggars Can't Be Choosers: Compulsion and Contract in Postbellum America." *Journal of American History* 78, no 4 (March 1992): 1265–1293.

———. *From Bondage to Contract: Wage Labor, Marriage and the Market in the Age of Slave Emancipation*. New York: Cambridge University Press, 1998.

Stansell, Christine. *City of Women: Sex and Class in New York, 1789–1860*. Urbana: University of Illinois Press, 1987.

Steinfeld, Robert. *The Invention of Free Labor: The Employment Relation in English and American Law and Culture, 1350–1870*. Chapel Hill: University of North Carolina Press, 2002.

Strickland, Arvarh. *History of the Chicago Urban League*. Urbana: University of Illinois Press, 1966.

Tannenhaus, David. *A Century of Juvenile Justice*. Chicago: University of Chicago Press, 2002.

———. "Growing Up Dependent: Family Preservation in Early Twentieth-Century Chicago." *Law and History Review* 19, no. 3 (2001): 547–582.

Teachout, Terry. *Pops: A Life of Louis Armstrong*. New York: Mariner, 2010.

Tomlins, Christopher. *Law, Labor, and Ideology in the Early American Republic*. New York: Cambridge University Press, 1993.

———. *The State and the Unions: Labor Relations, Law and the Organized Labor Movement in America*. New York: Cambridge University Press, 1985.

Trotter, Joe. *Black Milwaukee: The Making of an Industrial Proletariat, 1915–45*. Urbana: University of Illinois Press, 1985.

Turkel, Studs. *Hard Times: An Oral History of the Great Depression*. New York: Free Press, 1970.

Tushnet, Mark. *The NAACP's Legal Strategy against Segregated Education, 1925–1950*. Chapel Hill: University of North Carolina Press, 2005.

Tuttle, William. *Race Riot: Chicago in the Red Summer of 1919*. New York: Atheneum, 1970.

———. "Some Strikebreakers' Observations of Industrial Warfare." *Labor History* 7, no. 2 (1966): 193–196.

"Use of Vagrancy-Type Law for Arrest and Detention of Suspicious Persons." Note. *Yale Law Journal* 59, no. 7 (June 1950): 1351–1364.

Vapnek, Lara. *Breadwinners: Working Women and Economic Independence, 1865–1920*. Urbana: University of Illinois Press, 2009.

Wacquant, Loïc. *Prisons of Poverty*. Minneapolis: University of Minnesota Press, 2009.

Waskow, Arthur. *From Race Riot to Sit-In: 1919 and the 1960s*. New York: Anchor Books, 1967.

Welke, Barbarra. "Law, Citizenship, and Personhood in the Long Nineteenth Century: The Borders of Belonging." In Grossberg and Tomlins, *Cambridge History of Law in America*.

White, Luise. *The Comforts of Home: Prostitution in Colonial Nairobi*. Chicago: University of Chicago Press, 1990.

Wiecek, William. *The Lost World of Classical Legal Thought: Law and Ideology in America*. New York: Oxford University Press, 1998.

Willrich, Michael. *City of Courts: Socializing Justice in Progressive Era Chicago.* New York: Cambridge University Press, 2003.

Winkler, Adam. "A Revolution Too Soon: Woman Suffragists and the Living Constitution." *New York University Law Review* 76 (2001): 1456–1526.

Wood, Gordon. *The Creation of the American Republic: 1776–1787.* New York: W. W. Norton, 1969.

Yeamans, Robin. "Constitutional Attacks on Vagrancy Laws." *Stanford Law Review* 20 (April 1968): 782–793.

Index

Numbers in italics represent pages with illustrations.

Wilson, Robert, 178n89
Wine, George, 90
wine rooms, 82–83, 186n56
wives. *See* women
women
  and adult probation, 34, 36
  African American, 98, 99–100, 110–
    111, 114, 142, 192n2, 198n56
  as breadwinners, 151, 181n8, 198n56
  and Court of Domestic Relations,
    38–39
  and the courts, 79–93, 165n85
  criminalization of "immoral"
    practices, 72–73
  danger of wage work, 74
  dangers outside the home, 90
  department store work, 76, 77–78,
    85–86, 94, 186–187nn65–66
  dependency, 10, 21, 70
  domestic work, 76–77, 102, 184n34,
    194n15
  equality, 70–71, 135, 137–138, 147–148
  exploitation of, 73
  and health, 92
  and minimum-wage laws, 134–135,
    136, 151–152
  moral conduct, 72
  and moral crimes, 170n135
  and Morals Court, 40
  and the New Deal, 151–152
  occupations in Chicago, 183n26
  participation in economic activity,
    212n72
  pensioning, 96–97, 192nn112–113
  relief programs, 215n8
  tramps, 73, 137, 210n51
  and vagrancy laws, 18, 70
  and virtue, 40, 69
  wages, 135
  and wage work, 70, 72–73, 74, 78,
    183n26
  white, 3, 24–25, 71, 128
  See also sex workers; workingwomen
Women's Christian Temperance Union,
  73–74, 182n18, 186n56

Women's Model Lodging House, 193n3
work and workers, 6
  African Americans, 142, 212n75
  casual, 102, 194n15
  compulsory, 61–62
  department store, 76, 77–78, 85–86,
    94, 186–187nn65–66
  and domesticity, 11
  domestic work, 76–77, 88, 102,
    184n34, 194n15
  evolving conceptions of, 16–17
  foreign, 129
  garment trades, 184n32
  laws, 100
  manual labor, 126, 129
  menial, 33
  regulation of, 92
  seamstress, 21
  tramps' conflicting views of, 46–47
  and virtue, 91–92, 137
  See also workingwomen
Workers, The (Wyckoff), 54
workhouses, 46
workingwomen, 10, 71–72
  African American, 142, 198n56
  as cheap labor, 72
  commitment to protection of, 94–95
  compared to male wageworkers,
    181n8
  conditions of, 97–98
  contracting (*see* contracting
    workingwomen)
  and court system, 87–88
  defined by sex, 73
  journalists' opinions about, 74–75
  laws limiting hours worked, 91
  leisure spaces, 94
  and liberty of contract, 141
  minimum-wage laws, 134–135, 136,
    138, 210n42
  and needlework, 76
  reformers' opinions about, 75–76
  regulation of, 92
  "ruin" of, 74
  social scientists' opinions about, 76

wages, 170n133
Works Progress Administration, 151,
    215n7
worth, 2, 20–21, 50
Wright, Carroll D., 23, 75
Wright, Richard R., 103, 194n15
Wyckoff, Walter Augustus, 43, 44, 50,
    54, 67

Young, Louis, 58

zoning, racial, 198n50
Zorbaugh, Harvey, 130